WELCOME TO DEATH ROW

The Uncensored History of the Rise and Fall of
Death Row Records in the Words of Those Who Were There

S. LEIGH SAVIDGE
with
Steve Housden & Jeff Scheftel

XENON PRESS
Los Angeles

Nonfiction | True Crime | Rap Music | Music Business | Film | Performing Arts

First Edition

Published by
Xenon Press
3521 Jack Northrop Ave.
Hawthorne CA 90250

Prologue

In the spring of 1998, I made a decision to finance a documentary entitled *Welcome to Death Row,* which examined the most dangerous story in the history of the music business at the time: the story of the rise and fall of Suge Knight and Death Row Records. Ultimately, *Welcome to Death Row* led directly to my ability to write the initial drafts of *Straight Outta Compton,* the F. Gary Gray directed / Dr. Dre and Ice Cube produced feature film released by Universal Pictures in August 2015.

When people try to pigeon-hole the Death Row story as a Black story, I always correct them. It's an *American* story about politics, greed, ambition, epic success and epic failure and those who seek fame and fortune in the music business.

Death Row had done something that no record company had ever done before: They had released six consecutive albums that had shipped between two and six million copies. Label founder Suge Knight was a former bodyguard who had ripped superstar producer Dr. Dre from Eazy E's Ruthless Records, entered into business with billionaire, Ted Field, and superstar producer, Jimmy Iovine, and their then-fledgling label Interscope Records and had built a hit machine that was being run like a street gang, complete with Crips and Bloods, where office violence was a frequent occurrence. The label's biggest act, Tupac Shakur, had been gunned down in Las Vegas in a drive-by shooting and Knight was one of the suspects. Frosty relations between Knight and Bad Boy Records CEO Sean Combs, had led to violence, gunplay, and an ongoing war of words between rappers on both coasts.

All this had caught the attention of political conservatives like William Bennett, who had joined in an unlikely union with activist C. Delores Tucker to decry "gangsta rap" as irresponsible and an evil force that was polluting the minds of America's youth. Interscope had recently been purchased by Time Warner at a deal that valued the company at $400 million only to later divest their stake when Bob Dole and other high profile Republicans began applying political pressure for them to do so.

But these details weren't even the biggest piece of the story.

By 1998, Dr. Dre had left Death Row minus his equity after what many said was a violent confrontation with Suge Knight. *Los Angeles Times'* music journalist, Chuck Phillips, a Pulitzer Prize winner, was writing weekly stories about imprisoned drug kingpin, Michael "Harry O" Harris, being the funding source behind Death Row Records. There was a federal investigation into Death Row's funding sources and general business practices. Finally, Suge Knight's lengthy criminal record had finally caught up with him. He was serving a nine year prison sentence, the result of a violent episode involving a member of the Crip street gang at the MGM Grand Hotel. The incident was captured on the hotel's security cameras and had occurred just prior to the murder of Death Row's biggest star, Tupac Shakur.

Was the most successful Black-owned record label of its era largely a criminal enterprise where the White guys had gotten rich and the Black guys were mostly dead, broke, or in jail? Black, White, or otherwise, this story stoked people's worst fears and assumptions about haves and have-nots and the price of making it in America. The Death Row story was the talk of Los Angeles in all circles and *the* water cooler story in much of America.

I'd started a company with $17,000 and had worked 90 hour weeks for 12 years. I had a million dollars in the bank, a million dollar credit line, no debt and had built a distribution company that distributed Black entertainment. I'd made measured, strategic decisions with limited funds to get where I was.

But all that ended with this project.

2

For the next three years, I engaged in a sometimes inspiring, but mostly grueling, inexorably dispiriting process that endangered my life and the lives of my employees, depleted my financial safety net, and left me questioning who I was, what my motives were and, apart from the people my film examined, what my own capacity for ruthlessness was.

I would come to see *Welcome to Death Row* as the ultimate pyrrhic victory: A film that is a testament to a time period in American history but whose production process and expenditures would never allow it to make any real money. It was a film that could only have been done in that context, with Suge Knight in prison, and brave interviewees (many of whom have since died) willing to speak for our cameras despite the specter of threats to their personal safety and the government's investigation into Death Row. It was a film that energized and inspired many of the people that saw it and made me and my company *persona non grata* with a number of powerful people who did not want the story told.

Even so, this is a film I would never undertake given the same circumstances today.

In 2007, sometime after New Line Cinema made the initial deal for *Compton*, we asked Susan Self, a Los Angeles-based public relations executive to do a preliminary assembly of the transcripts from some of the interviews we had captured and sourced on the Death Row project and put them in a chronology of sorts that fit the narrative flow of the film. It was no surprise that 95% of the material we captured didn't make it to the final version.

Later, in 2013 as the *Compton* project headed for a production start date, the *LA Weekly* used excerpts from these transcripts as part of an article commemorating the 20 year anniversary of Death Row's defining album, *The Chronic*. The reaction was strong enough that I began to think that some synthesis of the oral history we captured and the long ordeal Xenon Pictures, myself, producers Steve Housden and Jeff Scheftel and others endured to make the film might make for interesting reading, especially for the many people looking to tell a story where the obstacles appear completely untenable.

The original tag line for the *Welcome to Death Row* film says it all:

"It Started in Compton. It Ended in Infamy."

Machine Guns in Malibu

When I arrived at the California State Prison at Lancaster to meet Michael Harris for the first time, I was immediately ushered into a side room and asked to disrobe. A prison official then put on a rubber glove and performed a cavity search. Traditionally, at least in terms of public venues, my ass has been kind of a no-fly zone - the exclusive province of the doctor that performs my annual hernia examination. But that was news to Lancaster's version of Inspector Clouseau. Throughout the process, he bore the blank look of someone who had done this a thousand times -- like sticking a finger in somebody's business looking for a baggie of crack represented just another day at the office. Even so, when he came up empty, there was a palpable look of disappointment on his face. I was told to finish signing in and was then released to the facility's 75-seat visitor waiting area.

There had been a violent incident between Black and Hispanic factions at the prison a few days before, and the facility was emerging from a *lockdown* phase. On site security had been ratcheted up and I was advised that I'd need to pass through two more security checkpoints before I got to the lunchroom area where my meeting was to take place.

Three hours passed.

At some point, a woman turned to me and asked why I was there. When I told her I was there to see the man whose street name was *Harry O*, it turned into the moment from the old EF Hutton commercial from the 70s - every head in the waiting room turned and looked at me.

It was clear that Michael Harris was the celebrity prisoner in Lancaster - *The Big Kahuna.*

****

I had decided that my company, Xenon Pictures, needed to deliver a film that would set it apart from any other company that was operating in the independent Black media space at the time. And though it frightened me to think about, I couldn't take my eyes off the story of Suge Knight and Death Row Records. There was a phrase that I'd been hearing from Black filmmakers for years: *"Our Stories Are Not Being Told."* And this was one that America was both velcroed to and terrified by.

In my initial examination of the Death Row story, I tried to put myself into Suge Knight's shoes. In Dr. Dre, he's got the most talented producer in the hottest new genre in the music business in the fold. There is the presumption of money and success in the offing. But he's a former bodyguard with a number of battery cases pending and he's got legal stuff coming from what he had to do to get Dre out of Ruthless Records. Dick Griffey at Solar Records is giving him studio time. But Griffey's got a limited appetite for funding the venture and he's almost broke. So where's he gonna get the dough to make it all happen? *Goldman Sachs? Uh uh.*

My thought process kept going back to *Isn't this the type of story that is really what America is all about? The kind of story America was built on?* One of my favorite quotes is from the writer Alexander Dumas: *"Behind every great fortune, there lies a crime."* When discussing this subject, people I knew often wheeled out the backgrounds of guys like Joe Kennedy or Walter Annenberg. But I knew those weren't isolated cases. I'd sat in country clubs in places like Greenwich, Connecticut and Watch Hill, Rhode Island and listened to guys wearing tweed jackets and bow ties who'd attended Exeter and Harvard Business School wax nostalgic about their grandfathers or uncles who had used brass knuckle tactics and broken some heads before eventually building their companies.

They'd always smile and say *"He was a real character."*

Wasn't the Death Row story all this but skewed inner city Black? Was it less relevant because it had skipped a generation and was happening in a segment of the Black community that had been completely underrepresented in the annals of business history? Wasn't this story the embodiment of the struggle of America's inner city youth looking to get a seat at the country's economic table? Was it less relevant because it was this samurai, in your face, story happening in the here and now?

In the white-hot summer of 1998, this was my thought process. But how would anyone get at this story?

My friend, Jeff Silberman, had left a big job at Viacom and had hung out his shingle as an independent producer. He had put me in touch with a Nigerian director named Ifeanye Njoku who had been making trips down to the California State Prison in Lancaster, California to talk to Michael Harris about his story. I had a few conversations with Ifeanye and quickly determined that he and I were not a good business match. A short time later, Silberman arranged for me to meet Michael's wife, Lydia. But before he did he wanted me know that I would be walking into a dangerous situation.

"Do you know who these people are?"

The fear surrounding the Death Row story had touched the whole of Los Angeles from South Central to the tony enclaves of the city's wealthy elite. Attendees at events at Interscope Records CEO, Jimmy Iovine's Malibu Beach house had been greeted by guys with machine guns at the door. Suge Knight had moved into the neighborhood and had dragged the security detail of a small country with him. Local residents were terrified. The government's investigation into Death Row's funding sources meant that the feds were turning Interscope upside down looking for information. Jeff said that for CAA and most of the major talent agencies in town, anything connected with Death

Row Records was untouchable. Serious money had been made and there had been serious consequences. Death Row artists and employees had been beaten up or killed. The company, which had been doing $150 million a year at its zenith was careening toward bankruptcy. From Jeff's standpoint, it was not a story anyone in town wanted to touch.

Jeff had had a number of meetings with Lydia Harris and knew her better than anyone I knew. He told me, *"She calls herself a singer. But she's really a gangster's moll."*

My own impression of Lydia was that she was a woman whose defining quality appeared to be her dedication to securing her husband's early release from prison. Everything in her personality seemed to accrue from that need. While living in the Houston area, she'd known some people connected with a label there called Rap-a-Lot Records. Michael Harris had had an early affiliation with that label and Lydia had met Michael through those associations. She'd fallen in love with him and he'd brought her to Los Angeles before he'd gone to prison. I sympathized with her because I got the sense of a woman trying to do right by her husband who was also very much out of her depth.

When I think back on it now, I marvel at how effective Lydia was in that initial meeting. She told me I was the only person she wanted to be in business with. *"Everything's in place. You've done documentaries and have your own distribution company."* She said things like *"Mike's a money making machine"* and that any film I did with him would be Xenon's version of Dr. Dre's seminal album, *The Chronic.* She knew how to make you sympathize with her. She was a woman all by herself, fighting wars in the jungles of the music industry. She told me that she and Mike had put together one of the biggest partnerships in the history of the music business and had gotten screwed out of millions.

It was a very compelling story, heads and shoulders better than virtually any true life story I'd ever heard.

Even so, people always ask *"Why did you go forward?"* And, to this day, I don't have an explanation that satisfies me or anyone else. It just comes down to the root of what operates in the beating heart of any entrepreneur: a certain naïve hubris.

At that point in my life, I'd followed my instincts on several projects that no one else in the United States had been able to accomplish before me. And in each case my instincts and thinking had been correct. I'd done Jay Leno's first live concert. I'd done the first full biography on Dr. Martin Luther King Jr. that had been authorized by the King Foundation. I'd built the first independent infrastructure and developed the first label to distribute independent Black Cinema in the U.S. home entertainment market. And in each case, before I'd embarked on the journey, I'd been told that the task was impossible.

This leitmotif seemed to define my life.

I wasn't that sure about everything Lydia had told me. She had an edge to her and she seemed very impatient. But I knew I could never do this story without Michael Harris' help. And Michael had all his eggs in Lydia's basket. Suge Knight was in jail and there was no way things were going to work out with him. Did I want to put my lot with a fearsome megalomaniacal control freak with a truckload of skeleton's to hide? Or with a fearsome legendary O.G. who'd provided the guidance and capital that had gotten Death Row off the ground? Not a lot of analysis was needed there. Additionally, it was clear to me that if this story was going to be captured, the time was now. There was a short window of time, when the story was still fresh and people loyal to Harry O were still willing to talk.

In a few short years, many of the key people we would interview would be dead.

The die was cast. If we were going to go down this road, we had to be in business with Michael and Lydia Harris.

In assembling my team for *Welcome to Death Row*, my first choice for producer was Jeff Scheftel. Jeff was a well-respected documentarian whose personal connections ran everywhere, especially in the music industry. Jeff had directed Xenon's previous documentary, *Mahalia Jackson: The Power and the Glory* and had a good relationship with Steve Housden, Xenon's Chief Operating Officer. Jeff was also an excellent interviewer and apart from being good at what he did, he was good company. He was fun to be around. People liked him.

But there was another reason I felt I needed Jeff for this film: *He had balls of steel.*

When I called him about the project, Jeff said, "*It's a great story. But if you start this project, they'll be a price on our heads. If we survive this, it will be a miracle.*"

And then he added "*I'm in.*"

South Central Los Angeles '80-'86

Gangsta rap, the music genre that propelled Death Row Records into the national spotlight, emerged from the West Coast hip hop scene of the 1980s. Receiving almost no radio play or mainstream promotion, it was truly a word of mouth phenomenon.

Fed up with the soft platitudes of the so-called "Jheri Curl R & B" that was the predominate trend of urban music at the time, a number of mostly unknown artists began recording songs on mostly low quality home recording devices that captured the grit, personalities, and pathology that existed in their inner city Los Angeles neighborhoods.

Like much of early 80s hip hop, gangsta rap was spread by radio DJs who moonlighted at house parties and public dances held in skating rinks, small convention centers, and veterans halls, assisted by street promoters who advertised the events through posters and flyers. Many of them participated in "record pools" which gave them access to advance copies of LPs from both established and smaller labels. In exchange for free records, the DJs provided feedback on the public's responses to different songs and styles. The overwhelming reaction of younger Black consumers to rap beats and lyrics of this new brand of story-telling convinced promoters they were on the verge of a new era in music.

ALLEN GORDON: I became interested in rap music in 1979. I listened to the Sugar Hill Gang's *Rapper's Delight* on a Bay area radio station. Ever since then, I had a hunger for anything that sounded like rappers or rap. I started going to house parties with the older guys in the neighborhood and a couple of them had relatives in New York. They would bring back tapes of parties that were being played and it was just different. The sound was like… a whole new world opened up.

11

MATT McDANIEL: Everything was underground. Not a lot was available in record stores. (The records) were mainly available at swap meets or out of the trunks of people's cars.

ALLEN GORDON: I was interested in how the guys were talking, how they were puttin' their words together. It was different from listening to disco, R & B, or rock. I was a big fan of Fleetwood Mac, KISS, AC/DC, and Michael Jackson and it was totally different. And when I moved to LA, my first experience with actually seeing rap face-to-face was with gang members. They'd be passing the time in those neighborhoods, just rapping back and forth.

DOUG YOUNG: The promotional aspect of the music game was my niche. One of my friends once told me that I could talk a cat off a tuna truck. I was always able to go in and talk to program directors or music directors and get records added or go into clubs and get 'em played.

SNOOP DOGG: My earliest recollections of hip hop was probably King T. He had a song called *Payback is a Mutherfucker*. Ice-T *Six in the Morning*. I liked *Rockberry* by the LA Dream Team. Songs like that just started breaking through for me. I felt it was easy to do that. LA Dream Team was doing nursery rhyme raps and Ice-T was doing hard core street rhymes. I felt like I could do both of them. If I put them both together, I could create my own style.

KEVIN POWELL: I was born in Jersey City, New Jersey. Working class, single mom, welfare - whole nine yards. I was a graffiti artist, a writer and a breakdancer. I started hanging around the hip hop community working with a lot of different people like Public Enemy, Sister Soldier, Doug E Fresh. By the late 80s, I was pursuing a career as a news reporter.

RUDY PARDEE: At the time, the East Coast had L.L. Cool J and

Run DMC. Their music was more drum machine, more beats with some scratchin' and samples here and there. Whereas the West Coast music was more electronic - we were more musical. You heard more keyboards. It was more of an upbeat, danceable type-thing and I think that's where the East Coast / West Coast rivalry came from; the East Coast guys would say *"Your music's too musical. "* But out here, they was diggin' it. I remember one L.L. Cool J album that was nothin' but drum machines and rapping with some scratching.

GARY JACKSON: A lot of people didn't get it. They hadn't realized that the phenomenon had been growing for so long in New York. By 1984, it had gotten a little clichéd despite the efforts of Grandmaster Flash, Cold Crush, Treacherous Speed, or Kurtis Blow. But when Run DMC came about and sort of married rock and rap together, that made it more of a viable entity.

ALLEN GORDON: Run DMC. Fat Boys. Houdini. I just listened to them over and over again until '85, '86, '87 when the twelve inch rap albums started coming to California. We'd go down to Leopold's Records and pick up a W Fresh single or Steady B, anybody that came out at the time. It didn't matter if they were good or bad, just as long as it was rap. It was the thing to buy.

DOUG YOUNG: Back in those days, you had a lot of clubs. So they tried to tell me *"Well, you could come into this club as long as what you're promoting ain't rap."* I'd say, "Well, they ain't rap, if that's what you want me to tell you. Okay. It ain't rap."

JEFFREY JOLSON COLBURN: There's a whole circuit of little Friday night parties where they spin records and the DJs and the MCs come out and play. It's the equivalent of playing nightclubs if you're a rock band. But here, you just go out and rap at these parties with your MC. You have little two and three man teams that go out to the parties, usually at a warehouse. And then there's street plastering, where they put up posters at whatever level they can afford, nice color pictures or just a logo on a piece of mimeograph paper.

S. LEIGH SAVIDGE: During this time, future N.W.A. members Dr. Dre, Eric *Eazy E* Wright and DJ Yella had a small entity called High Powered Productions. Eazy would organize the venues, often borrowing them without the owner's knowledge and Dre and Yella would present the music on an elevated stage.

SNOOP DOGG: I was always one of the most popular kids in school because I was more like a clown. We had this thing called *bagging*. I was bagging on people like a comedian because I was good at telling jokes. I was known for clowning. I went from bagging to rapping and getting a lot of attention in school. Getting suspended.

MC REN: I was in a little group and we'd go to house parties in matching outfits, our hats on the side…thought we was doin' something. I wrote battle rhymes about myself, like everybody else, cuz that's all people talked about in those days.

DOUG YOUNG: With rap music, there was no (payola). If it was good, you didn't have to spend a single dime. If a (club) DJ knew you was gonna always give him first dibs on your good stuff, he would put your music on immediately. And that's where your credibility came in. If you say that something is good, it has to be good. Because if it's not, after a while people gonna be smirkin' – "*Ah, here come that fool with his hands full of white junk.*" When I was out promotin' N.W.A. and stuff like that, people knew that I always had good records.

TRACY KENDRICK: There's this thing called record pools where DJs get promotional copies of records for paying a fee. I joined a pool of DJs that later would make a difference in rap business….wanting to do what they were doing in New York.

ALLEN GORDON: The process of albums going from region to

region is by word of mouth. Nobody that I know in California has parents that were born here. My parents are from Alabama, Ohio, by way of Philadelphia. Many people have grandparents from Louisiana and Texas, and you don't want to be bored with your relatives on summer vacations or family reunions so you take your tapes with you. You're playin' music, and people ask, *"Hey, what's that? Let me duplicate that."* So you go for the double cassette recorder or you lend it to them and they'll send it back to you. And we'd ride around in cars with kids from Louisiana, Chicago, Detroit, Alabama, New York. Everybody would bring the tapes they had at home.

MASTER P: If you couldn't get into the swap meets in LA, you was in trouble.

SNOOP DOGG: I used to sneak into a lot of house parties. I was young. I'd get a chance to rap on the microphone against some of the older cats and the word spread. You know, *"Snoop is tight."* We had a few concerts in Long Beach - The Fresh Fest - but they ended up violent. It was gang bang mayhem. Run DMC was there. Houdini. There were no West Coast artists there (except me). All East Coast. Everybody tripped out.

South Los Angeles-based KDAY became the first radio station in the country to play non-stop hip hop. An AM station with a 50,000 watt directional signal, KDAY was run by musical director Greg Mack, and has been credited with helping put the then unknown group N.W.A. on the top of the Billboard charts.

LAMONT BRUMFIELD: When did radio start to accept rap music? It goes back to the KDAY days. FM stations weren't really (playing) rap until they heard that everyone from L.A. was tuned into this one radio station called KDAY. It sounded all staticy - you could barely hear it. Only between Crenshaw and Western Avenue and you could barely hear it even there. KDAY played the rap stuff that everybody liked. So I guess all the other stations got hip to it and it just grew. I guess they had to adapt -

everybody was about makin' money and rap was makin' money, so they started playin' it.

RUDY PARDEE: The music director at that time was Greg Mack. And that guy was really instrumental in the development of West Coast rap music. A lot of people forget about that, but I'll never forget that he was the guy who gave everybody out here (on the west coast) a chance.

JERRY HELLER: (1) It was a lo-fi, low rent, low rise kind of enterprise. I'd be tuned into KDAY in the car on my way home to the Valley, 1580 on the AM band and as I would drive over the Cahuenga Pass, the signal began to drift. One second I'd be listening to the World Class Wrecking Cru doing *Juice*, and all of a sudden I'd hear Kenny Rogers break in from a more powerful Country station in the Valley.

MATT MCDANIEL: KDAY ended up being the place where the whole L.A. hip hop scene was born. At that time, you could walk in off the street, get your record heard and played on the radio the same day. If you had KDAY playin' your record, it's a whole different story. The whole city knew about it.

DOVE C: KDAY created the *Mix Master Show*. They went out to the community. (Greg Mack) would be settin' up there in Watts, in L.A., Inglewood, Carson, Long Beach. They'd be out there with their vans broadcasting live and then they'd take it to the clubs.

GREEDY GREG: What opened up the radio to rap music was its popularity in the clubs. And the danceable beats really made it open to radio, cause radio was kinda bogged down with the ballads. And kids don't like to hear ballads - they want to hear somethin' up, up tempo that they can dance and party and have a good time to.

Lacking any major label connections, many rappers would press *their own records and sell them at local swap meets. A well-known duplication facility was Macola Records in Hollywood, where $1,000 would buy 500 LPs. For many L.A. rap artists, Macola served as a de facto record label.*

RUDY PARDEE: I found out about Macola Records. (It was) located on Santa Monica Boulevard in Hollywood. They'd say *"You pay us a thousand dollars and we'll give you five hundred records to put in the trunk of your car. And we'll take another two or three hundred and ship 'em to our guys we distribute to."*

DOUG YOUNG: I had a bunch of the old N.W.A. stuff, *Straight Outta Compton*. I got three dollars for a 12 inch record because it was in the Macola jacket. And now I hear the 12 inches sell for like 50 bucks if you got the original Macola stamp *Distributed by Macola Records*. And a 100 bucks in Europe. This is for vinyl.

RUDY PARDEE: Macola Records gave me the opportunity to start my own record label. And the opportunity to put something on vinyl and be able to hand it to somebody and say *"Here's my record."* Now, we go to KDAY and say *"Here's our record"* and Greg Mack would decide whether it was good enough for air play. KDAY used to have a thing called *Lunch Time Jams*, where the station would do a remote every day at different high schools. I was the mobile DJ for KDAY. I knew everybody. So when I did a record, I felt comfortable taking it to him.

Alonzo Williams was a local entrepreneur who owned a nightclub called Eve After Dark. He was one of first entrepreneurs in South Central Los Angeles to understand how the wholesaling of quasi-legal or bootleg records could inform the kind of new music that would appeal to those in the inner city. Bootlegging became one the chief methods of advertising promising but largely unknown records or emerging artists. Pressing plants and audio cassettes made bootleg recordings easier to make, trade, ship and sell.

ALONZO WILLIAMS: We were bootleggers. Serious

bootleggers. We did all the mixes. Originally, we saw a couple of bootleg records in the record stores. So, I did some investigating to find out how I could make my own records. And my partner, Unknown, found this company in El Segundo that made records called Bill Smith's Custom Records. Unknown said *"Hey man, all we need is a four track recorder and a couple of these twelve hundred turntables and we can do this."* Twelve hundred turntables at that time were four hundred bucks a piece. And me being a businessman - I'm like *"That's too damn much money for some turntables. I have some Sanyo belt drives that work real well."* But he talked me into buying these turntables, and we started making these bootleg records. And we made a lot of money selling 'em. Before my club would open on Saturday night we'd make seven, eight thousand dollars - just sellin' bootlegs. But later we wanted to go legit.

GREEDY GREG: The bootleg actually helps you promote the record. So it's good that bootlegs are out there.

ALONZO WILLIAMS: Because of my bootlegging connections I was able to go back into the stores with my legitimate record and sell directly out of my truck to the stores. Our first real record was called *Slice* and it was a knock-off of Run DMC's, *It's Like That*. We sold about four or five thousand copies locally. For us that was a major achievement. Then we decided to make another twelve inch. It was called *Surgery*. Featured this little skinny little kid named Andre, supposedly a real dope DJ. And his mix was like the bomb - it was like something nobody'd ever heard before. You have two records that were totally different, and he made 'em match up beat for beat because of the twelve hundred turntables. And that was the introduction of Dr. Dre.

MATT MCDANIEL: Ice T would go to New York with a little palmcorder and tape DJ battles and come back to L.A. with the tape. It was just raw uncut footage. They started bootlegging this raw tape of the battle and selling it for $25 a copy.

WILLIE MOSS: You flood the neighborhoods and the streets with tapes, samples, and it pays off.

Record promoters would play the music for street kids to gauge its potential and then flood the neighborhoods with tapes and cds to drive demand.

DOUG YOUNG: There's certain stores around the country that Black people own that I try and keep secret. If (a record) starts doin' something in these particular stores, you're about to have a huge hit on your hands.

ALLEN GORDON: There are big car cultures all across the country and everybody sits around and plays their music loud. All these big sound systems. When somebody comes by and plays something at a certain baseline, that grabs the attention and you end up finding out who the artist is.

MASTER P: On the West Coast, you gotta have a beat because of a lot of low riders. They chillin' with the girls and they want to hear that music pounding. If you ain't creative enough to make sure the trunk's going to rattle, you ain't going to get the love out there.

DOREADOR: The streets are important to rap music because there's nothing to do but listen to music. It keeps you out of trouble. It makes you wanna make enough money to buy tapes.

LAMONT BLUMFIELD: How do you market to the streets? You just let the little kids listen to it and if they like it, they be shaken' their heads and you know you got something. So long as we be bobbin' our heads, the hits are gonna keep coming.

ALLEN GORDON: Hip hop has its own little caste system. And the cool kids are the hard knocks, the graffiti writers, the gang members who dance and the gang members who run, the most street-oriented kids. That's where all the cool comes from. What they play, everybody else plays. What they do, everybody else wants to emulate because that's the measuring stick of coolness in the neighborhood.

SNOOP DOGG: When I went to jail, I didn't lose focus. I just figured it was a down period in my time and I (could) come up as long as I had people believing in me. When I would rap in jail, everyone would tell me, *"Snoop, you got it. You need to get out of here and do something with yourself. "* So I took what they told me and put it to use.

The lucrative crack trade of the mid 80s fueled the explosion of Black, Latino and Asian street gangs, the most notorious being the rival Crips and Bloods of South Central Los Angeles. The house party and gang scene soon became intertwined, with drug dealers featured in the story lines of rap songs. The often out-sized audio systems in a number of cars served as traveling radios in a number of the South Central Los Angeles neighborhoods.

STUDIO TONE: It was a heavy drug scene in Los Angeles and there were a lot of guys experiencing that and they took it to their music. And in the drug scene, you have a gangsta mentality.

S. LEIGH SAVIDGE: During our interviews, many people emphasized how important the loud, booming, in-car, sound systems were to driving sales on some of the music that the driver would choose to play. One guy who watched a number of our interviews for *Welcome to Death Row* claimed to have the best equipped in-car sound system in South Central. He suggested that, for a time, he'd single-handedly been responsible for most of the music that was sold at the Roadium Swap Meet in Torrance.

STUDIO TONE: The relationship between crack and record sales is a major thing. From like 1985-1990, there's a major crack gang goin' on out there on the streets. And all the dealers had major sound systems in their cars - major fancy cars and they (played) all the latest releases. Puttin' that stuff in their cars and (people asking) "*Hey, what's he playin'? That sounds good.*" And then they'd go buy it.

DOVE C: You couldn't roll in your car if you didn't have no cool shit playin' in it. Just as long as you had the sounds, you'd have the bitches. You could be rollin' along on buckets and a hose - but the sound was everything.

STUDIO TONE: It doesn't exist that way anymore. You don't see as many cars riding around with the big sound systems booming, with the big fancy spoke wheels. And it's reflected in the record sales. If you listen to the lyrics on a lotta gangsta rap, they're talking about "*my turf,*" and "*my block, my yay yo*" -- that's cocaine, "*my nine*" meaning my weapons. These things are all associated with selling drugs. And I guess a little pimping here and there. It's the illegal stuff in life.

In the mid 1980s, the city of Compton, California, a once-thriving suburb of the Black middle class, succumbed to the crack epidemic and became the epicenter of Los Angeles gang violence. Against this backdrop, Alonzo Williams was bringing together the artists that would later make up the rap group N.W.A. and seed the genesis of Death Row Records. Future N.W.A. members Dr. Dre and DJ Yella were part of William's dance group the World Class Wreckin' Cru and Dre moonlighted as a DJ at Eve After Dark. The Wrecking Cru had a small hit called Turn Out the Lights.

ALONZO WILLIAMS: I opened Eve After Dark in 1979. I was twenty-one years old. We were still playing R&B at the time, but rap was starting to move. We were promoting dances - everybody was promoting dances. That was how you made your money. There was no dope game at the time so everybody was a promoter. My partner was Unknown DJ, a buddy of mine. The club started out off a little slow because we were in a real rough neighborhood. It was a whole different scene; everybody wore skinny ties and suits to work every day at the club. We made money on Friday and went shoppin' Saturday morning to wear something new at the club on Saturday night. I started promoting concerts to get the club rolling. I promoted Run DMC. They came out, they did a good job. But we realized they had a different vibe. We picked 'em up from the airport. And these guys got on leather pants. And this is December. But for us it's hot! And they looked at us like we was a bunch of faggots. We had on ties and shirts and suits. So there was no real bond there.

JOHN KING: Dre used to be a DJ in a nightclub, so he knew what people wanted to hear.

KEVIN POWELL: The World Class Wrecking Cru is really the foundation for N.W.A. Alonzo Williams was very important to Dre's early development.

S. LEIGH SAVIDGE: In his book, *Ruthless*, Jerry Heller, who managed the World Class Wrecking Cru, describes Alonzo as someone who wanted to be *"The next Berry Gordy."* By the early eighties he owned a club, a record label, Kru-Cut Records, controlled his own publishing, had a wholesale-only distribution deal with Macola Records and fronted the World Class Wrecking Cru.

ALONZO WILLIAMS: The World Class Wrecking Cru got a lot of flack and got laughed at cause we wore sequins and I had a long Jheri curl with a weave. But remember, our predecessors were Prince, Morris Day, Rick James, and Bar Kays.

JERRY HELLER: (from Ruthless) Lonzo dressed the Wrecking Cru in the style of Prince Rogers Nelson (a.k.a. Prince), in matching outfits of lavender satin, with sequin touches and lace gloves. Since Lonzo had started off as a dancer, he paid particular attention to choreography, modeling his groups after The Temptations.

ALLEN GORDON: Dre started off as a member of the World Class Wrecking Cru.

RUDY PARDEE: I thought Dre was good, always. He was the one musically behind The World Class Wrecking Cru. A lot of people think it was Alonzo. It was his group. But Dre was the creative force behind a lot of the music.

ALONZO WILLIAMS: Dr. Dre produced most of the songs (for the Wrecking Cru). My function was financier. We collaborated on the lyrics depending on what the song was. We often bumped heads on different things because I'm actually nine years older than everybody in the group so I came from a different era and a different mind-set. We always had conflict about what we were gonna do, how we were gonna look. That's what eventually broke us up.

STUDIO TONE: When he first started out, Dr. Dre was a DJ. And when he began producing music, he incorporated a lot of scratching stuff into it. And then he was sampling and doing a lot of replays, you know, and basically had a different style.

DOUG YOUNG: My job was to get the record out there - goin' to swap meets, goin' to schools, to barber shops, to the cruisin' spots, to the hangouts. I was one of the few brothers that could hang out with the Crips and the Bloods. 'Cause they all knew me as *"The CD Man."* I could be in Rialto hangin' out with Bloods and then roll over to Fontana and hang out with the Crips. Cause I always had tapes and cds for them. When the Los Angeles riots started, I was promotin' some records when they were snatchin' brothers out of their trucks. And these fools was about to get me, too. Well one dude remembered me , *"Hey, that's the tape man -- don't take his car!"*

ALONZO WILLIAMS: Soon stores were asking for three or four thousand of our records every week. I heard about this guy named (Don MacMillian) over on Santa Monica Boulevard. And I went and talked to him and I gave him the record. Next thing I know, I'm getting calls from Texas, Sacramento, all over the country for us to come perform these records. Again we were just four DJs from Compton that were just trying to do something locally and it turned into a regional thing. We're selling records up and down the coast, and now we have to go on tour. We had no show, no idea of what we'd do on stage and we just got in a U-Haul Truck one day, we started rehearsing first, and drove up to Sacramento and did what we called *our show* in Sacramento. It was myself, Dr. Dre, DJ Yella, and a brother named Clientele. And people loved us. We started doing shows every weekend.

NATE DOGG: I hooked up with Dre through his brother Warren G. We used to do demo tapes all the time, me, Snoop and Warren. We must have sent Dre about ten of 'em before he listened to one.

ALONZO WILLIAMS: Dre was always a ladies' man. When I met him he had three or four kids, at seventeen years old, and he's callin' hisself *"The Love Doc."* And he was Doc so we named him Dr. Dre. And that was the beginning of his career. I always felt like I was his big brother. He would come to me with all his girl problems, his D.A. problems - I tried to school him. He was makin' babies like a rabbit.   I often lied for him when he had problems with his girls – I'd cover for him. We'd spend a lotta time talkin' together. We would always hang out together during the week, cause it was always good to ride with somebody. With him I can get in the Diamond Lane. He'd get in the car, close the door, and before you'd put the car in drive and pull out of the driveway, he'd be asleep. But it was better than havin' one of them dummies in the passenger seat.

Lured by the promise of glitz and glory in the music business, future Ruthless and Death Row promoter, Doug Young dropped out of San Jose State and moved to Los Angeles. He began promoting an album called Sex Appeal from the recording artist Giorgio, who was a childhood friend. Sex Appeal was pressed at Macola where Young met owner Don MacMillian, who hired him to promote some Macola releases and Jerry Heller, who was managing a small stable of artists including The World Class Wrecking Cru.

JERRY HELLER: (from *Ruthless*) Don MacMillian had been kicking around the manufacturing end of making music forever. At Macola, he was using his expertise to service the needs of hordes of aspiring artists from all over Los Angeles.

Artists whose records were distributed through Macola during this period included future superstars Ice-T and MC Hammer.

DOUG YOUNG: Don and Jerry were pretty tight friends. Jerry used to cherry pick artists. They would get an inside scoop on who was doing what. Don would tell him how much the record was selling so (Jerry) could go in and tell the artist, " *Look, I could do this, that and the other for you."*

S. LEIGH SAVIDGE: Doug told us that he had worked out an arrangement with Giorgio to get a significant share of the proceeds from a multi-million dollar deal that Jerry Heller had executed with Motown in the wake of the success of *Sex Appeal.* When Giorgio refused to pay him, Young, who had a wife and a new baby on the way, went to Don MacMillian at Macola and asked him for a job. McMillan gave him some records to promote. One of those records was *Turn Out the Lights* from the World Class Wrecking Cru. The song was produced by Dr. Dre and featured a singer named Michel'le. Later, MacMillan introduced Young to Jerry Heller.

DOUG YOUNG: Jerry Heller couldn't believe what happened. I told Jerry the story that Giorgio didn't pay me. I didn't make no money from that...that I got it (*Sex Appeal*) on all the radio stations - got it in all the clubs. Jerry just could not believe it. He felt real bad And he said, *"I got something for you."*

Living to Testify

Though it was not contractually mandated, Michael and Lydia Harris made it clear early on that they wanted a Black director and a Black editor for the film. My response was *"Fine. But who we hire is a skill issue not a race issue."* For years, I'd been posing a question to people *"Okay, what's the hardest thing to do in the world?"* Then I'd answer my question: *"Number one: curing global poverty. Number two: climbing Mt. Everest. Number three: Making a great documentary film."*

I'd seen hundreds of documentaries and 98% of them simply didn't work. It took a special mix of people to do it well.

To find a director, Steve Housden and I spent weeks calling around to filmmakers we had done business with. The response was almost a universal *no*. There was a certain amount of intrigue in the project but a pronounced reluctance to be involved in any way with the Harrises or Death Row. The typical response was *"You guys are fucking crazy."* We finally settled on Chicago-based filmmaker, Darryl Roberts, whose enthusiasm stood out from the rest of the people we'd talked to. Darryl had been a local entertainment reporter in Chicago and traveled in celebrity circles that included Michael Jordan and D.L. Hughley among others. But at his core, Darryl was a journalist.

Darryl had directed a highly regarded independent film, *How U Like Me Now* and had worked previously with cinematographer Michael Goi, who had a reputation for shooting interviews in a highly stylized way. Darryl and I agreed on a weekly salary and we hired Goi, who would later be nominated for an Emmy for his work on AMC's *American Horror Story*. Then we hired Karl Slater, an editor who Lydia really liked, who'd done some very stylized music videos. Later, an Avid editing machine was moved into Karl's house in North Hollywood.

I knew I couldn't afford to put Darryl up in a hotel for what looked to be a lengthy production process. So I moved him into the spare bedroom in my Santa Monica condo. He would be my roommate for the next year.

****

My first meeting with Michael Harris took place at a table in Lancaster's prison lunchroom. He was a tall imposing man, 6' 5," and about 250 pounds, and possessed the musculature of someone who had spent a lot of time in the prison's gym. Michael was smooth and very engaging. There is an expression I sometimes use when I encounter someone who is unusually verbally gifted: *Butter*. Michael was Butter. He had a way of disarming you, like you'd gotten the hype about him all wrong. He studied me fairly closely before presenting three different business concepts. He talked about an article about me that had appeared in *The Los Angeles Times* earlier that year and said "*We need to be in business together.*" When I mentioned that were already in business, Michael said "*Yeah. But we need to take it to another level.*"

The business venture Michael appeared to emphasize the most was called UGN, which referred to *Underground Network*. He suggested that the business would distribute music and DVDs in inner city markets throughout the U.S. He suggested that the entity would utilize inner city residents and would operate outside of traditional channels. He told me that UGN could rival the physical disc distribution infrastructures of the major entertainment concerns and be the dominant player for urban-themed entertainment products. It soon became clear that he wanted me to invest in these businesses.

Then he asked me for an advance on our contractually mandated payment schedule.

Butter.

It soon became apparent that indulging Michael in long free-associations relating to prospective businesses in the urban space was going to be part of my business process to get the film done. He had a keen intelligence, and was a master manipulator in that he could make you feel like you were saving his life on one hand but you needed him to stay alive on the other. *"My people have your back."* In many ways, he reminded me of some of the corporate executives and lawyers I'd dealt with. There was little doubt in my mind that if things in his life had cut a different way, he'd be on the street hustling to build a company. He was hungry for knowledge he didn't already have and talked ceaselessly about constructing a major enterprise from behind prison walls. When I told him I was backing the first Black-run film distribution company in South Africa he said *"Too early. It will never work."* And it turned out he was right.

My contract with Lydia had included a list of people the Harrises had represented that they could deliver who would speak on the subject of Michael's association with Death Row Records or because of Michael's involvement in the project. Michael said, *"I'm gonna give you a ghetto pass."* But determining what that meant wasn't very easy. I spent much of my initial meeting with him trying to understand the timetable in which interviews with these people could be secured and he kept deflecting the subject. His agenda on this day was focused on the businesses he wanted to build with Xenon as an investor. Throughout the meeting, he kept referring to *"my people"* which he indicated was this large network of people who were lined up to work for him.

In time, I would come to understand that most of Harry O's legendary resources had dried up and that *"my people"* referred only to one person - Lydia Harris. Most of Harry O's key associates had long since moved on.

****

As we dove into our interview process, I quickly found that Michael Harris and I were at cross purposes. Darryl, Jeff and I wanted people that could give us specific information about the process by which Death Row had evolved. We were especially interested in people that could give us information about the business dealings that hadn't been reported on in the media and were known only to a few insiders. For his part, Michael saw the film as a vehicle for his re-entry into the entertainment business. So his focus was on securing interviews with people he wanted to impress or do business with, in particular known or unknown recording artists that he was hoping to sign. Already in the fold was a producer named Battlecat, who would go on to have a major career.

Almost immediately, Jeff Scheftel started getting pressure from Michael to take a crew to Oakland to film some artists in that region. We spoke to Jeff and Darryl about it. *"Why Oakland? We're flying 20 people up there? Who are we getting?"* And they responded, *"We don't know. This is what Harry O wants."* Michael had told them that he had arranged to get some artists that were known to Tupac. But when Jeff and Daryl got there, they found very few people that were worth filming. Later, I got a call from Scheftel that one of our interviewees had pulled a gun and threatened to crush the skull of a hotel clerk at the hotel where the crew was staying.

The contretemps had come because Lydia had been dissatisfied with her suite. Jeff told me it was a really ugly scene. Some of Lydia's associates had physically threatened Ian Haufrect, our associate producer, when he refused to hand over some petty cash. Darryl Roberts had threatened to walk off the production unless an apology was given. Later, the crew had gone to a concert featuring rap artists E-40 and Too Short and at a post-concert party, shots had been fired and everyone had cleared out. Jeff said *"There was no reason to be here. We have to change our process here or we'll never get this done."*

One of the people we met in Oakland was a singer turned music producer named Jay King. In the late 80s, King had fronted a group called Club Nouveau and had won a Grammy covering Bill Withers 70s hit, *Lean On Me*. He would turn out to be one of the few people we'd meet who knew Michael well and could speak in a very succinct and concise manner about who he was and what had happened to him before, during and after his involvement with Suge Knight and Death Row.

During a trip to Los Angeles a few weeks later, Jay came to my office and we spoke for a while. I asked him if he knew the circumstances behind Michael's attempted murder conviction. He told me that a relative of Michael's, James Lester, had stolen money from him. A duo of kidnappers that may or may not have included Michael had kidnapped Lester, driven him out into a remote part of the California desert, shot him several times in the chest and left him for dead. King told me that after the kidnappers had left the scene, there was a dramatic weather change from (hot to cold) that had had the effect of closing Lester's wounds and reviving him. Subsequently, Lester crawled on his hands and knees several miles to a remote farmhouse, got the inhabitants to call the police and lived to be the government's star witness in the attempted murder case against Michael. Lester's testimony had put the gun in Harry O's hand.

King told me *"Mike doesn't trust anyone."* I soon learned that most of our conversation, minus the details about his murder case, had been relayed back to Michael.

Straight Outta Compton

The gangsta rap era essentially began with the group N.W.A.. Comprised of a variety of artists during its five year lifespan, the group's two most influential members, included Ice Cube, who would soon leave the group to pursue a solo career and Dr Dre, who would become the music genius behind Death Row Records. N.W.A. was founded in 1986 by a Compton drug dealer named Eric Wright a.k.a. Eazy E. who then formulated a record label called Ruthless with Jerry Heller. Originally called N.W.A. and the Posse, the group's first hit was the Ice Cube-penned Boyz in the Hood, which had originally been released as a single on Macola Records. Eazy E then released a solo album, Eazy-Duz-It which was quickly followed by N.W.A.'s debut album, Straight Outta Compton, released in 1988. The album took the nation by storm and, in spite of almost no radio play, sold over a million copies.

DAN O'DOWD: Something really special was coming out of that neighborhood. It was a fresh, really volatile time in music. I liken it to Elvis Presley, when rock and roll started, to when The Beatles came.

KEVIN POWELL: To understand *Niggaz With Attitude*, you've got to understand the 1980s in the Reagan era. I remember when crack hit our communities in '82, '83, and '84. Kids who had no money all of a sudden had huge houses and the best cars. And they had guns. I remember reading about police battering rams in Los Angeles going into people's houses. Real crazy stuff. It was like this all over urban America. N.W.A. would start to make the kind of music that reflected what was going on in these cities.

JERRY HELLER:(1) Imagine your own streets, your own city, your own neighbors under assault by a drug that basically makes people lose their minds. Crack cocaine hit Compton with a vengeance. A few short years later, an itinerant troupe of Compton street poets calling themselves N.W.A. records the horrors they have seen in their own lives, using their own language, rendering the images that have been indelibly seared upon their young eyeballs by the crack epidemic.

DOUG YOUNG: After a while, Michael Jackson didn't work. People didn't believe the hype. They didn't care. They didn't feel it with all that 'trying to be shy' nonsense. Rap was gritty.

SNOOP DOGG: My original rap name was Snoop Rock Ski. I was trying to be like Kool Rock Ski from the Fat Boys. My first rhyme was Snooper Rhyme.

ALONZO WILLIAMS: All over the country, they had pockets of young brothers who sold dope and had to carry 9mm pistols who had a wad of money who were linked.

JEFFREY JOLSON COLBURN: N.W.A. were more like street reporters. To the people writing and rapping this, it was very real. There were gunfights outside their window.

GREEDY GREG: N.W.A. to me was like anti-establishment.

MASTER P: I was listening to N.W.A. -- Ice Cube, Dr. Dre - that was the whole West Coast. N.W.A. had the whole scene locked down.

JAY KING: They had a message that was clearly heard and felt by young people.

JEFFREY JOLSON COLBURN: Dr. Dre was one of these guys that could take this raw street sound and turn it into the kind of magic and would hit to a wide audience. He could relate to street rappers and take their stories and tell them in music that would be acceptable to both Black and White audiences. White audiences loved the beats and they loved the gritty stories.

RUDY PARDEE: N.W.A. was bringing South Central to the forefront with drugs and the whole shot - hitting an element of society that no one had touched on.

SNOOP DOGG: When I went and got N.W.A., I bought them as a fan. I wanted to hear what Cube was gonna say, how Eazy was gonna talk bad about a bitch, how Dre was gonna break the beat down and how Ren was gonna grove the track and be hard.

DOUG YOUNG: You had an all-star cast of people: Eazy E was the mastermind, Cube the rhyme writer, Dre laid down the tracks and the producer and Ren played the supporting cast. That made them one of the greatest groups in hip hop.

JEFFREY JOLSON COLBURN: As most rap fans know, N.W.A. was the first band to breed sub-bands. Now everyone has their spin-off acts. This whole model was set up by N.W.A., whose four core members all went off and had projects on their own.

SNOOP DOGG: The songs that really inspired me were *Dopeman* by Ice Cube, *Eazy Duz It* by Eazy E, King T's *Mixmaster Spade* and Breeze. He had a song called *Just Clownin'*.

JEFFREY JOLSON COLBURN: N.W.A. was hard core. *Straight Outta Compton* was like in your face. It wasn't like taking an Aerosmith song and putting a hip hop beat to it like Run DMC did.

KEVIN POWELL: Eazy made up the fact that these were hard core gangsters. Dre, Eazy, Cube - none of these guys were gangsters. They were able to create this image and sell it.

JOE ISGRO: N.W.A. was a phenomenon. (They had) an album that sold a million units that was never played on the radio. And I had to ask myself *"How did this happen? What went on here?"* It was done purely through street promotion and word of mouth.

KEVIN POWELL: I was in Elizabeth, New Jersey with some of my friends. One of them had a big car stereo system and started playing this record. I was like *"Where'd you get that from?"* Run DMC had set the stage for this kind of edgy rock attitude in hip hop and N.W.A. fell in right with that - talking very bluntly about the conditions in the community. As Chuck D said, *"It was all word of mouth."*

JAY KING: N.W.A. sold over a million albums. With rap music, once you're past five or six hundred thousand units, you've gone outside of the Black community. At that point you have Asians, Latins, Whites, Filipinos, Middle Eastern - you have different segments buying a record.

RUDY PARDEE: You had little White kids out there that was, you know, grew up in pop's country club and they wasn't havin' it. They wanted to hear N.W.A..

KEVIN POWELL: You can't talk about American music without talking about Black music. Why do we go from a Louis Armstrong to a Benny Goodman? Why did music that started with Louis Jordan and Big Mama Thornton and Little Richard and Bo Diddley become this phenomenon with Elvis Presley? When the Rolling Stones and The Beatles got to America, they didn't want to meet Elvis. They wanted to meet Little Richard and Chuck Berry.

JEFFREY JOLSON COLBURN: It became clear there weren't just 10 thousand kids listening to this. There were hundreds of thousands in each city.

MOBB: Everybody around the world was wearin' khakis and shades trying to be like N.W.A..

SNOOP DOGG: When I seen, you know, regular homies from the neighborhood that was just putting down real street rhymes, you know, it made us feel like we could do it. I had to be 17 or 18 years old. Trying to get mine.

DR DRE: (2) It's not what you know, it's what you can prove.

MC REN: (2) I think we're successful because we're telling it like it is, and you know, that's what people want to hear. Because they're sick of hearing about fairy tales and stuff like that.

TONE DEF: They talked about being gangstas. *Gangsta, Gangsta* was a big hit. *Fuck Tha Police* was a bigger hit.

EAZY E: (2) We don't tell you what to do and we don't tell you what not to do. You got your own freedom of choice. They're trying to hold us back because this record has cursing on it, or it said something, where you are talking about raping somebody.

MATT MCDANIEL: Eazy represented the hardcore little gangster on the street.

JEFFREY JOLSON COLBURN: Every kid wants something that's forbidden. Certainly this kind of imagery was. They couldn't even hear it on their regular radio stations.

DOVE C: Some of us really did live that criminal life. We called it gangster rap. The approach, the vulgarness - we didn't play by the rules. We didn't come in sayin', "*You can't cuss - you gotta make records for the radio.*"

TRACY KENDRICK: I remember getting a record by N.W.A. and it was called *Gangsta, Gangsta*. The quality of the record was just incredible. I don't think they was cursing just to be cursing. And I was shocked they could put it down like that and make it work musically and lyrically. And how they're able to make a clean version, but still give you the same idea. It gave you the same picture - the same message - using two different languages - the street language and the radio language.

ALONZO WILLIAMS: At the time, all the rappers were claiming their home towns - South Bronx, New York, Queens. We were from Compton. Nobody wanted to be from Compton, OK? "*Oh man, we can't be from Compton. We gotta be from Carson or Gardena.*" I said, "*You went to Compton High School. How you gonna be from Gardena?*" A few years later it was, "*Yeah, we're from Compton!* "

DR DRE: (3) Coming up in the ghetto, period, builds character man. You know what I'm saying? It can definitely build character in a positive way.

ALONZO WILLIAMS: Dre was never a bad ass. I remember him telling me at the dining room table that he'd never had a fight in his life. Okay, now these guys are *Niggaz With Attitude?* When I first met Eazy, he was holding his eye cause his girlfriend, Joyce, hit him in the head with a G.I. Joe lunchbox and gave him a black eye. So I knew he wasn't a real tough guy. Yella was cool, but when the fights broke out in the club, he wasn't in the middle and Dre left the club completely.

MATT MCDANIEL: I knew Eazy was selling drugs. He was like a lotta other young people in the 80s, when cocaine was off the hook. People were selling cocaine and making a lot of money. He was the first person that came out and admitted it and boasted about it on a record.

ALONZO WILLIAMS: I first met Eazy when he used to come to my club. Eazy used to wear tennis shoes and white T-shirts all the time. At the club, everybody would be wearing those skinny ties looking like Morris Day and the Time. So he couldn't come into the club. Plus he looked like he was 13 or 14 even though he was the same age as Dre. The club was 18 and over and Eazy didn't fit the make-up. He would always get on my nerves. One day, he came back and put on a tie and a shirt. I let him in because he was Dre's buddy.

JEFFREY JOLSON-COLBURN: Eazy E turned out to have some business savvy.

ALONZO WILLIAMS: Eazy was a local crack slinger, okay? Made him some money. And because I was one of the few guys he knew that had a studio, he wanted to get with me. He was not intending to be a rapper. He was going to be a financier. Then he started to get a grasp of the music industry,

A near death experience during a drug run was probably the titular event in Eazy's life that led him to examine music creation and distribution more carefully. Drive-by gunfire had killed a drug associate of Eazy's, a close friend named Anthony, who had been sitting in the passenger seat while Eazy was driving. Eazy had driven into a district in South Central that was allegedly the exclusive province of a rival dealer whose minions had decided to exact retribution. Eazy escaped without injury but many people I spoke to said he never forgot that incident, taking it as a sign that he needed to leave the game.

ALONZO WILLIAMS: (Eazy) and I had a love-hate relationship. We would talk shit back and forth. I didn't dislike him. He was nothing spectacular to me. As Dre started getting more popular in the record scene, Eazy would start to come around more and more.

S. LEIGH SAVIDGE: According to Tomica Woods - Wright, the association between Eazy and Dre went back a number of years beginning with their partnership in High Powered Productions. But their home lives were different. Eazy's parents were together and both worked. Dre was the product of a broken home. Dre's mother was not enthusiastic about his pursuit of a career in music and Dre often slept at Eazy's house when he wasn't getting along with her.

ALONZO WILLIAMS: Dre was producing for me at Crew Cut Records and the Wreaking Cru. Dre started getting in trouble. He was going to jail for warrants on a regular basis.

S. LEIGH SAVIDGE: Lonzo told me that Dr. Dre was always in hock to him during the Wrecking Cru period and this was the issue that eventually caused a permanent schism between the two. He told me this story about coming out of Eve After Dark one night with Dre and Dre's car, which Lonzo had arranged for him to buy, and was in Lonzo's name, was parked on the street with several parking tickets on it. Dre just scooped up the tickets and threw them on the ground. Lonzo saw himself as a guy who took responsibility for things and saw Dre as a talented fuck-up who was always going to be broke. He said that the pivotal change in the relationship came when Dre got picked up on another warrant. He called Lonzo from jail and Lonzo wouldn't put up the money to get him out.

ALONZO WILLIAMS: Dre started getting in trouble. He was going to jail on a regular basis. Dre would wait until a ticket turned into a warrant, go to jail and then call somebody to get him out of jail. We're talking about $600-$700 bucks. This happened about 3-4 times during the CBS (Records) era. We were making little or no money. \ Every time he goes to jail, I'm digging in my pocket to get him out. I got tired of it. One Friday, they were about to ship him off to county jail and he asked me to page Eazy.

DOUG YOUNG: Eazy got him out of jail. It was only a couple thousand dollars.

ATRON GREGORY: The Wrecking Cru eventually split up but Alonzo also had a recording studio behind his house where he was developing other artists. And Easy E paid for some studio time and so did Dre. Dre had other things that he was interested in doing that were different from what Alonzo wanted to do. So he started working some with Eazy, who asked him to do more music for him.

KEVIN POWELL: Dre was like a lot of kids from the ghetto. A tremendous amount of raw talent. Zero knowledge of the music business.

ALONZO WILLIAMS: I wasn't going for a partnership. I was putting up too much money and information. Dre wanted his own label and (to) be one of the bosses.

DOUG YOUNG: Eazy knew that Dre was a dope producer.

ALONZO WILLIAMS: They cut a deal that Dre would do some tracks for Eazy in my studio. Eazy was not originally a rapper. He was going to be a financier for another rapper. But Eazy and the guy had a falling out over some money that hadn't been made yet.

Eazy met Ice Cube through Dre and the Wrecking Cru and was aware of Cube's growing reputation as a strong performer in local area groups like CIA. The relationship crystallized when the then 17-year - old Cube presented Eazy with the lyrics for the song that became Boyz in the Hood. Dre had invited a New York based group called HBO out to Los Angeles to record the song. But when conflicts arose between the HBO group members and Cube, Dre, and Eazy over a number of stylistic issues including the song's lyrics and meaning, Eazy asked them to leave. Dre then encouraged Eazy to try the song himself.

ALONZO WILLIAMS: Eazy figured he had tracks, he had money. It was like *"Shit, I'll do it myself."* That's how he got in front of a microphone. *"Just give me a shot."* We all laughed. It was like Mickey Mouse makes a record. You got this little guy talkin' all this gangsta shit, and you know this guy is like 5'1. There's no way anybody's gonna believe this shit. I used to call him Jimmy Cagney. It really worked for him.

S. LEIGH SAVIDGE: As is portrayed in the *Straight Outta Compton* film, Eazy required a lot of hand holding by Dre in that initial session for *Boyz in the Hood*. But against anything that anyone might have anticipated given his lack of formal training, Eazy soon demonstrated that he had innate, God-given abilities as a rapper.

ALONZO WILLIAMS: The initial demos were recorded in my studio on my MG 1212. I still got that locked away in a safe place 'cause I know it'll be worth some money one day.

MATT MCDANIEL: People were recording in sixteen track studios, pressing up a box of records and selling them out of the trunks of their cars.

The finish work on Boyz in the Hood was done at Audio Achievements in Torrance. The owner / engineer was Donovan Smith.

ALONZO WILLIAMS: That was our spot. Donovan was the man that was the *go to*. He was like a sick individual when it came to sound. He loved it so much. That's why the records sound so great. He made sure. That was his thing. He was an old biker cat. He'd make some of the worst shit sound fantastic. We all loved him.

S. LEIGH SAVIDGE: Lonzo told us that the money tendered from Eazy to Lonzo for the newly produced tracks reconciled all the debt between Lonzo and Dre. At the time, Lonzo saw this as the best way to get back the money Dre owed him.

ALONZO WILLIAMS: Because of my bootlegs and my connections, Eazy came to me to try and help him get into the local swap meets. I was the king of the swap meets. So I took him around to Mr. Chang and Mr. Park and all the guys I dealt with. But they couldn't play it because there was cussing. So he had to go back and do an edited version.

During that period, there were certain parallels to the business of localized drug dealing and the localized pressing and selling of records to local stores, swap meet vendors, and key individuals. In both cases, the key to success was to establish a network of people to sell to which was inextricably linked to having the best (the most dope) product.

KEVIN POWELL: There's a very fine line between street hustling and music industry hustling. Both worlds are peddling product as quickly as possible.

ALONZO WILLIAMS: We sat there in my living room and thought (Eazy) just might sell some records. *"Yeah, right. Not gonna happen."* We laughed about it. (Eazy) wanted me to take it to my friend Greg Mack at KDAY. It took him forever to play it. But they finally got a little spin on it. So I'm doing little spot promotions and he's starting to get a little buzz. Now it wasn't funny anymore. Instead of me going to the swap meet to drop off 300-400 records, now Eric is doing it. Then three to four hundred turns into two to three thousand and the guys I was selling to started buying from him. He was making money on the streets.

DOUG YOUNG: People always wondered how that stuff got played. Well, it was by my cleverness, my sneakiness and underhandedness doin' whatever it took. My rappers were killing those R&B fools. We got in the trenches of every 'hood.

ICE CUBE: (2) We used to ride around in Eazy's jeep all day and sell records at swap meets.

EAZY E: (2) I used to make people buy records…with a gun.

ALONZO WILLIAMS: Ruthless Records, that's another story. When Eric (Eazy) came to me wanting to form a label, he had several different names like Righteous Records. But he wanted something that was scandalous. Eazy and Dre were supposed to be partners in Ruthless. Dre was gonna do the beats and make the music and Eazy was gonna put the money up. They cut the deal in my living room. I'm the witness to everything. I'm like Forrest Gump!

ALONZO WILLIAMS: N.W.A. started off with maybe fifteen or sixteen cats, and all of a sudden fourteen cats are gone and Arabian was still there. All of a sudden Arabian got kicked to the curb. If you listen to some of the first N.W.A. records, Arabian Prince is there. Ice Cube wasn't there. Then they dropped Arabian and bought in Ice Cube. And Ren, I can't even tell you where Ren came from - he just showed up one day.

SNOOP DOGG: I wanted to be in N.W.A.. I felt I could be the missing link or fill a spot if anybody was to leave.

ALONZO WILLIAMS: They had several different names they kicked around and they came up with N.W.A.. That kinda stuck. It was *Niggers With Attitude*. And they're like niggers. And their attitude was shit. (They figured) *"Well, we're cussin' on our records so we might as well throw niggers in our name."* To make it cool, instead of spelling it with an *er* they added the *az* and it was *niggaz*. I guess that took some of the edge off when they changed the spelling. For awhile it was hard for them to say what it stood for. But once they got used to it and started getting some popularity, their chests started swelling up so they felt comfortable.

While managing the World Class Wreaking Crew, music industry veteran, Jerry Heller had been introduced to Eazy E by Alonzo Williams. The meeting happened at Macola Records. Eazy paid Alonzo $750 for the introduction. Jerry Heller grew up in Shaker Heights, Ohio which, in the late fifties, when he graduated from high school, was on its way to becoming one of the wealthiest communities in America. He attended Ohio University, and later USC, where he got a master's degree in finance. In his late twenties, with partner, Don Fischel, Heller established a management firm that represented major artists like Marvin Gaye and Creedence Clearwater Revival and *arranged tours for a who's who of high profile rock bands from that era including ELO, Crosby Stills and Nash, Led Zeppelin, Elton John, Pink Floyd and The Who. Heller was not afraid to mix it up with other up and coming music people of that era - clashing famously with other emerging moguls like David Geffen.*

DOUG YOUNG: Everybody that talk all that shit about Jerry got the story twisted. Jerry was there from the gate.

JEFFREY JOLSON COLBURN: Jerry Heller was a rap entrepreneur. (He) realized
very early that this kind of street poetry had a place. As head of Ruthless Management and Ruthless Records he helped N.W.A. find a larger, Whiter audience.

JERRY HELLER: (1) Joe Smith or David Geffen might have looked at me as if I were nuts, but I couldn't help it. I was down in the trenches with the little guys. This was just my kind of thing.

ALONZO WILLIAMS: I met Jerry Heller at Macola Records. He was a well-respected manager, a rock and roll manager. He was an older Jewish cat. He knew all about the record business.

S. LEIGH SAVIDGE: Heller told me he had trouble navigating the transition from disco into the punk era in music. Amid a bad divorce and alcohol dependency, he went into free-fall and his career hit the skids. By the mid-eighties, he was crashed on his mother's couch somewhere in the San Fernando Valley and talking about a comeback. During this time, he had an office down the hall from where future Priority Records founder, Bryan Turner, had an office. Jerry told me that at his lowest ebb, he came into work and found a padlock on his office door for unpaid rent. After an long time associate, Morey Alexander, told him about the emerging scene at Macola, he contacted owner, Don MacMillian, and took a shoebox sized office there.

ATRON GREGORY: I moved down to Los Angeles after I got out of school. My only relationship I had in the music business was with Jerry. Jerry was managing the World Class Wrecking Cru. They had an independent label called Kru-Cut Records. He introduced me to Alonzo and Alonzo and I started running Crew Cut Records together.

JERRY HELLER: (2) I was managing a group called the World Class Wreaking Cru, through a guy named Alonzo Williams, and Dre and Yella were in that group. They were involved tangentially with a group called CIA or the Stereo Crew and Jinx and Ice Cube were in that group.

S. LEIGH SAVIDGE: In a short period of time after settling in at Macola, Heller had been able to completely rebuild his career. In addition, to the World Class Wrecking Cru, Heller was managing most of the artists and groups on Lonzo's Kru-Cut Record label. One of those groups was C.I.A. (Crew in Action) which featured Ice Cube. Another artist was a young female singer named Michel'le (Toussant).

ATRON GREGORY: I ended up being the World Class Wrecking Cru's road manager as well. And when we were home, we'd work at Kru-Cut on sales of the World Class Wrecking Cru. We ended up doing C.I.A. and the Michel'le record *Turn Off the Lights*. CIA was Ice Cube's group.

ALONZO WILLIAMS: (Heller) was one of the few guys I met in the industry that would call you back, okay? And for a Black man from Compton, that makes you feel really good.

JERRY HELLER: (2) Eazy actually paid Alonzo 750 bucks to introduce him to me and to set up a meeting. So, that's how I met Eazy. He played me a track called *Boyz in the Hood*, which I thought was the most important song I had heard since the beginning of rock and roll.

S. LEIGH SAVIDGE: Jerry told me he was very burned out on the economics of the record industry at that point. Major labels were paying a fortune to retain or secure established acts and 90% of the industry's releases as a whole were either breaking even or losing money. Suddenly this *street guy* is playing him music that he loves that was created for a few thousand dollars and, as an added bonus, he's already got people locally that are buying the record.

DOUG YOUNG: Jerry saw Eazy's vision. That's when we were doing a hundred thirty beats a minute style, L.A. stuff. The real fast stuff, the supersonic stuff. And Eazy was about to slow the whole thing down.

JERRY HELLER: (2) I didn't know that (Eazy) was an artist, nor what N.W.A. stood for. I thought it stood for *"No Whites Allowed."*

The meeting of Jerry and Eazy was a perfect storm, a confluence of timing and need for both men. Heller knew most of the key people in positions of power at the record labels, he knew publishing and he understood the infrastructure that had to be put in place to get a label going. On Eazy's side, he knew - whether it was Jerry or someone else - he needed someone to help him with that.

KEVIN POWELL: What Jerry brought to the table was a knowledge of the music business. I don't think it matters what genre of music you work in. Once you know the business, you know the business.

RUDY PARDEE: And Jerry basically explained (to Eazy) that *"You guys are selling a lot of records, you guys are known. We want to take you to the next level."* He felt he could get a deal for us at a major record label.

S. LEIGH SAVIDGE: Heller understood, first and foremost that Eazy wanted his own label and he didn't want equity partners. So he played an important card by messaging early on, *"This is your company, I'll set up your company and get everything in place. And I'll take 20% for my services."*

DOUG YOUNG: In retrospect, Jerry Heller brought all the real money to rap. People can call him a cheap Jew all they want. But Jerry Heller taught me a lot of my game. I always say to myself when I'm in any business deal, *"What would Jerry Heller do?"* Jerry Heller brought all the real money to this game. New Yorkers know…they wasn't makin' shit.

S. LEIGH SAVIDGE: Jerry knew instinctively that to get the relationship with Eazy, he had to go *all in* which meant that he had to sever ties with the Wrecking Cru and everything else he was doing with Lonzo. Additionally, he has always maintained that he found critical funds to get Ruthless Records going and functioned as a financial partner to Eazy in the beginning. But Jerry probably also understood that he didn't want an ownership stake in Eazy's company. Eazy's life was chaotic. He had multiple kids by multiple women and already had a lot of people relying on him for money. Though he never said it to me explicitly, he probably deduced that he wanted his piece of the puzzle to be separate from all that.

ALONZO WILLIAMS: We didn't feel that Jerry Heller should be representing us and gangsta rap. I didn't have a problem with gangsta rap personally. But my partners did. What we were doing and what gangsta rap represented were two different things.

JERRY HELLER: (2) I called a meeting the next day at Martoni's restaurant in the back room. I told everybody that I was gonna be representing Ruthless and Eazy E and I'd help them find new management. But from that day forward, it was just gonna be Eazy E and I.

ALONZO WILLIAMS: We gave Jerry an ultimatum. Us or them. It reminded me of a Godfather movie. It was an Italian restaurant. We were in this private room and we got so loud they had to tell us to be quiet. So Jerry decided to cut us loose. And I respect him for that. From then on, we became distributors.

DOUG YOUNG: Jerry Heller told me *"I got a guy named Eazy E. He's about to put out a group. Here's some records; I'm gonna let you listen to some of this stuff and whichever ones you want to promote I'm gonna let you."*

After being turned down by any number of major distributors, Heller persuaded Bryan Turner at Priority Records to take over the release of N.W.A. and the Posse and release Eazy's solo album, Eazy Duz It, and Straight Outta Compton. Turner had formulated Priority after working at K-Tel, a direct response seller of music compilations on television. Prior to these releases, Priority had released two rap-oriented compilations but had developed only one act, the novelty group, The California Raisins. The group's recording of the Marvin Gaye song "I Heard it Through the Grapevine" and other well-known songs had landed them on the Billboard Hot 100.

S. LEIGH SAVIDGE: Heller encountered some headwind as he circled around to some of his old school cronies in search of a distributor that would embrace N.W.A.'s music. He told me about a meeting with legendary Capitol Records chief, Joe Smith. Heller played a few tracks for him and Smith had ordered him to turn the music off. Heller said Smith pointed to the iconic globe on top of the Capitol Records building and said *"See that globe? That is the home of the Beatles and some of the greatest music ever recorded. No way does this garbage ever get distributed by this company."* (In a few short years, Bryan Turner's Priority Records would be distributed by Capitol.)

DOUG YOUNG: At my first meeting with him, Eazy pulled up in a Suzuki Samurai with MC Ren - it was just them two. And they had on white t-shirts and blue khakis - I think Easy had on some gray khakis - lookin' like gang bangers. I said, *"Oh my God! Somebody hooked me up with some gang banger cats."* And Easy gave me a demo, and on that demo was a record called *Boyz in the Hood* and *Dope Man.* If I liked it, Eazy was gonna pay me five thousand dollars for four to six weeks to promote it. I told him *"Man, I love this."* I thought it was the dopest, the craziest stuff I ever heard in my life. Dre kicked in the bass. He's cursin' and talkin'. I'm like, *"Who are these crazy idiots?"* But it was clever - it was dope. The beat was bangin.' From there, everything started changing in L.A. hip hop.

Eazy and Heller broke ties with Macola after Eazy discovered that copies of N.W.A. and the Posse had been sold out the back door and not accounted for.

DOUG YOUNG: (Jerry) would ask for something outrageous. And he usually got it. I mean he got an outrageous deal for Ruthless with Priority. Remember Priority was only doin' the fuckin' *Raisins.*

S. LEIGH SAVIDGE: Eazy often wore dark sunglasses at business meetings. I asked Heller about this and he suggested that when negotiating, Eazy didn't want people to see his eyes - that it was an old hustler's trick to not let the person you were negotiating with understand what you were thinking. (In the late 90s, I had a meeting with Fubu CEO Daymond John. He came into Xenon's conference room wearing dark sunglasses, positioned himself at the opposite end of the table and was expressionless for most of the meeting. I remember thinking, *"He's channeling Eazy E."*)

The success of Ruthless Records began in 1988 with JJ Fad, an all girl R & B group that Jerry and Eazy were aware of because of the group's prior affiliation with Macola Records. Jerry Heller arranged to put the group's first album through the Atco unit of Atlantic Records and it quickly went platinum. Next up came the one-two punch of Eazy E's solo album, Eazy Duz It which was quickly followed by Straight Outta Compton. Both albums reached the market via Priority Records. Dr. Dre would produce all of these recordings. Eazy Duz It and Straight Outta Compton would both hit multi-platinum status.

JAY KING: Jerry Heller and Eazy were pretty brilliant at what they did.

KEVIN POWELL: Eazy was a business genius. Eazy is the one who started the process of setting up the artist. The fact that he could put out an album, *Straight Outta Compton* and each album could tease a new artist - *Straight Outta Compton* had DOC. And then you had DOC's album and he'll tease Michel'le or someone like that. That's the savvy marketing stuff that Death Row Records would eventually copy.

ATRON GREGORY: Easy E had a huge female following. There's always been a huge female base.

KEVIN POWELL: I went to Eazy's office in Woodland Hills. We were sitting in his office and there were lots of pictures of kids. And I said, *"Are those all your kids? How many do you have?"* He had these really little fingers and he counted one, two. He couldn't remember if it was five or six.

The DOC (a.k.a. Tracy Curry) was a singer and lyricist from Dallas who had been discovered by Dr. Dre and had become Ruthless Records second major solo act with an album called "No One Can Do It Better" which sold over a million copies. He was also the principal songwriter for much of the N.W.A. and Ruthless recordings.

ALLEN GORDON: Dre heard a tape of the Fila Fresh Crew (which was a group DOC was with in Dallas). He told DOC if you really want to make something happen, you need to come out to Los Angeles. DOC came to L.A. and stayed with Dre and helped form the Eazy E album (*Eazy Duz It*) and the *Straight Outta Compton* album.

THE DOC a.k.a. TRACY CURRY: (4) When it comes to making music, those guys (Eazy and the other artists) didn't know how to build songs back then. For the lack of a better word, they was just kind of street guys. And even though it was street music, music is like writing a book. It has to have a beginning, middle, and end.

MC REN: Everybody had to try to outdo each other. That's why it was so tight in those days. That's how you get tight. You have to have somebody back at you -- *"What you got?"*

ALONZO WILLIAMS: N.W.A. had just booked a tour. I went with them to the Carson Mall, to HQ - which is a sporting goods and gun store and these guys are buying automatic semi-automatic weapons to go on tour with. I'm like *"Shit! What kind of tour you guys going on? Vietnam?"* And these guys are buying serious artillery to go on tour! I said, *"I don't want to live like this."*

S. LEIGH SAVIDGE: Jerry Heller told me that he and Eazy went toe to toe over Eazy's decision to bring automatic weapons on the N.W.A. tour. Ultimately, they struck a compromise, agreeing that the weapons would be transported on a separate bus that carried the group's equipment.

Shortly before the first and only N.W.A. tour, Ruthless, and Priority Records received a letter from the FBI condemning its classic protest song, Fuck Tha Police. Written by assistant FBI director, Milt Ahlerich, the letter suggested that songs like Fuck Tha Police openly advocated violence and assault against policemen and requested that N.W.A. refrain from singing it in the future. The letter was sent to a number of law enforcement agencies throughout the country. As the N.W.A. tour kicked into gear, promoters in any number of American cities warned Jerry

Heller and Eazy E that there would be trouble if the group chose to sing the song. Many police departments on the various tour stops refused to provide security at NWA shows. The infamous N.W.A. / FBI letter can now be seen in the Rock and Roll Hall of Fame in Cleveland.

ATRON GREGORY: N.W.A. said something that everyone wanted to say. Everyone probably at that time period wanted to say *Fuck Tha Police.*

MASTER P: (*Fuck Tha Police*) kind of caught me off guard. It made you feel like you were part of it. Getting pulled over. Getting mishandled. A lot of people could relate to that. It was so real it made you open your eyes.

S. LEIGH SAVIDGE: Heller told me that getting security for the N.W.A. tour was a nightmare due to the infamous FBI letter. Law enforcement and off-duty cops simply refused to provide security at the shows in many of the cities.

ATRON GREGORY: N.W.A. had their last show in Detroit. The first and last show is always the scariest since everyone's energy is up and anything can happen. Now part of their contract stated they wouldn't perform *Fuck Tha Police* and *Straight Outta Compton*. No city wanted anyone to come in and say *Fuck Tha Police.*

S. LEIGH SAVIDGE: In a meeting I had with DJ Yella and Madeleine Smith (who handled publishing issues for Ruthless and later Tomica Woods-Wright), Yella suggested that prior to entering the stage in Detroit, Eazy had made the decision not do *Fuck Tha Police.* But when he got onstage and was able to gauge the sentiment and energy of the crowd, he changed his mind - shooting a signal to Dre, Cube and the other group members that suggested, *"It's On."*

ATRON GREGORY: When it was time for them to go on stage, I

was watchin' Ice Cube and Dre - they kept lookin' at each other and finally they just said *fuck it* and the song *Fuck Tha Police* came on. And the whole crowd went crazy. All of a sudden you heard boom - boom - boom in the audience. And one of my security guys saw people throwin' cherry bombs. And then the stage was stormed, and the security was fighting them off. Turns out that they were plainclothes cops. And to make a long story semi-short, the cops came back to their hotel and surrounded it. And the police really couldn't do anything except say *"You can't do this song in our town."* They ran a background check on their driver's licenses. And nobody had any warrants, so they had to let 'em go.

S. LEIGH SAVIDGE: The detainment and ultimate release of the N.W.A. artists in Detroit represented another close call for Eazy and Ruthless Records. Jerry told me that during the detainment, he worked furiously to get a driver to get the equipment bus that carried the automatic weapons across Michigan state lines.

In the wake of the explosive success of Ruthless Records, with JJ Fad's Supersonic, Eazy Duz It, and Straight Outta Compton all shipping platinum, key artists in the Ruthless Records roster began to view Jerry Heller as someone who was being overpaid versus what the artists were making and trouble began to brew. Ice Cube was the most vocal of the dissenting voices.

ALONZO WILLIAMS: When it looks like success is about to happen, that's when the shit starts. That's the characteristic of rappers, though. As long as we're doing local gigs, we're all homies, we're all buddies, drinking forty ounces. As soon as we can afford a bottle of Moet, we ain't buddies no more.

JERRY HELLER: (1) The first $250,000 slugged into Ruthless was mine and then I put up another million over the first few years of the label's existence. Thus I went against the sage advice of one of the smartest men I had ever met, David Geffen, whose business mantra was always OPM - other people's money.

JONATHAN CLARK: Most artists are taken advantage of because they're stupid. They're uneducated, dumb, chicken-shit and selfish. And somebody can come up to someone like that and offer 'em fifty dollars and they'll do anything.

LAMONT BRUMFIELD: They get ripped off because they're impatient. They're from the ghetto. Everybody know their situation. When somebody offers you a little money and you wanna be a rapper, what are you going to do? That's your opportunity.

HANK CALDWELL: I used to say *"We don't give advances, we give chances."*

DAN O'DOWD: N.W.A. could have lasted forever had there not been outside people, lawyers, finger-snappin' record label executives and people wanting a piece of the action. (N.W.A.) was selling out of the back of cars and they were making money and they were going to the top one way or the other. Add a few lawyers and business types and it started pulling apart.

Ice Cube and Heller were oil and water from the get-go. Cube was a budding entrepreneur in his own right, with the highest level of education of anyone in N.W.A., having attended Taft High School in the San Fernando Valley and later, an architectural school in Arizona. Cube saw the arrangement that Eazy had made with Jerry as a slap in his face. "I wrote Boyz in the Hood. Who is this guy? Why do we need him?" Eazy and Cube had been running buddies doing their small time business selling records at the swap meets and suddenly Eazy's in business with Jerry who's taking a dollar one percentage of everything that comes in from N.W.A. and Ruthless. Cube is being told he now works for Eazy and Jerry. Given the strong personalities of all three men, the center was probably never going to hold.

ALLEN GORDON: Ice Cube was making his solo album. He

was supposed to have the album after *Straight Outta Compton*. Then he got pushed back and the DOC's album came out. Then, when they were supposed to go into the studio and record Ice Cube's album, Jerry Heller, I'm told, interrupted that session and said *"No. We're trying to put out the Above the Law album - they need the studio time."* (That's) when Cube got frustrated and decided he was going to do his own thing.

MC REN: We was on tour and we was in Phoenix and Jerry Heller blew into town. He was like the one who signs the contracts. You know, we dumb. Give us $70,000. Everybody else had signed a contract but me and Cube.

S. LEIGH SAVIDGE: Cube's relationship with Jerry worsened as time went on. Heller told me there were physical confrontations between the two. In my discussions with people close to Cube on one hand and with Jerry on the other, the principal issue can be summed up in one word: Respect. Neither man felt the other person respected him. Neither man felt the other person understood their value in the success that had happened. Additionally, the relationship between Heller and Bryan Turner had become frayed. Heller chose to put DOC's album *No One Can Do It Better* through Atlantic Records and Turner began jockeying behind the scenes to steal Ruthless talent. The bad blood set the stage for a publicist at Priority Records named Pat Charbonnet to develop a relationship with Cube and eventually lure him into the fold there with Bryan Turner. By the end of 1989, Cube was out of the group.

MC REN: (Cube) was like *"Don't sign a contract! If me and you don't sign 'em, they can't do nothing. They have to do what we wanna do."* I was mad. I needed that money. And I was thinking about E. I grew up with him - just flip on him like that. I had a kid on the way, young, all by myself. So I did it and he didn't do it.

S. LEIGH SAVIDGE: It is significant to note that when the N.W.A. tour landed in Phoenix and Jerry Heller had flown into town with contracts and advance checks of $75,000, Dr. Dre signed his contract with Ruthless. While Cube has said publicly that, at that juncture, he'd only been paid $32,000, Dre, who had produced everything that Ruthless had released had been paid substantially more than Cube, and like MC Ren, had kids he needed to provide for. In his book, *Ruthless* and in various interviews, Heller points out that, aside from Cube's personal animus for him, the real reason for not signing his contract with Ruthless was Cube's understanding that he could make a lot more money as a solo artist who was writing and performing his own songs. During his tenure with Ruthless, he'd co-written songs and was one of five members of N.W.A., so his earning potential had been more limited. Eventually, he would receive substantial funds from Ruthless beyond the $32,000 he'd received by the end of the N.W.A. tour. But Cube was not going to wait on Ruthless' timetable and when Priority offered him a deal for a solo album, he grabbed it. Heller suggested to me that the deal Cube signed with Priority was less economically advantageous than the one Ruthless offered him.

ATRON GREGORY: Whenever you have a five member group and you have agents and managers - you have someone that's taking 20 percent and someone who's taking 10 percent. So that leaves 70% for the group members. Or 11 percent each. Some of the members of the group see someone making more money that isn't actually a group member - even though that's the way it always works - and there tends to be a problem. You see something you don't like and as an artist, you want to make a change. That's pretty much what happened.

DICK GRIFFEY: What the artists really don't understand is that these guys with the small distributor labels, they don't really have anything to give. Because the deals they make or what they are offered as so thin.

Angela Wallace served as Dre's attorney during his time with Ruthless.

ANGELA WALLACE: Ice Cube was the one who initially left, because (he) realized that Jerry Heller had essentially screwed over all of them. By *them* I mean the initial members of N.W.A.. There was money that N.W.A. had coming that they never knew about.

DOUG YOUNG: When we lost Ice Cube, I remember bein' at a marketing meeting and sayin *"I don't know how you let the nigga with attitude get out of N.W.A.."*

KEVIN POWELL: I remember being in a studio in New York City when Cube was working on his first solo album (*Amerikka's Most Wanted*). "The Bomb Squad" - Public Enemy's crew - were putting it together. He was really hurt by what had happened because these are guys that had spent a considerable amount of time together. He kept saying *"The business, the business, man. You can't make any money."*

ALLEN GORDON: N.W.A. would probably still be together if Eazy had just paid people a little more attention and kept 'em happy.

MC REN: In the beginning, (Heller) was cool because we weren't making any money and he was trying to make us money. But when we started making real money - because his name - he used to sign the checks. I'd tell Eazy, *"This fool is signing your checks!"* Bill Cosby once said on TV *"Don't let anyone sign your checks. "* And I asked him why he let Jerry Heller sign. This nigger didn't even know why.

KEVIN POWELL: I don't know anyone who hasn't signed a bad contract. It's a user friendly business. *"I have something you want so you have to sign to me so I can take you to the next level."* That's the nature of the business. That's the way the music industry is.

DOUG YOUNG: Jerry Heller taught me to go ask. He said,

"You're gonna have to ask for what you want up front or you're not going to get it in the end." 'Cause no one is gonna volunteer you no lotta money. Gotta ask for it.

Many people collapse the time tables between the departures of Ice Cube and Dr. Dre from N.W.A. and Ruthless. But there was an 18-month window between when Cube left in the late fall of 1989 and when Dre left in the early months of 1991. In the wake of Cube's departure, N.W.A. minus Cube began taking shots at him, attacking him in tracks like 100 Miles and Running which Dre was producing. So, at least for a while, there was no love lost between Cube and Dre.

ALONZO WILLIAMS: I gonna say this and he'll call me a liar but I was there when Dre told me he'd sell his soul to the devil for a million bucks. And I swear right now, the devil's gotta have a receipt for his ass.

Norman Winter's Client

Back channel communication to Michael Harris became a recurrent theme with some of the key interviewees who had agreed to speak on his behalf. Many were loyal to Michael and many of them simply didn't like or trust me. Conspiracy theories ran rampant throughout our interview process. Rumors were floated that the project was really an elaborate ruse - that I'd been hired by the federal government to assist them in their efforts to bring down Death Row Records. It mirrored the same kind of crazy misinformation that had, in part, contributed to the demise of the label.

One day, I had a meeting with publicist Norman Winter. I'd paid Winter a retainer to help secure interviews for the film and saw myself as his client.

Winter's place in the history of the music industry had long since been sealed due to his long standing relationships with legendary CBS Records chief, Walter Yetnikoff and a host of major artists including Elton John, Michael Jackson and Bob Dylan. He'd also represented Michael and Lydia before, and during, the partnership arrangement between Michael and Suge Knight.

When I got to Winter's office, I was exhausted. We'd gotten our asses kicked up in Oakland and I was very worried about the level of co-operation I was getting from the Harrises. And I made my first big mistake since filming had begun - Winter asked me how things were going and, thinking that I was talking to him in the context of a client relationship where I was the client, I began to unburden myself to him. I told him that I was concerned. We'd already spent $200,000, most of it paid to the Harrises, and we had virtually nothing. It was now clear that the Harrises had their own agenda and wanted us to film a bunch of artists that knew virtually nothing about the Death Row story. And they wanted us to film them because they wanted to sign them as artists. *"The whole thing is crazy"*. Winter appeared to be sympathetic.

But after the meeting, when I got back to my office, Lydia was there waiting for me. She was not happy. She handed her cell phone to me and said, *"Here Mike."*

Michael went absolutely crazy on me. *"You stupid, motherfucker! My eyes and ears are everywhere! How you gonna speak to my people like that! Do you know who Norman Winter is, motherfucker! You think you're gonna tell him something that he isn't going to spit back to me word for word?"* It was a bone-chilling moment that made the crazy calls from Jay Leno's manager, Jerry Kushnick, years before seem almost soothing by comparison.

I got the message. I was not Norman Winter's client. I would never speak to him again.

After Jeff and Darryl returned from Oakland, we all went out to dinner. It was clear that we'd all deluded ourselves that Michael was going to be in any way beholden to us just because we were going to be giving his life and story with Death Row a voice. Jeff and Darryl were being pummeled with calls from a cell phone Michael had access to. He was bullying them, threatening them. *"My people are watching you."* Darryl told us that Lydia had a gun in her purse and had taken to following him by car everywhere he went. The communication between the two had devolved into psychological warfare where Lydia would call Darryl and tell him where he had had lunch and where he had stopped for gas. It was a sobering revelation that production funds were being used to pay people who Lydia had charged with spying on our director. Jeff Scheftel was getting pummeled with calls from Harry O. *"He thinks he's running the show. He thinks we work for him. This show is going to be hard enough anyway."*

Then Jeff said something we all knew but probably needed to be reiterated: *"This guy built a nationwide drug operation. This is how he deals with people."*

I determined from the meeting that I needed to take point in the relationship with Michael and Lydia. I had a company to run and this was going to be a major distraction. But I had to figure out how to protect Jeff and Darryl and create an environment that would allow them to work. There was no way I was going to be able to prevent the interface between Darryl and Jeff and Michael and Lydia. But if there were battles to be fought with the Harrises, the point person needed to be me.

Welcome to Death Row was becoming a full-time nightmare for all of us.

Jeff found a production space in the basement of the old ICM building on Beverly Boulevard in West Hollywood and we began conducting many of the key interviews that would appear in the film. On the first day of shooting, Lydia walked up to Jeff and opened her purse. There was a pistol inside and she indicated that it was loaded at all times. Then she squinted her eyes and told him that she'd hired *security* in the form of current and former gang members to watch the set. She indicated that she needed two for herself.

All this was just the dress rehearsal for the main show. The film's production life would continue to imitate the story we were trying to tell.

A Bodyguard Goes to Work

Suge Knight was a former college football player and bodyguard who moved in the same circles as Dr. Dre. Looking to establish business ties in the growing rap scene, Knight assisted songwriter, Mario "Chocolate" Johnson, with collecting royalties due him from a popular white rapper named Robert Van Winkle a.k.a. Vanilla Ice. After allegedly making physical threats to Winkle, Suge enlisted the aid of Dick Griffey, the founder of Solar Records, which had once been one of the most successful Black-owned music labels in America. Intrigued with N.W.A.'s financial prospects, if not the music they were creating, Griffey suggested that Suge, Dre, and rapper and lyricist The DOC leave Ruthless Records and start their own label.

MATT MCDANIEL: Suge Knight was always around. He was around in the days of N.W.A. I just never noticed who he was.

JOHN PAYNE: I can give you my first impression of him - just a big kid. He was, at that time, a total nobody. He was actually somebody that you could miss.

VIRGIL ROBERTS: Here's a guy who's a college graduate, who's a football player. When they had the football strike in 1987, he was a replacement player for the Rams.

DICK GRIFFEY: I met Suge Knight previously because I had a driver named Big Wes, and Suge would always be with him. Everybody likes to be around show business, regardless of what career they're involved in.

VIRGIL ROBERTS: In the 1980s, Solar was probably the most successful Black-owned record label in America. Motown was the most successful in the 60s, Philly International in the 70s and Solar was the most successful in the 1980s. Dick Griffey, who was the founder of the company, was one of those men who had the rare ability to identify talent in people. We're the company that discovered Babyface.

ANGELA WALLACE: Mr. Griffey had a wealth of knowledge. The Whispers, Babyface - a lot of people went through Solar Records similar to the way a lot of people went through Motown.

DICK GRIFFEY: I was kinda born into the music business. My mom was a gospel singer and pianist and she and her sisters were kinda like the Black Andrews Sisters. So I come from a show business family. I'm a musician; I'm a drummer and a singer. I evolved from the nightclub business into a concert promoter. I became the premiere African American concert promoter in the country. All of the big names, you name 'em, I did em. Stevie, The Supremes, Jacksons, all the big major acts. I got involved with Don Cornelius as the talent coordinator for *Soul Train* and became his manager. And as his manager and advisor I said *"Don, why don't we do some other things?"* And I started out by saying, *"Let's do a record company."*

KEVIN POWELL: Suge was a bodyguard, bodyguarding Bobby Brown.

HANK CALDWELL: When I first met Suge Knight, it was through Dick Griffey at Solar. At that particular time, Suge was a security guard and was involved with security as far as going out on tour with the acts.

SUGE KNIGHT: (5) People used to say I was Dick Griffey's bodyguard back in the 70s when Solar was hot. Well, that's a compliment. Because if I'm somebody's bodyguard when I'm ten years old I must be doing a good job.

KEVIN POWELL: Being a bodyguard is probably one of the best music industry schools that you could go to because you're going to learn everything about the business.

By 1990, Suge Knight already had a lengthy criminal record.

ANGELA WALLACE: Most of the instances Suge was involved in -- the alleged batteries and assaults -- stem from when he was a bodyguard.

DOUG YOUNG: Suge was DOC's bodyguard. He and DOC played football or something at the University of (Nevada) Las Vegas. I used to see Suge back in the N.W.A. days doin' security.

THE DOC a.k.a. TRACY CURRY: He (Suge) wasn't my bodyguard. I used run with him.

KEVIN POWELL: A lot of people in the industry talk around a lot of security and bodyguards and think "*Oh, these guys are stupid.*" They think they're just big guys with a lot of muscles who must not be very intelligent.

MC REN: I remember when DOC's album blew up, Suge was bodyguarding for him. He always used to holler but he would do his job, stay close to DOC. He had a big truck, A big black Blazer.

KEVIN POWELL: Suge Knight was taking in what was going on at Ruthless - hearing the grumblings from Ice Cube and Dre and watching and listening to what was going on with Eazy and Heller.

SUGE KNIGHT: (5) I was up there looking and learning, you know. And I seen the different people complain. I seen artists. I seen people trying to be artists. I seen people talking about songs. And I'm just listening and hearing it all. I investigated and found out who do the writin' and the music and how do they get paid? So that's when I started my publishing company and signin' writers

KEVIN POWELL: I know a lot of broke rappers -- singers

who've gone double and triple platinum - because they don't own their publishing rights. Suge learned somewhere during this period that publishing is tremendously important because that's where the money is.

DICK GRIFFEY: (Suge) was always entrepreneurial. He had his own little company and was trying to do things. Suge was a leader. He was a winner. He was smart. He kind of reminded me of a hip hop Dick Griffey.

MARIO JOHNSON a.k.a. CHOCOLATE: (On Suge) My first impression? He got money. He gonna take care of us.

KEVIN POWELL: Suge is a very intelligent man. When I interviewed him, I was struck by his knowledge of the business. He was a savvy interviewee. Every question I asked him, he had an answer for. I walked away saying *"He has this mythological thing about being an intimidator -- but he's a smart cat."*

SUGE KNIGHT: (5) One of the songs I owned was *Ice, Ice, Baby* and six other songs on that album (*Hooked* and later, *To The Extreme*) with Vanilla Ice.

VIRGIL ROBERTS: There were a lot of young African Americans who were interested in starting companies who would come and ask questions of Dick Griffey. They would seek his advice.

DICK GRIFFEY: What I'm interested in really is teaching young people how to be in business for themselves.

VIRGIL ROBERTS: Suge first came to see Dick because he was managing a young guy named Mario Johnson, p.k.a. *Chocolate*, who had written a number of songs on a Vanilla Ice album.

MARIO JOHNSON a.k.a. CHOCOLATE: I did all the songs at his kitchen table at his house. Me and Quake would do the tracks, and I would go to his house and write, give him the songs and he would learn them.

VIRGIL ROBERTS: Chocolate had gotten some credit on the album, but they hadn't paid him and they wouldn't return his phone calls.

MARIO JOHNSON a.k.a. CHOCOLATE: The album (initially entitled *Hooked*) was actually released on Ichiban Records in 1989. I couldn't get in contact with (Vanilla Ice) but the record wasn't doing anything at the time. When the video hit BET, the record took off.

JAY KING: The problem for Vanilla Ice was that he was Blacker than most of us. And he put himself in a world he was never gonna get out of. He was too Black for White folks and he was never gonna be Black enough for Black folks. But he sold 12 million albums before it stopped working. (*To The Extreme*) was one of the best-selling albums ever.

JEFFREY JOLSON COLBURN: Suge didn't have a strong label background in the conventional sense, but he proved capable of playing hardball with the big boys.

During his college football days at UNLV, Knight was known as a dirty player. Former teammates have said that his favor maneuver was the head slap.

MARIO JOHNSON a.k.a. CHOCOLATE: I remember bein' at Vanilla Ice's attorney's office. I found out his album had two million pre-orders before it was (released) so I knew we had a big record.

SUGE KNIGHT: (5) The thing happened so fast, it blew up so quick, they tell me *"Look, we'll give you a couple of dollars if you'll let bygones be bygones."* I wouldn't go for it.

MARIO JOHNSON a.k.a. CHOCOLATE: Suge didn't know how

to handle a big potential lawsuit like that - a record of six, seven million, at the low end. When we started the lawsuit, the record was still climbing like hotcakes so we needed somebody to consult with us, instead of just tryin' to do it ourselves.

VIRGIL ROBERTS: Dick asked Suge *"How do I know this guy wrote the songs?"* So Suge brought Chocolate into the office. And I interviewed Chocolate and he was able to produce handwritten sheets for songs like *Ice Ice Baby* and explained how he and Vanilla Ice had actually worked together in a club in Texas. And he had a girlfriend who'd been at the kitchen table when he'd written these songs. He put together a pretty good case that he was entitled to be paid for these songs and hadn't been. So Dick and I ended up making a fairly substantial deal for them, and when I say *substantial* I mean hundreds of thousands of dollars to Chocolate for doing this publishing deal. And that was the first business transaction we did for Suge.

While this was happening, Suge was looking for Vanilla Ice.

SONSHINE: (Suge's) a hard businessman. He takes action. He goes after what he wants. Everybody doesn't agree about the way he does things. But he gets it done.

ALLEN GORDON: Apparently, (Chocolate) wrote the song for Vanilla Ice and didn't really expect anything from it.

VANILLA ICE: (3) Suge came to me at the Palm Restaurant first and sat down and said *"Hello."* He was kind of nice, you know. It kind of scared us because he was really intimidating. He had six or seven guys with him that looked like a football team.

MARIO JOHNSON a.k.a. CHOCOLATE: We knew where (Vanilla Ice) was staying because I was supposed to be hearing some tracks he was doing. He wanted me to come by myself. And Suge was like *"Why do they want you to go by yourself? They already tried to beat you out of money, beat you out of songs. I'm going with you. "*

VANILLA ICE: (6) I went to my hotel room and Suge was in there with several people. He let me know he wanted to get some points off the record *Ice Ice Baby.*

ALLEN GORDON: When Suge found out that Chocolate wrote the song, it was like he needed to grab some of that money. Not necessarily for Chocolate's sake, but to fund his own ideas and goals.

MARIO JOHNSON a.k.a. CHOCOLATE: I went to go talk to him about why my songs was on the album and I wasn't (paid) for them. He didn't want to talk about it. It was me and Suge and Ron Brown who went over there.

ALLEN GORDON: Any time you can conquer someone that appears weaker than you - that's almost the nature of Man. Suge wanted to be king so you gotta conquer certain land. If you can get three or four points off an album that's gonna sell ten million copies - *Why not?*

SUGE KNIGHT: (5) Their whole attitude was *"Look, we're just going to go in there and tell him we're gonna do it like this and give him a check."* I had a different program when we met. I'm like, *"You can't give me nothing. It's what I'm going to give you because you didn't get the rights to put it out there; because I haven't got paid and my client hasn't got paid."*

VANILLA ICE: (6) Suge took me out on the balcony, started talking to me personally. He had me look over the edge, showing me how high I was up there.....I needed to wear a diaper that day.

MARIO JOHNSON a.k.a. CHOCOLATE: I don't know what he's talking about. But like him saying that Suge hung him over a ten story floor - that's bullshit. I was standing right there. Suge just came in like a man, told him we could be here for a few minutes or we could be here all day. *"My boy done put in a gang of work for you. Your record's out. Your shit's like six million sales already."* And he took (some) money out of his pocket to try to pay Suge for my flight.

KEVIN POWELL: It was funny for a lot of Black people to watch this because historically a lot of us feel that Blacks were the ones that were ripped off in the music industry and hung over the balcony by White label executives.

ALLEN GORDON: Okay, Vanilla Ice was not hung out the window by his ankles but he was suspended in mid-air, eighteen floors above sea level. Now whether Suge Knight actually had his hands on him himself or it was one of his goons, it still points to Suge Knight.

KEVIN POWELL: That was the beginning of Suge's mythology - that this man could be so bold and go into there and get the publishing rights from this White cat who had become hip hop's Elvis.

MARIO JOHNSON a.k.a. CHOCOLATE: When we went to the hotel that day, it was strictly for conversation. Nobody got pushed - nobody argued, no shoving - nothing. When we got there everything was peaceful. Attorney David Kenner showed up, took a statement, and we got all our paperwork together. We didn't make (Vanilla Ice) sign papers. Our attorneys, through Sony, fought my case against Vanilla Ice. His (version) was a publicity stunt and he knows it.

Later Vanilla Ice would change his story.

VANILLA ICE: (3) He didn't hang me off from any balcony, okay? The story's been kind of blown out of proportion and I want to clarify that Suge and I have no bad feelings towards each other.

S. LEIGH SAVIDGE: When I watched the footage that VH1 sent of Vanilla Ice's story change, the most interesting part was at the very end. Thinking that the camera had stopped running, Vanilla Ice continued to talk. He was positively terrified of Suge Knight. It was clear that regardless of what had actually happened that night at the Hotel Bel Age, he still very much feared for his life. On balance, his new interview made me think of the POWs in Vietnam who were forced by the Viet Cong to say they had been treated well.

MARIO JOHNSON a.k.a. CHOCOLATE: Vanilla Ice made so much up in his mind, he actually started believing it. Cause I was there - no threatening, no nothin'. We had a normal conversation. He tried to pay Suge for my flight ticket for comin' out there to produce stuff.

DICK GRIFFEY: We had to sue BMI and Winkle (Vanilla Ice) to recover that money. They never voluntarily gave up a dime.

VIRGIL ROBERTS: It was more than a year in the settlement of that lawsuit that Chocolate finally got paid. Doesn't mean (Vanilla Ice) didn't get hung over a balcony, but if he did, it didn't make him go pay.

MARIO JOHNSON a.k.a. CHOCOLATE: We sued using normal courts and attorneys. You just heard it from me.

VANILLA ICE: (3) You could say I was an *investor* in Death Row Records with no return on my money.

DICK GRIFFEY: I made a deal for Chocolate, an administration deal, which is the best there is. The people that collect the money only take ten percent. Usually it's a co-publishing deal and they have ownership. And he (and Suge) got a huge advance. So I guess Suge said *"Wow! This old guy here is a miracle worker. Now I got another problem…"*

DOUG YOUNG: In Dre's eyes and even in my eyes at the time, I thought Eazy and Jerry wasn't paying Dr. Dre enough money.

Sonshine is a recording artist who worked with both Dr. Dre and Tupac Shakur and was once Dre's girlfriend.

SONSHINE: Dre was unhappy about the money situation at Ruthless. He couldn't even go buy a car without Jerry Heller being there or signing some papers.

In his book Ruthless, Jerry Heller talks about going to Dre's house one day and finding tens of thousands of uncashed checks from BMI and ASCAP in a drawer.

NORMAN WINTER: Suge, despite the fact that he was a football player or a former football player, was very astute at business. He's the one that masterminded the entire situation for Dre and found a loophole to get him out of his deal.

SUGE KNIGHT: (5) I'm from Compton. It wasn't no puzzle. I know how to get a brother. I said, *"Let them have this. Let's start something new which will be bigger and better."* And that way, it'll be something we'd definitely own…something that we actually own the masters.

JEFFREY JOLSON COLBURN: Dre said that Jerry and Eric Wright were keeping too much of the money so I want off of my contract. Eric Wright was not about to let his star producer out of his contract and said so. At that point, Dre gets some help in the form of Suge Knight.

ALONZO WILLIAMS: Several big people wanted Dre on their label. I had been asked if I could sway Dre over to a couple of labels. I had been told that if I could get Dre somewhere, there's a production deal and $100,000 for you. 'Cause Jerry and I were cool and Eazy and I were cool, I'm not gonna do that.

ANGELA WALLACE: Inasmuch as Suge and Dre are probably perceived as opposites, they were good friends in the beginning.

MC REN: Suge started hanging out with Dre and going to clubs. That's how him and Dre got down. Suge hooked him up with somebody that was checking his paperwork out.

DR DRE: (3) (Suge) was an aggressive person that cleared the way for me to go in and do what I had to do. By any means necessary.

SUGE KNIGHT: (5) They (Ruthless Records) had Dre doin' all this work and makin' all these great songs and they wasn't payin' him what he was worth. Matter of fact, they weren't payin' him at all.

ALONZO WILLIAMS: Dre went from working for me (where) he might have been making, if he was lucky, $15, $20 maybe $30 grand a year between the gigs and whatever checks we got. Eazy gave him $100 grand a year to produce records for Ruthless. But he may have been doing 10 records a year. So he was getting $10 grand a record. So he was actually getting less than he was getting from me. That pissed him off and no one wanted to negotiate.

DOUG YOUNG: Now Eazy can say in retrospect that he maybe shoulda paid Dre more. They shoulda talked about it more like businessmen. But then here comes that street thing
that comes back. *"You know that mutherfucker's playing with my money."* And then the homies talkin' about *"This fool's got three, four cars, where're your three, four cars?"* And Dre's starting to look at all them chips stacked and he's the one doing everything. He did the DOC's album. He did Michel'le's album. He did Eazy's whole album. He did the *Straight Outta Compton* album.

KEVIN POWELL: If you don't know you're worth one hundred

thousand or five hundred thousand - you can be happy. It wasn't until people said *"You're the foundation of this thing"* that he realized he should be making a lot more money. Dre was just a staff producer the way he was being paid.

ALLEN GORDON: Suge asked him to check his contract and DOC said *"Hey, fine by me."* And it wasn't what it should have been. Dre was content with what he had at the time. He was buying new houses and cars and spending money. And after a few talks with Suge and DOC, he figured that somebody should check into it.

JOHN KING: Suge is kind of a secretive dude. Whenever he and Dre would talk, he would get in (his) ear and whisper.

ALLEN GORDON: After he (Dre) found out that his contract wasn't what it was, in comes Suge Knight whispering in his ear, *"You need to come with me. I can check your contract. I can do this for you. I can do that for you."*

JEFFREY JOLSON COLBURN: (Suge) was a no-holds-barred person that would go in there and accomplish something.

KEVIN POWELL: Suge was calling Ruthless Records, calling Eazy and Jerry to find out what's going on with this contract that Dr. Dre has - saying that he is now representing Dre - and apparently he is being rebuffed. For whatever reason, Jerry Heller and Eazy thought they could ignore it. Jerry had been around the business a long time. *We got a contract.*

S. LEIGH SAVIDGE: Jerry Heller told me that eventually Suge began making unannounced visits to Ruthless' offices in pursuit of the contracts for The DOC, Dre, and other artists. Heller recalled coming into the office one day and finding Suge there waiting for him. Suge was starring very intently at the chair behind Heller's desk. Heller said to Suge, *"You want that chair, don't you?"* In response to this, Suge brandished a gun. Later,

Heller arranged for the contracts to be made available to him.

VIRGIL ROBERTS: After that first deal, Suge mentioned there were other clients who'd also written songs and produced records and hadn't been paid either. Specifically, Doc and Dre. Solar hadn't been involved in rap music and we weren't particularly interested in doing rap music. So we didn't know who Doc and Dre were.

MC REN: One day Dre was telling me to check my paperwork out. 'Cause Suge had hooked him up with somebody that was checking his paperwork out.

DICK GRIFFEY: Suge shows up on my doorstep with these two guys called DOC and Dre.

VIRGIL ROBERTS: So Suge brought them to the office and they explained they'd written and been involved in producing a number of hit records for acts that were signed to Ruthless - N.W.A., JJ Fad, DOC - and they'd never received a royalty statement. I asked them to bring me copies of all their contracts.

DICK GRIFFEY: I'm telling DOC and Dre - I don't know who you guys are - I don't know your music. I don't particularly care for it. But if somebody's selling it, you deserve to be paid. You deserve to maximize your opportunities. So let me show you how to do this.

VIRGIL ROBERTS: I called the attorney for Ruthless, Ira Selsky, and asked him about the agreements that Doc and Dre had with Ruthless and he confirmed the situation.
I looked through their agreements and said it seemed contracts had probably been breached. But you're gonna have to hire a lawyer if you want to get paid.

As important as Dre was to a new, prospective entity, at that juncture, The DOC was critical as well. Ruthless had become reliant on The DOC for the lyrics to much of their music.

DICK GRIFFEY: Doc was the storyteller. He was probably the most influential person in gangsta rap.

ALONZO WILLIAMS: Someone wanted Dre on his team and Suge could deliver him. Well, he had to go through The DOC, 'cause at the time Suge was DOC's bodyguard. (Suge) had a direct tie to Dre. DOC and Dre met at my house.

ALLEN GORDON: Dick Griffey has his label. He's looking for something new because Solar isn't putting out anything that the public wants. Suge felt *"This is the individual I need to bond with to make something happen. I have the best writer in hip hop at the time besides Ice Cube, which is The DOC and I'm gonna take the best producer in hip hop which is Dr Dre from (Ruthless)."*

VIRGIL ROBERTS: Doc and Dre had been principally responsible for much of the success of Ruthless and so we thought we could get them a million dollar advance. And we did make that deal. And Dick said *"Look, I'll show you how to start a company. And you won't have to worry about people paying you -- you'll have a company that you will own and control."*

VIRGIL ROBERTS: Jerry Heller was running the business operations for Ruthless. And I don't think he foresaw that DOC and Dre were really talented songwriters. The contracts they were doing were single song agreements. When they would turn in an album, they would do a contract for some of the songs that were on the album. But they didn't have a term contract. A term contract would be a contract where you have a songwriter or an artist under contract to you for a period of years and you get the benefits of everything they did. That's what allowed us to be able to go and make a publishing deal for DOC and Dre with Sony. It didn't violate any of their agreements.

DR DRE: (3) I was owed money, but they wasn't paying it. I

think they were trying to starve me out. As hard as you work for your money, there's at least two or three people out there working just as hard to get it from you.

DICK GRIFFEY: Fortunately for Dre, (Ruthless) didn't have him signed as a songwriter. They just took his songs on a project by project basis. So I was able to get take Dre and DOC and get them a large, seven figure advance from Sony.

VIRGIL ROBERTS: They weren't prohibited from starting their own company. So you could start your own company and work with your own artists and that would be a way to get paid without violating the contracts. It looked like it was going to be a fight (from Ruthless) for back royalties.

S. LEIGH SAVIDGE: Ruthless had paid many thousands of dollars to settle a lawsuit stemming from a violent encounter Dre had had with Dee Barnes, the host of *Pump It Up,* a television show that focused on the hip hop music world. The Dee Barnes incident had emanated out of a war of words between N.W.A. and Ice Cube and the legal dollars Ruthless had spent fighting the claim were significant.

ALONZO WILLIAMS: Dre was supposed to be a 50/50 partner in Ruthless. He was gonna do the beats and make the music and Eazy was gonna put the money up. When Dre realized that he worked for Eazy and he did not own part of the company, that's when they fell out.

S. LEIGH SAVIDGE: In *Ruthless,* Heller says that Suge's unannounced visits to Ruthless' office and direct intimation of himself and Eazy had led to the hiring of businessman and former Mossad operative, Mike Klein, as Ruthless' head of security. Klein's first move was to install former Israeli soldiers wielding Uzi machine guns at the office entrance. By chance, I had visited the Ruthless offices during this period to secure an interview with Eazy for another project. Seeing guys with the machine guns as you walked in let you know right away that this was a very unconventional business. It felt like a military zone.

SUGE KNIGHT: (5) Dre basically made Ruthless Records. I mean he did the music. He knew how to work with the artists. And it was supposed to have been his and Eazy's company together. But then when Jerry met Eazy, Jerry came in and ex-ed Dre out and said, *"I'll give you a little bit more money. We'll just use Dre basically as a slave."*

S. LEIGH SAVIDGE: My relationship with Jerry Heller started off very badly. When I called him and asked him to do an interview for the film, he demanded $100,000. When I came back with a number that was a small fraction of that, he was insulted. I fought to keep him on the phone. I told him that the film would be like (Kurosawa's) *Rashomon*, that the people who chose to speak would be heard and that those who didn't would be silenced. The viewer would draw his or her conclusions about what happened based on who they believed. I told him I needed his voice because, from what I'd heard thus far, he didn't have many defenders. He told me he didn't care and hung up.

DOUG YOUNG: I said, *"Well, What's goin' on with Dre? You mean to tell me you want Dre to go?"* (And Eazy said) *"He just wanted to get paid some more money and he already got all of his money."* I remember saying to Jerry and Eazy, *"If you let go the Michael Jordan of hip hop production, you guys done lost all y'all mind. You guys probably coulda regrouped from Cube and just found another dope rapper. But if you lose Dre, this company is through."*

S. LEIGH SAVIDGE: Jerry and Eazy were at a critical juncture with Dre. Many people I spoke to felt that if they had offered a little more money to him that he might have stayed. But Dre was now firmly under the guidance and spell of Suge Knight and neither Jerry nor Eazy could envision a scenario where a workable relationship that involved both of them could exist.

KEVIN POWELL: Jerry Heller has got to be one of the most fascinating people I've ever interviewed. He admitted that he probably did pit Eazy E versus Dre - that he made a mistake paying more attention to Eazy than Dre - that he probably made some mistakes in his business maneuvers with Ruthless.

DICK GRIFFEY: They had the worst contracts I've ever seen in the history of the record business. The contracts that Ruthless and Heller had with N.W.A. and Dre - I guess if I said Draconian that would be a kind word. I suggested *"Why don't you talk to Eazy and see if you can make a deal where Dre continues to produce for Ruthless, for N.W.A. and other acts?"*

KEVIN POWELL: I know from talking to various sources who don't like to be quoted on record, that (DOC) was grossly underpaid by the Ruthless camp.

ALLEN GORDON: When an artist signs a contract, that's what he signed.

VIRGIL ROBERTS: Eric had what he felt were valid contracts. That's what the dispute was over. He hadn't accounted and stuff. So in my view, the guys were gonna be able to get out of their contracts.

JERRY HELLER: (1) The idea of the artist as a sinless, blameless little lamb wandering among record label wolves didn't exactly jibe with the picture I had formed, working, representing and hanging out with musicians during my decades in the business. A lot of artists weren't lambs at all. They were wolves in sheep's clothing. I wouldn't want to run up against them in a dark alley.

KEVIN POWELL: A funny thing happens when people become addicted to money and fame. You start to believe your own hype. You start to believe you really are a gangster out of Compton, California. You start to live out this fantasy world that you created and carry guns onstage. (Eazy) was this little dude.

It was a Napoleonic kind of thing. You start to think that you are the bomb and everyone should follow you.

ANGELA WALLACE: Jerry was being paid two to three times the normal amount. (N.W.A.) initially paid Jerry to manage them which is absolutely absurd.

JERRY HELLER: (1) At that point in my career, I earned the commission of all top managers, which was 20%. In fact, I was known as H20 meaning Heller at 20%.

S. LEIGH SAVIDGE: The central issue that seemed to stick in the minds of the DOC and Dre and ended up becoming the battle cry for the many folks that now wanted a piece of these guys was the notion that Heller had engineered the contracts with Ruthless so that he could take 20% off the top from all of Ruthless' revenue and another 20% from the earnings of each artist as a management fee. When I asked Heller about this, he was adamant that this was fiction, that it was, in his words, *"The type of shit people say to get an artist after you've done all the work to make them successful"* and that he would pursue litigation against anyone who tried to label the so-called 20 and 20 issue as fact. Even so, word circulated among Ruthless' competitors that Eazy had struck an untenable deal with Heller.

JERRY HELLER: (1) There isn't a single instance of Jerry Heller, stealing, taking money under the table, or cheating artists out of payments rightfully due to them. You can't do it, man. So once and for all, shut the fuck up.

ATRON GREGORY: Whenever you have a lot of success, there's always people coming in and saying *"Well hey, if you're with me, I can do it this way or Why didn't you do it this way?"* I'm a manager. Where were all those people who could've, would've, and should've - where were they when you first started?

VIRGIL ROBERTS: In the process of having a number of

conversations with DOC and Dre, the question came up about *"How can we be assured that we're going to get paid in the future?"* Dick said *"Look Dre, if you can make records the way you make records, I'll show you how to start a company. You won't have to worry about other people paying you. You'll have a company that you own and control."*

On a fateful early morning in the spring of 1991, moves were made to take DOC and Dre and other acts including Michel'le from Ruthless. The incident unfolded on the third floor of the Solar Building. Jerry Heller was no stranger to mobsters, tough situations, and tough people. Growing up in Ohio, he had known notorious Cleveland mobster, Moe Dalitz. His second job in the music industry was working for Associated Booking, a talent agency in the early sixties owned by Sidney Korshak, who was the Chicago mob's go-to guy in the Los Angeles entertainment world. While arranging tours in the 60s and 70s, he'd interfaced with the toughest names in the business: Bill Graham, Led Zeppelin manager, Peter Grant, and David Geffen.

ALONZO WILLIAMS: It didn't go down the way it was supposed to and so Eazy had to be persuaded to make some moves and make things happen.

S. LEIGH SAVIDGE: Jerry told me that Eazy E was intent on killing Suge Knight, something he also discusses in his book, *Ruthless.* Initially, when Jerry tried to talk him out of it, Eazy took it as a sign of Jerry's naiveté - that he didn't understand that this had to be done – that since Suge was trying to destroy everything they had built - killing him was in line with the code of the street. Eventually, Jerry talked him out of it.

MC REN: It just went down so quick, man. And you know I was thinking *"I can't shake on E like that."* Because I didn't have no proof. E's probably seeing it. Dre's probably seeing it. I didn't see nothing.

KEVIN POWELL: Contracts don't mean anything in hip hop. If

you want to get out of a contract, you can figure out ways to get out of it.

JEFFREY JOLSON COLBURN: According to court papers, Suge and his friends basically came in and told Eric and Jerry that Dre was leaving and they couldn't stop him and that this was not just legal - it was physical. It was personal. The story went that Suge and others came in with baseball bats and forced him to sign the papers.

JERRY HELLER: (7) Under threat of his life and telling him that they would kill his mother and that they were holding me hostage, under those kinds of duress, got him to sign releases for Dr. Dre.

JEFFREY JOLSON COLBURN: The people I spoke to were afraid of talking about it. Jerry Heller did not want to talk about anything on the record that would come back to haunt him -- if some crazy guy, not even Suge but someone trying to impress him decided to get rid of (Jerry).

S. LEIGH SAVIDGE: Sometime in 2006 I had an eight hour meeting with Eazy's widow, Tomica Woods-Wright. Among the subjects we covered was the infamous night at Solar Studios. Her version of the events as related to her by Eazy was that Eazy was lured to the Solar offices by Dr. Dre after Eazy answered his late night page. Eazy had told her that Dre told Eazy he was looking to patch up the relationship and that he had a solution that would resolve the issues between them. Eazy had suggested to her that Dre wanted to discuss how he could continue working for Ruthless and pursue his own projects separately. But when Eazy arrived at Solar, Dre was either in another room or not there at all. Instead, Eazy was met at an elevator by Suge, who led him into a room where there were several men who were carrying bats and pipes. It was 2 am and the room was soundproof. Suge allegedly told Eazy that they were holding Jerry Heller hostage and knew where his mother lived and were prepared to kill her.

ANGELA WALLACE: It was a rather unpleasant event. And (Eazy and Dre's) friendship was put to the test.

JERRY HELLER: (1) I couldn't grasp the idea that two people could be that tight, could have that much history, could reach the pinnacle of fame and success together and then have one turn around and betray the other.

S. LEIGH SAVIDGE: At this point in our interview, Tomica stopped talking and got very morose. Then she emitted a laugh and said that when Eazy was allegedly forced to sign the paper that would release Dre, DOC, and Michel'le from Ruthless, he wrote *Mickey Mouse* on the signature line. Then she went silent again. From what I could deduce, she felt that the darkness and betrayal Eazy experienced that night changed his spirit and his very way of being for the rest of his life. She said that after that incident, he was angry and broken. Eazy had refused to give her specifics about what had happened. Tomica took me to the edge of a very emotional cliff - but ultimately did not want to discuss the specifics on this either. Her demeanor and body language suggested to me that something very dark had happened. You could tell that images were coursing through her mind like it had happened yesterday. I'd heard that the guys in the room with Suge had gang affiliations and had been in prison and watching her I got the sense that she felt that Eazy might have been raped. I got as far as *"Was he…?"* And she put her hand up and stopped me while fighting back tears. Only the people in the room know for sure.

DICK GRIFFEY: I wasn't there. I wasn't in the room. But when Eazy said (in a deposition) that me and the chairman of Sony, Tommy Mottola, was in the room with bats and pipes, he's obviously a liar.

VIRGIL ROBERTS: The story I got from Suge was that Eric

agreed to release DOC, Dre, and Michel'le and, in return, Dre would produce some tracks for Eric. There was an N.W.A. record which Dre was producing and had stopped working on. He agreed that (Dre) would finish the N.W.A. record. Suge said he would meet with Bryan Turner of Priority and get an additional advance and an increased royalty rate for N.W.A. and ownership of N.W.A. masters from Priority. Suge did that re-negotiation with Bryan. There was an advance of money that was paid to Dre - and the record was finished and turned in. So Suge felt that he'd lived up to his part of the bargain by getting Ruthless free of some of the obligations they had with Priority.

After the incident at Solar, Jerry Heller would take drastic measures to insure his ongoing safety.

JERRY HELLER: (1)   When I rolled up to my house in the northern L.A. suburbs, one of my bodyguards would usually go in first, to make sure the place was secure. Only then would I be able to enter my own home. I kept loaded guns all over the house - a .25 Colt double-action automatic in a secret drawer in a Chinese prayer table near my front door; an ivory handled .32 caliber within reach of my backyard Jacuzzi, a 12 gauge Remington standing upright in my bedroom closet. I slept with a big .380 Beretta underneath my pillow.

JEFFREY JOLSON-COLBURN: (Later) In October of 1992, Eric Wright / Eazy E filed a RICO lawsuit against them. RICO's a racketeering lawsuit.

VIRGIL ROBERTS: I went to a settlement meeting at the offices of the attorneys for Ruthless. Suge was at the meeting. DOC and Dre were there. Eazy was there and Jerry Heller was there. The question of releases came up and somebody asked Eazy *"Were you coerced to sign anything?"* And he said *"No. We had a deal and I lived up to the deal."* That was before the lawsuit came out.

JERRY HELLER: (1)   I couldn't see the conference as anything but a funeral wake for N.W.A.. Eazy stared across at Dre for the whole duration of the sit down. Dre shifted in his seat uncomfortably. For once he wore sunglasses and Eazy left his eyes uncovered. *"Did you know about this, Andre?"* He responded with a single word to Eazy's question: *"No."*

S. LEIGH SAVIDGE: I asked Kevin Powell why Eazy would say that everything was copacetic given what had happened to him.

KEVIN POWELL: People are scared of Suge Knight-period. Even with him in jail. People are scared. I told people I was doing this interview -- this documentary was happening and they're like *"That's crazy. Why are you doing that?"* I come from the inner city and you got that one cat that pops up who's like Richard Wright's Bigger Thomas -- that one bad Black man that everybody's afraid of. And that's what Suge Knight represents for a lot of people.

MICHAEL BOURBEAU (Ruthless' lawyer): (8) There is no question that we have substantial documentary evidence of a conspiracy here.

JEFFREY JOLSON COLBURN: Eazy E's lawsuit contended that there was money laundering, extortion, threats, and violent intimidation. Not only was it charged against Suge and Death Row for stealing their top producer, Dr. Dre, it was charged against Sony Music who was part of the group that was going to distribute Death Row Records. So you had Eric Wright and an East Coast attorney claiming that Sony had used strong arm tactics to gain advantage in the music industry. This is something that Sony's boss's in Japan didn't like hearing.

S. LEIGH SAVIDGE: Shortly after we finished *Welcome to Death Row* I discovered that I was in business with the guy who had been the lawyer at Sony who had drafted the document that released DOC and Dre from Ruthless. When he learned that I was going to show the legal document pertaining to the RICO action which bore his name, he begged me to digitally obscure his name. He told me, "*I don't want my kids to see that.*"

JEFFREY JOLSON COLBURN: It was the first time RICO had been used in the music business. It's a thing they use to get the Mafia when they can't get them on anything else. The lawsuit never went anywhere.

S. LEIGH SAVIDGE: When I asked Heller why the RICO case had failed he shook his head and told me that Ruthless had hired Michael Bourbeau, one the best RICO lawyers in the country to try the case. When I asked if either he or Eazy had compromised the case by making problematic or unverifiable statements during their depositions, he didn't remember.

NORMAN WINTER: I was consulting for Ruthless, working through Jerry Heller. One day Dre and Suge came to my office in Hollywood and said they'd left Ruthless and were starting their own company.

DOUG YOUNG: Now what do I do? Do I drown (with Ruthless Records) or do I jump ship with Dre? That was a pretty easy one. Dre is the man who had the golden touch. Cube is gone; Dre is gone. Now me, being the smart savvy businessman that I am, I start lookin' to cut my losses. It's time to get off this Titanic.

JEFFREY JOLSON COLBURN: From day one, this label was born amid a controversy that involved violence.

Meanwhile, Across Town on the Sunset Strip

By December of 1981, I'd been out of college for about 18 months, had no job and was trying to find my way career-wise. I'd finished near the top of my class at Boston University's School of Public Communication and had completed a student film, *Lacoste*, which had only made a small ripple on the student film circuit. My hero in life was Doug Kenney, who had written *Animal House* and was one of the founders of *National Lampoon* magazine.

A friend in New York let me crash on the floor of his apartment. But the material I submitted to *National Lampoon* didn't get a response. I went to dozens of job interviews but only got one offer, a position as a security guard at CBS. I tried to imagine a life where I wore a uniform and greeted guys like Howard Cosell every morning. I couldn't.

I soon came to the conclusion that if I were going to pursue a career in the film industry, I needed to learn how to live on little or no money. And that was going to be very difficult in New York. So I flew back to my hometown of Seattle, packed up my car, drove to Los Angeles, and moved into a house where five other people were living. All the rooms were taken. So I was offered the couch. It was wasn't much. But I was off the floor.

Over the next four years, I tried a number of things in an effort to find where I might fit in the show business food chain. Initially, I had no real strategic plan other than to pay my rent and try to get in front of people who could help me or mentor me. I tutored athletes at UCLA. I sold shoes at Foot Locker. I wrote speeches for local politicians. I developed a comedy act and bounced around clubs like *The Comedy Store* and *The Improv* where I met people like Sam Kinison and Steve Oedekerk and saw a virtual who's who of the comedy talent that would define the next few decades while they were on their way up. I was a contributing editor at an all-comedy monthly called *Laff Track* where my editor was *Huffington Post* founding editor, Roy Sekoff.

Beginning in 1984, I started finding work as an assistant editor on a series of independent films including *Boys Next Door* which starred a young actor named Charlie Sheen. At night, I would work on *spec* screenplays. One of them, *Hancock Park*, got a decent review from someone at Fox.

But where was all this going? The hard truth was that no one wanted to hire me for even an entry level job at any kind of even semi-respectable company in the film or television business. People told me all the time, "*You've never had a real job.*" My father would say, "*You don't have health insurance.*" At my lowest ebb, the people at a show called *The People's Court* told me that I didn't have enough experience to help them select potential candidates involved in small claims disputes to appear on the show. A week later, a guy at Fox ended an interview early when he saw I was wearing a Star of David over my tie and I couldn't tell him which temple I went to.

My overwhelming sense after a couple of years was "*I have to create an asset. I have to do something that gives people a reason to want to do business with me.*"

In the middle of all this, I borrowed money from some friends and produced the first live concert featuring a young comedian named Jay Leno. Soon after, I discovered that Leno, who would soon become the permanent guest host of *The Tonight Show*, had regrets about appearing in the show and did not want it to come out. I began to hear that Leno's manager, Jerold Kushnick, was calling places like HBO and telling them that if they picked up the show, they'd never do business with Leno again.

As I headed into the fall of 1985, I was $25,000 in debt from an untitled show with Jay Leno and knew that my career as a film editor had run its course. I had just finished recutting a rape-revenge film called *The Ladies Club*, which involved women who had been raped teaming with a female surgeon to castrate the men who had raped them. I remember telling the guy I worked for that I was relieved that there were no close-ups of the severed penises. His response was, *"We've got 'em. But we decided to take em out."*

It was time to find a distributor for a show Jay Leno didn't want seen.

Dogg Days at Solar

The initial recording sessions for the new label happened at Dre's home where he had a studio. But when his house burned to the ground under somewhat mysterious circumstances, Dick Griffey allowed Suge and Dre use of his studios at Solar Records. Though initially, DOC and Dre were the label's only asset, Dre's producing skills attracted notable new talent, such as Dre's step-brother, Warren G, and his friend, Calvin Broadus a.k.a. Snoop Doggy Dogg, who immediately got attention with his unique rapping style. As this was happening, the DOC's influence in new arrangement began to fade. A car accident had robbed him of his voice and his lyrical abilities, while valuable, paled in the face of Dre's production skills. Additionally, the enterprise was struggling financially. The advances from Sony had been used up and Dick Griffey did not have the means nor the inclination to continue to bootstrap the new entity.

S. LEIGH SAVIDGE: When Dre effectively stopped working for Ruthless, he began working out of his house where he had a recording studio. But when his house caught on fire, Death Row's base of operation would move to the Solar building in North Hollywood.

DOUG YOUNG: I remember hearing a lotta of rumors about something goin' on with Dre - that he burnt down his house for insurance money. And one day, 45 Keene, a friend of mine from New York, was staying at the Mondrian when Dre was staying at there. And we were down in the lobby and I saw Dre, and said *"What's up man -- what you doin' over here?"* He says *"I've been stayin' here for the last couple of months."* And I said *"What happened to your house out in Calabasas?"* And he told me about the fire -- and I said I thought that was just a damn rumor. I said *"What's the word - you tried to burn your house down and collect some insurance money?"* He said *"Nah, I didn't do that, man."* So I asked him what was he workin' on, and he said he got his own label called Death Row.

SNOOP DOGG: Dre was getting ready to leave N.W.A.. But nobody knew but us. Dre had DOC, Lady of Rage, and Warren G and I brought RBX and Kurupt, Daz, and Jewell.

JEFFREY JOLSON COLBURN: They knew they had a superstar producer and one with a lot of street credibility which meant he could attract a lot of acts. Dre had some other people he could pull in and Suge had some people he could pull in.

NATE DOGG: I thought Dre owned Death Row records when I signed on.

VIRGIL ROBERTS: The initial understanding was that Doc and Dre and Dick and Suge would be partners in this company. And the name of the company was going to be Future Shock.

JEWELL: DOC was tryin' to name it Future Shock, but I was like *"That sounds like something from the Jetsons. We can't go out like that."*

John Payne was a studio engineer during Death Row Records' rise to fame.

JOHN PAYNE: Suge had just moved into the Solar building when he was with Future Shock. He was doing a publishing deal with the Sony label, DOC, and Dre.

VIRGIL ROBERTS: Solar had a distribution deal with Sony at the time and our anticipation was that (since) we were doing publishing deals with Sony that Sony would distribute the label.

In a transaction under the Future Shock label, Griffey and Virgil Roberts were able to secure a significant advance from Sony against future publishing earnings for DOC and Dre. Shortly thereafter, Suge and Dre settled on the name Death Row Records for the music that Dre would create going forward.

VIRGIL ROBERTS: I was the lawyer for Future Shock and it was agreed that Dick would supply recording studio facilities, that we would take some of the proceeds from the publishing deal and those funds would then be used to make records and sign artists. We began to sign artists and make records for the Future Shock label.

JOHN PAYNE: They were carried or financed (by) Solar at the time. But it wasn't a tremendous amount of money. It was more or less getting the phone bill paid and keeping the lights on.

JEWELL: We were in the studio and Dre and them were thinking about the name. And I'm like *"It should be Death Row cause we all got cases."*

DICK GRIFFEY: The guys liked the name. There was a producer that owned the name Def Row and we purchased the name from him.

ALONZO WILLIAMS: The name Death Row came from my partner, Unknown. Initially it was supposed to be Def Row as in Def Jam. D-E-F. And Dre bought the name Def Row and changed the name and gave Unknown some money for the idea.

JEFFREY JOLSON COLBURN: Death Row Records came about in 1991. There had been gangsta rap before and Priority Records and some other labels were active in it. But there wasn't a label that was totally dedicated to gangsta rap. There was hardly a name for it then. It was just hard-core street rap and N.W.A. summed up the scene the best.

SNOOP DOGG: Me and Nate Dogg went to high school together. Me and Warren G grew up selling candy and playing football. Warren G was my best friend and Nate Dogg was my best friend. So we formulated (the group) 2-1-3. Warren G was a

DJ, I was a rapper and Nate Dogg would sing the hooks. We didn't have drum machines back then. All we had was just records, turntables and a microphone.

SUGE KNIGHT: (5) Each one of the artists that was there in the beginning, I got a lot of love for and they will always be part of the family. Because they took that chance. It's not like we had a name out there. It's not like we had a lot of money to give them. The money I gave came out of my pocket.

SNOOP DOGG: We started making tapes around 1989. I had just graduated from high school and really didn't have no career. I didn't want to work at no job, no 9 to 5. We had a homeboy named Money B, a White boy. He was tight at making beats. So Warren G hooked me up with him and Nate Dogg was hooked up with him. So we got in the car and went to his house and put down a song called *Long Beach is a Mutherfucker*. And that was the first song we put down on cassette. We all got copies. About a week later, 200 to 300 people in the neighborhood had come up to us that had heard it. Before we knew it, we started selling them. Five dollars a tape.

NATE DOGG: I hooked up with Dre through Warren G who was his (step) brother.

SNOOP DOGG: We went back to Money B and made another song. Then we went to the eastside of Long Beach to VIP Records and started making songs with DJ Slice. He tightened up our song a bit. Added a bigger beat. Then we started making songs with him and LC, a producer from the Westside. He started producing beats for me, Warren G and Nate Dogg. Calvin (the owner) from VIP tried to take the cassette to labels. "*He doesn't have what it takes,*" they said. "*He's no DJ Quick,*" they said. "*He'll never make it.*"

DICK GRIFFEY: They were housed in my building, so they didn't have a lot of expenses. The greatest expense in making a record is the studio time. I had a six story building. They were down on the third floor. Whatever they did, they did it on the third floor. Since I didn't have a lot of experience in rap or hip hop, I kind of let them do their own thing.

KEVIN POWELL: What Solar gave Suge was legitimacy. You have this music figure in Dick Griffey who has a track record. That gives Suge instant credibility as a businessman.

SNOOP DOGG: Then I did another song called *Gangster's Life* with Nate Dogg crooning in the background. It was a real story. I mixed it with LL Cool J's song *Cars Ride By With The Booming System*. Now I had a song that everybody on the streets could relate to. And that was the song that got Dr. Dre's attention.

SONSHINE: I remember them talking about this guy that could rap so good and they brought Snoop around and everyone was amazed.

SNOOP DOGG: The first tape (of mine) that Warren G gave Dre was the one that hooked me up. When he finally got a chance to hear me, I was ready. I didn't want to rap for him until I was ready.

S. LEIGH SAVIDGE: Snoop came very close to aligning himself with Above the Law, a group and label then affiliated with Ruthless Records.

ALLEN GORDON: Snoop was the protégé of Above the Law. Warren G was hanging around. Because Snoop was in his group 2-1-3. They were working together.

SNOOP DOGG: Above the Law was one of the first labels that was interested. They brought me up there. They liked me and told me that they would put me out after their other artists, Kokane and Shelly. I was down with them. I was willing to wait and make it happen. We would catch the Metro and go to their studio in L.A. every day. They would give us a few dollars, then give us a ride back to Long Beach. They were looking out for us, keeping us inspired. Kokane was down with me. He told me it was worth the wait. I waited and waited and waited. But Warren G got tired of waiting. So he took the tape to Dr. Dre.

DICK GRIFFEY: I'm a *songs man*, you know? And rap music is, for the most part, sampling. And pretty soon they're going to be sampling samples. It's a storyline and some content. And a lot of the storyline I don't like. There's some I do like. But the main attraction to this art form (for me) is the story.

SNOOP DOGG: Warren G called me and was like *"Snoop, I got Dre on the phone, he liked the tape, he wants to work with us."* And I said *"Nigga, stop lying."* And someone said *"Hello?"* And I said *"Who's this?"* And he said *"It's Dre. Man. That shit was dope. I want to get with you. Come to the studio Monday."*

LAMONT BRUMFIELD: We was sittin' in Inglewood one day and this guy walked by and I was playin' this tape (of an artist I represented). He said he knew this guy Kurupt that was like this. So I went over to Kurupt's house -- he fresh off the plane from Philadelphia. You could still smell the mustard on him. I had him do a battle and he slayed my rapper right there.

NATE DOGG: Everybody was taking direction from Dre, as he knows what he's doing. He just finished doing N.W.A. albums, double and triple platinum so you have confidence. You've watched this man make money.

LAMONT BRUMFIELD: I had met Dre a few times, givin' him tapes of Kurupt. But when Snoop mentioned that Kurupt had slayed him at the Roxy, that kinda got Dre's attention.

SNOOP DOGG: I told (Kurupt) that we was having a pool party and to come down. And I told Dre, I got a homeboy who's tight. He damn near tight as me, if not tighter. I wasn't trying to hate. I was trying to get the best underground product we could get. So the party's like *"If he tight, I give him a record deal. If he weak, I throw him in the pool."* So it was somebody's birthday. They plugged the mike up and told Kurupt to bust a birthday rap. He bust a cold freestyle about the birthday boy. And it was like *"That Nigga's signed!"*

DOUG YOUNG: Everyone was following Dre, because people knew Dre was *The Man*. Everything he touched was gold or platinum or better.

MARIO JOHNSON a.k.a. CHOCOLATE: Dr. Dre likes to teach -- taught me a lot about the business. He used to come over to me and Doc's house and tell me *"Wake up, boy. You're sleeping too much. Need to be workin'."*

KEVIN POWELL: Dr. Dre brings Suge instant credibility in terms of being able to select creative people and talent. By this time, he's got ten years in the music industry. He's a cult figure on the West Coast. If it means hanging out in the studio with the possibility that you might make a record one day -- you'll just come.

JOHN PAYNE: The (influx) of talent was the result of people wanting to work for Dre and not a result of Suge going out and finding them. Dre was the only asset the company had. He was actually the most bankable person at that time -- pretty much in the industry - from the R&B and rap standpoint.

NATE DOGG: At that time, it was a dream to just be in the same room with Dre. Dre wanted us to come to the studio? I'd have jogged up there if I didn't have a car.

SNOOP DOGG: When I moved to Hollywood, my first apartment was $500 a month. There were seven of us staying there. DOC, Daz, Kurupt, my girlfriend, and some other people were always staying there. All in a one bedroom apartment.

Only $500 a month. But somehow we could never pay the rent on time.

MARIO JOHNSON a.k.a. CHOCOLATE: When my records started jumpin' off, Dre would tell me, *"Choc, you're at four million! Read Billboard, you're at seven million!"*

SNOOP DOGG: Back then, Suge was very behind the scenes and helpful and quiet, humble, non-visible. He didn't like cameras. He was invisible. The invisible man.

MARIO JOHNSON a.k.a. CHOCOLATE: Suge was the guy who was makin' sure all of us was in the studio on time.

DAN O'DOWD: I don't know Suge. Pleasant enough guy. Personally, I couldn't see him running a major corporation.

DR DRE: (3) Suge's role was handling the day-to-day business, dealing with artists, dealing with distributors and record companies. My job was to push these buttons and make the records happen.

DICK GRIFFEY: Here was a young guy who was obviously a decent hip hop / rap / A & R guy. He told me he was helping pick the material and pick the acts and so forth. I remember saying to him one day *"Suge, I actually believe you do know what you're doing - don't you?"*

ALLEN GORDON: DOC was going to be the biggest rap star at the time. He had sold nine hundred and seventy thousand units (of *No One Can Do It Better*) before his car accident.

S. LEIGH SAVIDGE: In the interviews he has given to the press, the DOC has been pretty vocal about how he was not in the proper mindset to exploit the opportunity he had during this period. By his own admission, he was drinking a lot, behaving irresponsibly and was depressed over a car accident that had damaged his vocal chords and ended his career as a singer. Heller told me that he'd tried repeatedly to get DOC to see Marty Hopp, a prominent ear, nose and throat doctor. Heller told me, *"I'd make appointments and he'd never show up."*

THE DOC a.k.a. TRACY CURRY: (4) All I wanted to do was be drunk and high. And talk shit to everybody. Which I did all the time. I would show up to meetings totally fuckin' inebriated and blow the meetings up, with Dre and Suge . So at some point, I don't blame those dudes for being like, *"Wow, this guy's losing it."*

JOHN PAYNE: Doc was supposed to be an equal partner with Dre. Doc had a successful album but then he almost killed himself in a car accident, lost his voice, really wasn't supposed to be speaking again. He was treated like a step-child and pretty much swept under the carpet. I think they used him for his writing value. They could get him to write some songs or something but his maximum earning potential didn't justify the cost.

S. LEIGH SAVIDGE: DOC's biggest contribution during this period may have been his mentorship of Snoop Dogg.

SNOOP DOGG: Me and DOC were tight. There would be no Snoop Dogg without DOC. He inspired me by letting me write songs with him. By critiquing each other. We would stay up to 2 or 3 in the morning at his house, playing video games and drinking beer. Then we'd go off and write rhymes and record them on cassette and deliver them to Dre the next day.

THE DOC a.k.a. TRACY CURRY: (4) Snoop would write a rap. This is when he moved in and was staying with me at my house. He'd write a rap and come upstairs, and I'd say, *"This part is good. This part ain't good. Take these lines out. Try to replace them with these lines over here. "* That's the way I helped Snoop. I helped him find out how to write a song."

SNOOP DOGG: I wanted to appreciate the game and accept everything that was offered to me and learn, and just be a student at the time.

During this time, money was tight. But being in the Solar building made all the artists feel like they'd made it.

JOHN PAYNE: The early days of Death Row were rather dismal, rather poverty stricken. It was like that show with Jimmy Walker, *Good Times*.

SNOOP DOGG: My first apartment was fun for me. I had a pet roach. We called him Gooch. He would always come out when we had company. We started feeding and taking care of him because he was one of the homeboys. Rent was $500 a month. Manager was named Wendy. Still owe you - I'll holler back at you..

NATE DOGG: The best records came out when we were starving.

DICK GRIFFEY: These guys were broke all the time. Nobody ever had any money. I was on the phone with Suge's wife, paying the house payments.

SNOOP DOGG: Dick Griffey back then was the chicken man. When we needed food, he'd break us off some (money) for some chicken. We needed a few hundred dollars for the rent and he'd come through. He was like Grandpa. Dick Griffey was good to us back then.

SUGE KNIGHT: (5) The money I gave em' came out of my pocket.

NATE DOGG: We moved from having free studio time to being in a studio where it cost money. So when Dre walked in, it was time to work. All work and no play.

SNOOP DOGG: It was a change from Dre's house to Solar Records. We were in an environment where real records were being made. We seen Dick Griffey every day and we knew what type of stuff he did for the industry. We knew that being around him and being with Dr. Dre, that the opportunity was real close.

JOHN KING: Death Row started out as a family. We used to have meetings sayin' *"We're gonna come up!"* When it got to be more of a business, where contracts had to be signed and documents had to be accounted for, that took the love out of it.

SNOOP DOGG: We used to stay up all night; didn't leave till five or six in the morning. There was a special vibe - you just wanted to be there. It was right in the middle of Hollywood and we'd never really been out of the neighborhood and we was getting a chance to see it all. This was the same studio that Shalimar, Lakeside, The Whispers, Babyface, The Deal all recorded their albums in.

DICK GRIFFEY: Virgil and I were there to handle business.

JOHN PAYNE: On a business level and on a day-to-day basis, it was merely existing. It seemed like they were trying to find somebody to put some money into it or somebody to help them out.

ANGELA WALLACE: Anyone who's ever started a record company understands that you have to have an influx of capital. Without it, it's just impossible because most artists don't maintain jobs. Individuals that start record companies, that's one of their biggest mistakes. They try to support the artist, which is an extremely difficult task.

SNOOP DOGG: Suge had this idea of bringing in someone who could make this a company - who could front the company. (Investment) money was hard to come by, because there was no structure, no label. Dre didn't have any money. He was leaving N.W.A..

Xenon Pictures

By the mid-eighties, the delivery of film content via videocassette to a burgeoning store network in the U.S. had transformed the entertainment business. As Eazy E, Ice Cube, and Dr. Dre were working to create the next major shift in the music industry, the videocassette had become the primary driver of revenues for filmed entertainment. This was true not only for Hollywood's major studios, but for a number of smaller entertainment companies as well. The videocassette boom was a gold mine for companies and individuals that owned film libraries, bringing a new life for films of all genre and budget that had been released years and even decades earlier.

In pursuit of a distribution deal for my Jay Leno project, I'd landed at a company called Video Warehouse Distribution. V.W.D., as it was called, was a wholesaler of VHS tapes to the burgeoning video store market. They were also the small company version of some of the films I'd worked on. The owner of the company was a British guy that was sleeping with the wife of the owner of his biggest supplier, who he wasn't paying. The sales director was a heroin addict who was a cold calling nut job who made the guys in the *Wolf of Wall Street* look like choirboys.

But the thing that really got my attention was the demand for some of the titles they were getting from some of their suppliers. There were horror titles from the 70s like *I Spit On Your Grave* and *Gates of Hell*. They had two Bruce Lee titles, *Fist of Fury* and *The Chinese Connection*. They had a women-in-prison film called *Escape* which was owned by a notorious B-movie producer named Charles Band.

They had something else as well. They had Black Cinema. All of the films were from the 70s and most of them were referred to as *Blaxploitation films*. A company called Unicorn Video had Jamaa Fanaka's film, *Penitentiary*, and films starring Fred Williamson like *Mean Johnny Barrows*. Melvin Van Peebles's 1971 classic, *Sweet Sweetback's Badasssss Song,* was on Magnum Video which was owned by a porn company.

Within a month of working at V.W.D., I was doing virtually all of the company's sales. I developed a very simple strategy: get the store owner on the line, figure out who the customers were and what was renting and sell them the best of whatever V.W.D. had. By the two month mark, I'd developed 250 accounts and new video stores were wiring money to V.W.D.'s bank and asking me to buy them a beginning inventory.

I knew I'd stumbled onto something. But this situation with V.W.D. was never going to last. They were stiffing all of their suppliers and my success there had only served to forestall their demise. When the marshals came and seized the copy machine, I knew it was over.

In my four months at V.W.D., I'd made nearly $40,000 which seemed like an obscene amount of money at the time. I paid off some of my debts relating to the Leno project, grabbed my newly established account base, found an office in Santa Monica, grabbed some of my chronically unemployed friends, and dumped $17,000 into a new company that would later become Xenon Pictures, Inc.

It was January of 1986 and I was 27 years old.

Years later people would say, *"How did you happen to become a distributor of Black film content?"* It just happened. I was in an office on a red, Radio Shack phone making a hundred plus calls a day to video stores. A number of store owners and buyers were singing the same chorus: *"We have Black customers and no films featuring Black actors."* If I was going to establish myself as a distributor, I had to have a niche of some sort. I was never going to be a distributor of high profile studio titles. With $17 grand? I needed something that could get me in the door.

And that something was Black cinema.

From its inception, the video industry, which would morph into something called the *home entertainment industry* was always much different from the music industry, both structurally, and from a marketing standpoint, when it came to Black content. The music industry had been releasing music featuring Black artists for decades and an infrastructure that included Black executives, Black salespeople, Black promotion personnel and Black publicists had formulated around it. But there was no such equivalent in the home entertainment industry. The studio supplier base was overwhelmingly White, the wholesale distributor base was overwhelmingly White, and the store base was overwhelmingly White.

The other issue was that there was simply a dearth of content featuring Black performers. There were newer studio releases with Eddie Murphy, like *Beverly Hills Cop,* and films like *Glory,* with up and coming actors like Denzel Washington. Steven Spielberg had done *The Color Purple*. Spike Lee had directed *She's Gotta Have It* and was on his way to becoming the first breakthrough Black director of his generation. There were films in the catalogs of MGM and Warner Brothers like *Shaft, Hell Up in Harlem* and *The Mack*. And there were television movies based on books, like Maya Angelou's *I Know Why the Caged Bird Sings.*

But the explosion in filmed content for Black audiences was still almost a decade away. It would need a catalyst. And that catalyst would be the hip hop music movement.

I began calling suppliers and buying and wholesaling the Black cast titles they had in their libraries. I started buying from Magnum and Unicorn who I knew from V.W.D. Karl-Lorimar, who'd released the *Jane Fonda Workout* tape, had *Bingo Long's Traveling All-Stars and Motor Kings* with Richard Pryor. Active Home Video had movies like *Petey Wheatstraw: The Devil's Son-*

in-Law and *Disco Godfather*. A company called Marketing International had a back door, closeout arrangement with Vestron Video. From them, I could get *Richard Pryor: Live in Concert* and *Redd Foxx: Video in a Brown Paper Wrapper*. Within a few months, I was wholesaling 200 Black cast titles from 40 different suppliers.

During this time, I had one experience that really defined where the industry for independent Black content was in 1986. The largest chain in Omaha, Nebraska was Applause Video, which would later become part of Blockbuster Video. The owner was a guy named Allan Caplan, who was also the head of the Omaha Chamber of Commerce. I'd called Caplan about 60 times and he kept blowing me off. So I pulled a Barnum and Bailey type move and hired an Omaha-based ranch hand to walk a donkey into Applause's corporate office. The donkey had four videos strapped to its back.

One of them was Melvin Van Peebles' classic 1971 film, *Sweet Sweetback's Badasssss Song*.

The donkey got Caplan's attention. *"You think I'm a horse's ass, don't you?"* We got down to business and Caplan admitted that at least 15% of his stores had a significant Black customer base. He put in an order for $2500 worth of product. Two weeks later, he was on the phone and he was hot. *"You sent me a film that has a fourteen year old kid fucking a hooker! Do you have a death wish? Do you understand the kind of community I'm in?"* He was referring to a scene in *Sweetback* featuring Mario Van Peebles, Melvin's son. He continued, *"This film has words in the title that aren't even in the dictionary."* I told him some easily verifiable facts about the film - that it was one of the most high-profile and historically significant cult films ever made. *"This film is studied at film schools all over the U.S.!"* Caplan didn't care and things got much worse. He told me point blank, *"I'm taking this to the D.A. I'm gonna shut you down."*

The issue would eventually go away. But it presaged what was to come with Death Row Records and the hip hop music movement.

Harry O

Dick Griffey offered to sell the Death Row label a recording studio, and Suge was able to finance the deal with money from a mysterious unnamed source, later revealed to be incarcerated cocaine trafficker, Michael Harris, a.k.a. "Harry O," who was serving back to back sentences for cocaine distribution and attempted murder. The initial meeting between Suge and Michael Harris took place in a downtown L.A. jail in 1991 and was arranged by David Kenner, a Los Angeles-based criminal defense attorney who specialized in federal drug cases and was representing Harris in his attempt to appeal his attempted murder conviction. Later, Suge, Kenner, and Harris agreed to set up an entertainment company named Godfather Entertainment, of which Death Row would be a subsidiary. The launch party for the new partnership - sans Harris - was held at the iconic Chasen's Restaurant in 1992.

VIRGIL ROBERTS: Dick had made a deal with Suge, Doc, and Dre to sell him a recording studio that he owned. And that was going to be something they'd own separate from the Death Row label. He made a deal to sell them studio equipment and other things.

S. LEIGH SAVIDGE: I was always curious why Griffey would sell a studio and studio equipment to Suge. A source at Sony told me that the reason was likely money. The source told me that Solar owed Sony unrecouped advances on prior business deals and that Sony had perfected a lien on the Solar building, which was one of Solar's principal assets. Regardless of any issues that might have existed with Sony, Solar's R & B focused music was quickly falling out of favor in the face of the emerging hip hop movement.

MICHAEL HARRIS: Griffey'd been robbing Sony for years. That building over there- (Sony) owned it. (Griffey) tried to sell me the building -- tried to sell it to 400 people. Sony came and sat down with David Kenner and said, "*Look, before you guys get caught up -- we own the building.*" So Dick is not really looking for this thing to materialize. He was looking for the short term.

VIRGIL ROBERTS: Suge said he'd found somebody to help them finance the purchase of the studio, David Kenner.   And we re-negotiated the studio purchase agreement with David to change the purchase terms and a few other things with respect to the studio.   In my mind, that's all (Kenner) had to do with Death Row -- the purchase of the studio.   That was it.

S. LEIGH SAVIDGE: David Kenner was, by all accounts, a brilliant criminal defense attorney. A former county prosecutor, he'd represented people like notorious drug dealer Freeway Rick Ross. Another client was Michael *Harry O* Harris, a former drug kingpin serving dual sentences for cocaine trafficking and attempted murder. Kenner was working on an appeal for Harris. But Kenner had other ambitions as well. He wanted to be in the music business.

JEFFREY JOLSON COLBURN: It's always been a subject of speculation where they got their original funding. However, rap by this point was selling millions of albums. It wouldn't be hard to fund it without outside money. It would have been possible to get an advance from your distributor, from Sony. A seven figure advance.

JAY KING: There are so many things you heard about this situation. I'll tell you this, Mike Harris was firmly planted in the middle of it.

S. LEIGH SAVIDGE: By the time he was 26, Michael Harris had built a nationwide crack operation from a base in South Central Los Angeles. Much of the business was conducted out of so-called *rock houses* - houses that were purchased in his name, but also in the names of relatives and people he knew.

KEVIN POWELL: Drugs has been the death of my community, but there's no better way to be educated about business. You can't be a hustler on the streets if you don't have a working knowledge of business, mathematics, networking, distribution, geography and the legal system. Transfer that to the music world - it's the same thing.

MICHAEL HARRIS: You had to understand that era. Growing up in that neighborhood, you are quite impressionable. We saw those movies, *The Godfather*, *Scarface*, dealing with a culture we knew nothing about: Cubans and Columbians. But we still tried to emulate them.

KEVIN POWELL: I don't know anyone that doesn't have someone who's a drug dealer in their world -- a relative or friend. There's a real thin line between the drug world and the music industry. Harry O is not the first drug dealer to put money in the music industry, and he's not gonna be the last. Can't get it from banks. This is the path of least resistance.

DAN O'DOWD: There was always the presence of another man, who remained nameless at the time. People were always waiting to hear this third person's opinion - this person nobody knew. I later learned who it was.

LYDIA HARRIS: On the news, they used to call Mike, *The Godfather*.

MICHAEL HARRIS: I come from a place called the *Low Bottom* -- east side of Los Angeles. That place exists in every city. It was a while before I even realized that I was living in what they called the ghetto. Because I had nothing to compare it to.

JIM LAMPLEY / NEWS REPORTER: (9) (Michael Harris is) man who tried to murder his best friend, at the same time he was attempting to win his way into Beverly Hills acceptance.

CHRIS BLATCHFORD / NEWS REPORTER: (10) Michael Harris (is) a man drug agents describe as a major cocaine trafficker. At the young age of 26, he had already made millions of dollars. (His roots are) the streets of South Central Los Angeles, where he started pushing dope on street corners and ran with a Blood street gang called the Bounty Hunters. In the drug world, he is known as Harry O.

MICHAEL HARRIS: I was not a drug dealer. I was a person who decided to sell drugs. I decided I didn't want to do that anymore, so I took the proceeds and invested in real estate and businesses that turned out to be quite profitable.

KEVIN POWELL: Most drug dealers put their money in something legitimate. Where I grew up, cats started laundromats, car washes - some cats became record label owners. That's part of the business.

S. LEIGH SAVIDGE: Michael saw himself as an entertainment impresario, in the vein of a Joe Kennedy or an Annenberg, men whose initial capital had come from illicit means. But his reputation was that of a ruthless drug lord, a guy who'd gotten rid of a lot middle men to deal directly with Mario Villabona. To those that knew him, this was a guy you didn't want to cross or mess with.

MICHAEL HARRIS: I despise drugs. I despise what it did to my community. I despise what it did to people I love. I despise my involvement in the dealing of drugs. I just think we all had the same attitude - somebody's gonna do it. So we might as well do it. When somebody doesn't have anything, they'll do anything to get it.

CHRIS BLATCHFORD / NEWS REPORTER: (10) Michael Harris built an organization that distributed cocaine in California, Arizona, Texas, Michigan, Illinois, Iowa, Indiana, Missouri,

Louisiana, Florida, and New York. Investigators say he dealt so much cocaine, that Columbian drug kingpins like Mario Villabona were obliged to deal directly with Harris. But like a mob godfather, Harris sought to legitimize his illicit fortune and gain Beverly Hills respectability.

JAY KING: Mike Harris was known in our community. He was in jail *doing things.*

SAM GIDEON ANSON: Michael was someone who had been in the entertainment business before he went to prison and stayed active in business once he was in prison.

JOHNATHAN CLARK: Mike is the kind of person that he'll believe in the impossible. You could sit up and talk to Mike and you could come up with some of the craziest shit that you ever thought of. Tomorrow, Mike's down at the county clerk's office, and registering the name of the business. That's the difference between Mike and most people -- he moves on what he talks about.

NORMAN WINTER: Mike Harris had a wonderful background in entertainment. I think he was the first African-American to produce a Broadway show that was a smash.

DICK GRIFFEY: *Checkmates* was the name of the play. The play opened on Broadway. Many of us, African Americans, have been on Broadway, out front, singing and dancing. But few of us had been there as producers.

S. LEIGH SAVIDGE: *Checkmates* was produced in conjunction with one of Broadway's most visible companies, The Nederlander Organization. At the time, Michael was 23- years-old. The star of *Checkmates* was Denzel Washington, who Michael told me he met when he owned a limousine service that he ran out of the L'Ermitage Hotel in West Hollywood.

LYDIA HARRIS: How did Michael get into the entertainment business? He had a limousine service. The people he picked up were in the entertainment field, a lot of celebrities – because everybody wanted limos.

MICHAEL HARRIS: I worked closely with people like Denzel Washington in the beginning when he was getting his career off the ground. But I didn't make him. I just worked with him. I was in a position to help him.

RON NEWT: Mike was managing Vanessa Williams and dealing with Denzel Washington. Mike was a nice guy. He had the limousine service. He was Mr. Hollywood.

DOUG YOUNG: I met Harry O at Jonathan Clark's house around '85 or '86. (Clark) was another player in the music game back in the day.

JONATHAN CLARK: I first met Michael when he owned a limousine company, a sandwich shop, and a beauty shop. He owned about three or four different businesses. That's when I met him -- when I was workin' over at KJLH.

DAN O'DOWD: Moves at Death Row were not made without calls being made to jail. And Norman Winter didn't believe his client was really in jail -- the man who was picking up the bills and taking care of things.

NORMAN WINTER: When I was introduced to Mike on the phone a couple of times, I thought he was an entrepreneur in New York. I knew he had a limousine company, and I was talking to him about Lydia. Because Lydia Harris was one of the premiere artists on Death Row at the beginning and he was trying to get a music video for her. He wanted to present her properly. So we talked to Mike probably two or three times during a two or three week period, giving him updates. We got Lydia on television -- we had news crews come out from ABC and other affiliates. And it went really well. The day before, I'd informed him that there was also an award being presented to Dr. Dre by a trade publication -- which got him very excited. And Mike said, "*So it's gonna be good?*" I said "*You should come see your wife. You can hang out in New York. So come on out.*" and he said, "*I'll try.*" He played me like a violin. And then, I found out later that he couldn't because he was incarcerated. We laughed about it, after that. But I had no idea that he was in jail.

DAN O'DOWD: My first recollection of Death Row was in the office of Norman Winter, who was retained as their publicist. I'm a video director. We were discussing a couple hundred thousand dollars for a video for Lydia Harris. Where's the money gonna come from? Then Dave Kenner set me up with an appointment at the jail downtown where I'd meet someone who could give me all the answers.

S. LEIGH SAVIDGE: From the beginning of the filming of *Welcome to Death Row*, I saw the relationship between Harry O and Suge Knight as the piece of the story puzzle that would intrigue people the most. Suge was a fearsome individual who came out of nowhere, using tactics that had never been utilized in the music industry to achieve his success. Desperate for cash, he decides to partner with, accept money from, and eventually betray, Michael Harris, who was equally fearsome and equally ambitious. What happens when two people like this have a falling out?

SAM GIDEON ANSON: We'd heard a lot of rumors early on about Michael Harris -- that he was involved with Death Row -- from colleagues who had covered his drug conviction in the 80s. And so one of the first stories we did was finding out who Michael Harris is and how was he involved with this label? We chased down documents and talked to people. And the while rumors kept getting stronger, it was very difficult to pin down his role. The break came when we called the Secretary of State's press office and asked for documentation about a series of companies that went by the prefix GF or Godfather -- there was Godfather Entertainment, Godfather Productions. And I remember standing by the fax machine as the Secretary of State's was faxing over these documents, and there was Lydia Harris' name next to David Kenner's on a document of a company that purported to be the parent company of Death Row Records. And this was astonishing to us. Here on paper was evidence of Michael Harris' involvement.

S. LEIGH SAVIDGE: I first learned about Harry O from reading an article about him written by Sam Gideon Anson in the old *LA Reader*.

DAN O'DOWD: After going through a major clearance arranged by Mr. Kenner, we went upstairs and into a private room. Michael Harris had his own private room. Clearly a man of power within this jail system. When we sat down, he asked the guard if he "*didn't have something better to do*?" and the guard subserviently left the room. I'm thinking, if Michael Harris is not *The Man*, why am I talking to a guy in prison about a budget for a music video? Who would not put that together?

SAM GIDEON ANSON: Michael's reach is considerable. Can he run a business from prison per se? Well, one can certainly have a lot of influence and involvement in business projects.

ANGELA WALLACE: Prior to his incarceration, he was very visible -- doing things in the community. Basically, he was a party animal until Lydia toned him down and then he did the right thing.

LYDIA HARRIS: I met Michael Harris at a club in Houston. One of my girlfriends named Kim, she's a rapper with Rap-a-Lot Records and she introduced me to him. Everybody was catering to Mike. So I'm like, "*Who is this guy?*" Nobody said anything. I asked my girlfriend, Kim, "*What does he do?*" She said he had a limousine service. And his limousines won a contest once - he had the cleanest limousine service. So everybody's running around trying to satisfy Mike. He said to me, "*Can I call you after work?*" I said, "*Of course.*" Later he said, "*I wanna fly you out (to Los Angeles).*" So that was my first trip to L.A. My aunt went with me, and my friend Kim and two other girlfriends. When we got to the airport, he had his limousine service out front. They picked us up in the car, and there were roses. Then we went to Fatburger, and then to his condominium in Cheviot Hills. He greeted everybody and I'd never seen a place like that before. He treated me like I was somebody special.

Michael Harris was arrested on federal drug charges in 1987. In a joint statement with Mayor Tom Bradley, federal drug agents called Harris' arrest, "the most dramatic move yet against major suppliers of cocaine in South Central Los Angeles."

PAUL PALLADINO: The first time I met Michael, it was a drug case involving Bo Bennett and Mario Villabona. Michael was sort of the secondary party here, along with several Colombian women. Don Re represented Mario. David Kenner represented Beau Bennett. That trial resulted in a number of convictions in Federal Court. After that case, Michael contacted David Kenner to represent him on his appeal. And that's how they built up a relationship.

Michael and Lydia were married after he was sentenced in the federal drug case in 1988. He'd been in jail for several months.

MICHAEL HARRIS: My most profitable businesses were my real estate investments. They made millions of dollars. It's public record.

S. LEIGH SAVIDGE: According to *The Los Angeles Times*, the government seized multiple homes, businesses, and a fleet of expensive cars from Harris before he went to prison. The businesses included Kartier Limousines, an exotic car company called Beverly Hills Auto Leasing, a deli, and a hair salon. They also seized a cigarette boat from Long Beach Harbor that sank in an accident that killed Harris' brother, David. Michael told me that cash that had been generated by these investments prior to their seizure was held by associates that remained loyal to him.

SAM GIDEON ANSON: Dave Kenner was a longtime Los Angeles criminal lawyer. By the late eighties, he had become part of a fraternity of top flight attorneys that handled a lot of federal drug cases. Kenner had a habit of getting very close to his clients and getting involved in their lives. Perhaps more so than might be wise for a lawyer.

MICHAEL HARRIS: I knew if David was head counsel for our case, I would go with his flow. And so we conferred and developed a respect for one another and became quite close.

SAM GIDEON ANSON: He became someone who was a confidant, a friend of Michael Harris and also involved in business with Michael Harris.

DAN O'DOWD: David Kenner clearly represented the interests of Michael Harris in the beginning.

JAY KING: Me and Mike started getting a rapport with one another. He understood that I understood the record business. Once I went down to see him in downtown Los Angeles, in a holding facility. I got a chance to sit down with him and David Kenner. For some reason, Kenner and I didn't hit it off.

S. LEIGH SAVIDGE: According to Mark Friedman, an ex-con and bail bondsman, who over the years has had extensive dealings with Michael Harris, Suge Knight and David Kenner - Mario Villabona told his lawyers and that Harry O owed him $3.5 million at the time Michael's assets were seized. Additionally, Friedman told me that Kenner had once represented Villabona.

MICHAEL HARRIS: To achieve the massive task of getting me out of prison, it took not just money but power and the proper timing. At some point, (David and I) talked about getting into the entertainment business

VIRGIL ROBERTS: (Kenner is) a lawyer who had a lot of money, and represented people with lots of money. It's not unusual for someone who represented people with money to say "*I want to invest.*"

MICHAEL HARRIS: At some point, we talked about getting into the entertainment business (together). I felt it might help me get out of prison. Creating a powerful company (would) put me in a position where I could vigorously fight for my freedom.

LYDIA HARRIS: David fell in love with Michael and they became friends. He was a friend to us. I looked at him like family. I was out in L.A. by myself, and he was like, you know, took me in, you know, him and his family. We'd go out to eat. We'd do everything together.

VIRGIL ROBERTS: Everyone wants to be in the entertainment business, and in the years I've worked, I've gotten tapes and offers from everyone from politicians to businessmen who want to be in the entertainment business.

MICHAEL HARRIS: A young man by the name of Eric had told me about Suge's background and that Suge was aware of my background and intrigued by my past and wanted to hook up with me in some fashion. We talked on the phone a few times. I think Suge knew who I was, but didn't care. I think he felt it was more a myth.

S. LEIGH SAVIDGE: The connection to Eric had come through Jonathan Clark, a former Marketing Vice President at Motown Records. At Michael Harris' request, Clark had taken at interest in Lydia's career as a recording artist.

LYDIA HARRIS: Jonathan Clark did my first song, *Wishing You Were Here*. His friend Eric said, "*Hey, if you want some hype on the song, I can hook you up with this guy they call Sugar Bear.*" I went down to Solar Studios and I met Suge. Suge said, " *I've heard a lot about your husband. I got a lotta respect for him.*" "That's nice," I said. He asked, "*Do you have any money?*" And I said, "*I'm not gonna tell you what he has. Evidentially he has something.*"

KEVIN POWELL: Anyone that comes from the background that Suge comes from is going to aspire, on some level, to be a Don. And on the street level, Michael Harris was a Don. He was a *baller*. He was a hustler. In the ghetto world, the cat who has all the money and the clothes and the beautiful women - that's as important as a little White kid in Iowa wanting to be president of the United States.

MICHAEL HARRIS: Once I found out that Suge was in the entertainment business, which I had been contemplating re-entering, we made the hook up and we talked on the phone a few times.

LYDIA HARRIS: We started talking with Suge, and Mike said, "*You got Dre?*" and Suge said, "*Yeah, the hit producer.*" And Suge said, " *I can get him to do a track for your girl.*"

S. LEIGH SAVIDGE: Before Michael had gone to prison, his brother David had died in an accident involving a cigarette boat the brothers owned. Michael suggested that Suge used his knowledge of this story to expedite a bond between the two.

MICHAEL HARRIS: Suge took (my brother's) place. We got very close, like brothers. We were visiting one another every night, and talking on the phone every day.

LYDIA HARRIS: Mike said, "*We need to meet.*" And Suge said, "*I can't get in to visit you. I got a couple of cases.*" And Mike said, " *I got this attorney. He's bad. He can get you in here."* And Suge was like, *" Wow!"*

SAM GIDEON ANSON: We knew that Michael had been David Kenner's client and that was one of the original connections we looked for - we figured that David had a role in putting Michael together with Suge.

MARK FRIEDMAN: Unless he was representing him, it would be very difficult for David Kenner, this White defense lawyer, to walk on the street and meet someone like Suge Knight.

LYDIA HARRIS: (Mike) called Kenner and said, *"David, I think we got a way we can get in the entertainment business."*

SAM GIDEON ANSON: David Kenner brought Suge Knight to see Michael at the Metropolitan Detention Center in downtown Los Angeles.

LYDIA HARRIS: Kenner wanted to get out of the criminal aspect because the business, the monies were slow.

S. LEIGH SAVIDGE: Lydia told me that initially Suge didn't trust Kenner.

LYDIA HARRIS: Suge said, *"I really don't trust White peckerwood - paleface."* Mike said, *"That's my guy. I trust him."*

Suge understood that Harry O's reputation could be useful in cementing Death Row's reputation as the most authentic gangsta rap label -- that Harry O's involvement, when matched with Dre's reputation, would be an additional catalyst for the artists Death Row was looking to attract.

MICHAEL HARRIS: When I asked the question, *"What does it actually take?,"* Suge told me we could be 50/50 partners for about a million-five.

S. LEIGH SAVIDGE: Chuck Phillips of *The Los Angeles Times* had reported that a significant part of the initial $1.5 million had come from another imprisoned drug dealer named Patrick Johnson. Harris later confirmed this but made it clear he didn't want me to talk to him. (Later, it was suggested to me that Harris and Johnson had an unresolved financial dispute.) In time, I learned that a number of people, most of them wealthy individuals, had also loaned money to Suge during Death Row's early, *Chronic* and pre-*Chronic* phase.

MICHAEL HARRIS: The $1.5 million was ear-marked for whatever had to take place to keep everybody secure. If the artists needed any money for room and board, they made that decision. If we had to fight criminal cases or lawsuits, they had the reserves to do that.

SAM GIDEON ANSON: They set down their business plan that they'd start a company called Godfather Entertainment and one division of it would be Death Row Records.

MICHAEL HARRIS: I suggested to David and Suge that I do not include my name in the corporation, and that these guys could go ahead and do the actual upfront managing and representing of the company. Kenner started off as my guy, watching my back, supposedly. And Lydia was there to represent my percentage of GF entertainment, which we decided would be the parent company of Death Row.

JOHN PAYNE: Mike trusted these guys.

JEWELL: I knew him as Michael Harris. But people referred to him as *Harry O*. From the beginning, he was there.

MICHAEL HARRIS: Suge had five or six cases pending, which Kenner was able to neutralize. That's why he wanted us to be his partners. David was the legal mind, Suge was handling the day to day stuff and I would provide the overall philosophy and legitimate connection to the streets.

JEWELL: Suge was all by himself. And once he talked with Michael Harris, a certain position started being filled.

SAM GIDEON ANSON: In the summer of 1991, Kenner started coming around. There was a lot of buzz about this company, a lot of expectations that it could be a successful company; and David was one of the people around at the time that was making a play to be Suge's partner and take care of business for Suge, to handle business for Suge.

JOHN PAYNE: One day I see these two people walking into the Solar Building who I'd never seen before. One was David Kenner and the other was Lydia Harris. And I was also told we'd be getting collect calls (from jail). And to accept them, find Suge, and connect him.

MICHAEL HARRIS: During this time, we were inseparable. David was the legal mind. Suge was handling the day to day stuff. And I would provide the overall business strategy and legitimate connection to the streets.

LYDIA HARRIS: Kenner said, "*Lyd, we'll tell people that Michael's in London.*" Michael didn't care (if people knew he was in jail). He wanted people to know he was doing business. (he wanted to) let everybody know what they're getting into when you get involved with him.

JOHN PAYNE: Michael is very smart. If Michael wanted to call you and say, "*I wanna do a record,*" he would have it laid out from a to z and beyond. Not just for today. But for the next five years.

DICK GRIFFEY: I saw a few little upgrades in the studio, some chairs, some speakers.

VIRGIL ROBERTS: I've heard that Michael supposedly put a lot of money into the company. If he did, I don't know where it went. It wasn't going to pay bills, and it wasn't going to make records.

JOHN PAYNE: A couple of days after Mrs. Harris and David Kenner came in, things started to change drastically. Immediately the studio gets carpeted, things start getting fixed. I start getting money to find apartments for the artists that didn't have apartments, that didn't have any money. I'm also given an allowance for them.

DICK GRIFFEY: I don't know anything about Michael and Lydia Harris as it pertains to Death Row.

MICHAEL HARRIS: The publishing deals with Sony? (Griffey) took the money and spent it. He done spent his half and what little money they had - and they was broke again.

JEWELL: We had these jackets with the Death Row emblem on it that said GF Entertainment.

DICK GRIFFEY: I don't know anything about Godfather Entertainment. Nothing at all.

LYDIA HARRIS: (Mike) would call Suge and wake him up. Cause Suge would get up late in the morning and Mike would say, "*To handle business, you got to get up early.*" Suge would get up in the morning and we would handle business. Mike would say, " *Go do this, go do that.*" And he'd do it.

MICHAEL HARRIS: (Suge) was the type of dude that didn't wake up until one or two in the afternoon. At eight in the morning, I'd call him up and make him go do whatever he had to do. I was kind of like a surrogate father to him. He respected me.

LYDIA HARRIS: Mike would get on the phone with Dre and talk to him about what the people wanted to hear -- the music, the lyrics and what he knew would sell. Because the guys listened to it all day in jail.

JOHN PAYNE: Lydia was always cool. She had an office. They came in and set up all the offices. And she very rarely came in. I think she was trying to give everybody some space. But anything we asked for, anything I needed, I talked to Lydia and she made sure that it was happening.

During this period, Lydia's house was broken into and Kenner allowed her to stay at his home in Encino.

LYDIA HARRIS: I wasn't trying to be involved. 'Cause David would come back every night and let me know what was going on. I knew Kenner would catch on better than me. That's who Mike put there.

JOHN PAYNE: At that time it seemed like (Suge) was very protective of her. It appeared to be cool, like he had respect for her. And it seemed like the way he talked about Lyd and Mike -- that they were really close. It was the utmost trust.

PAUL PALLADINO: Originally, David was handling a lot of the civil and criminal cases they had. And, as a result of them seeing that he was very competent, they brought him more and more into other areas of the business.

MICHAEL HARRIS: We were visiting one another every night and talking on the phone every day.

JOHN PAYNE: Kenner and Suge used to visit Michael all the time. All the time. I even went once. Course I didn't get in. I drove Suge there a couple times and just stayed in the parking lot. There's love and there's friendship, but it was too many fucking visits. People don't visit their relatives that much.

Mothers don't visit their sons that much.

S. LEIGH SAVIDGE: The frequent visits were likely something that Harris demanded. During the first two years on the *Welcome to Death Row* project, I drove down to Lancaster over 25 times to see him. It was never because I wanted to. He demanded it because, given his past experiences, if someone didn't make the effort to come see him he viewed it as a betrayal. My sense is that this emanated from when he ran several legitimate businesses and his drug operation. He was used to people reporting to him. He demanded attention. He demanded answers to thousands of questions. And in my case, each visit would involve lengthy and strenuous negotiations for additional money for Lydia.

A launch party for the Death Row label was held at Chasen's restaurant in Beverly Hills

SAM GIDEON ANSON: From September (1991) through the winter, you see a lot of activity -- GF Entertainment is a name that's floating around the business. In February of '92, they have a launch party -- GF Entertainment launches Death Row Records. It's the party at Chasen's.

LYDIA HARRIS: The Chasen's party was (about) introducing Death Row - who was starting the company.

DAN O'DOWD: So, Norman Winter came up with the brilliant idea to have the kick-off (party) for Death Row at Chasen's, and everyone would get *served* with (fake) subpoenas as an invitation. And we'd go into Beverly Hills and rub it in everybody's nose that Death Row is coming out.

NORMAN WINTER: Chasen's was *the place* in Los Angeles in 1992. All the superstars, and every president up till Reagan were at that place constantly. Presidents. Society. When you're unknown, you pick the best venue you can get. Even if they don't come to see your act, they come to see and be seen. And sometimes they come back with an earful and eyeful.

NORMAN WINTER: The invitation was printed on a one-sheet, folded to look like a subpoena. (It read) *"You are hereby ordered to appear before the honorable Dr. Dre and the offices of GF Entertainment as a guest of the court, witnessing the springing of Death Row Records."* We had it delivered by two large security gentlemen who walked in on people and handed them a summons that looked real. Dave Kenner helped me write the text.

DAN O'DOWD: Everyone showed up. It was a madhouse. Lydia played. Snoop was there. The whole ensemble was there.

At the Chasen's party, the DJ announced "Let me see somebody give Dre, Suge and DOC a round of applause. (Pointing to Dre) That bro' right there is gonna be the record company of the 2000s."

NORMAN WINTER: Not only did (everyone) have a good time, they could not believe the abilities of these performers. The service was impeccable, and there were great camera opportunities out front when you arrived. We wanted metal detectors out front, but (Chasen's) thought it could hurt their business.

MICHAEL HARRIS: I wanted to let the city know that we were on our way.

JOHN PAYNE: They had enough money behind them and they looked good. All the acts performed that night. Everyone was well-behaved. Mike made sure the all the girls dressed nice. They were wearing $600 dollar dresses. Even the bodyguards were in tuxedos. It could have been the next Motown. Motown groomed their people and gave them self-esteem and respect.

NORMAN WINTER: We invited virtually every major record

executive in Los Angeles and New York. We planned on spending $20 - 25 thousand but it turned out to be 35 to 50. We had huge screen monitors showing the Grammys, which were taking place in New York.

SUGE KNIGHT: (11) The market we're going after is mainly for the people. I mean for us, the West Coast has a lot talent around, guys that don't have the opportunity and haven't had the opportunity to prove their selves. So as far as GF Entertainment goes, with the studio and the films, we giving all the youngsters the opportunities from the neighborhoods where - basically we haven't forgotten where we came from.

JOHN PAYNE: Death Row came out of nowhere, and had a party at Chasen's on Grammy night, which was reserved generally for all the White people. You know, that's White Night. Even though the music is universal, that's *White night.*

DAN O'DOWD: I personally interviewed all the players that were there.

DAVID KENNER: (11) GF Entertainment is a multi-media company. We have Death Row Records. We have a movie production unit. Concerts. We're going to be doing pay per view concerts, and all kinds of exciting things.

DAN O'DOWD: The entire Chasen's event was paid for by Godfather Entertainment. Everyone got a microphone in their face. When it came to David Kenner, he toasted the man who made it all (possible), Harry O.

JEWELL: In the beginning, they were giving Mike his props. And they were recognizing that there was another entity that helped this be one major pow wow.

DAN O'DOWD: Everybody was nodding to a guy named Harry O.

DAVID KENNER: (11) The label started with Dr. Dre, who was gonna do his own thing. And it was a lotta help from Suge Knight, and Harry O, and a number people. And we got it all together.

DAN O'DOWD: And that's on tape, and the FBI confiscated that from me under very rude circumstances.

JOHN PAYNE: Mike thought everybody should look good. He got Suge a Benz, a 500 series. Dave Kenner got a car. I got a Lexus LS - I got David's (old) car. Before that, Suge had a Suzuki Samurai.

LYDIA HARRIS: The day we did the Chasen's party, they shipped Mike to Tehachapi State Penitentiary. It was sixty days before Mike could use a phone.

JOHN PAYNE: Godfather Entertainment is Michael Harris' company. Look at the *Deep Cover* soundtrack. It says *Godfather Entertainment*.

The Big Three

By 1987, Xenon was barely surviving as a wholesaler of VHS tapes. If I was going to build this business, Xenon needed to become a label that marketed content that would secure us credibility with Black consumers. We needed a catalyst.

That catalyst was a 1974 film owned by a Black comedian named Rudy Ray Moore. It was called *Dolemite*.

It should be no surprise that everyone in the Death Row story knew who Rudy Ray Moore was. Dr Dre would sample his audio recordings several times on his seminal album, *The Chronic*.

After getting out of the army in late fifties, Rudy had tried his hand as an R & B singer before becoming a comedian who did x-rated "party records" geared specifically for a blue collar, Black audience. If Redd Foxx was *Playboy*, Rudy was *Hustler*. On records like, *Eat Out More Often*, he'd appear naked on the cover, with a harem of naked women. One day, a Black classmate in my eight grade class showed me one of Rudy's album covers. At the time, I thought it represented the end of civilization.

There were two things that set Rudy apart from virtually every other Black performer.

First, he had virtually no interest in obtaining any kind of mainstream White appeal. He saw his audience as Black. Period. He was a heavyset man, with a dangerous look, who talked in very graphic terms about sex. He was a storyteller, who had developed a number of onstage personas that derived from a long tradition of stories told among working class Blacks in the south.

The persona that audiences remembered the most was a bad ass character named *Dolemite*.

Secondly, like Alonzo Williams, Ice Cube, Dr. Dre, Eazy E and Suge Knight, Rudy was an extremely self-determined man. He pressed his own records and eight-track tapes, and sold them directly to fans at the clubs where he performed. He never waited for a deal or an offer. He had a relationship with a small indie label called King Records. There were wholesalers he worked with. But Rudy would never allow himself to be beholden to them. He was never going to wait on anyone for his money.

By the early part of the 70s, between the notoriety of his records and his regular appearances on a coterie of clubs that catered to Black audiences known as the *chitlin circuit*, Rudy had made enough money and had enough of a fan base that he decided to produce, self-finance and star in a film called *Dolemite*. The film was released by a long-defunct company called Dimension Pictures, and opened to generally negative reviews.

But significant segments of the mostly Black audiences that saw *Dolemite* were just blown away. For many, the film was nothing short of transforming. The Dolemite character was doing something on film that audiences had never seen before. Here was an overweight, relatively unattractive Black man turning every died-in-the-wool Black stereotype that had ever been seen before on the silver screen on its ear. Dolemite was a Black super stud, with a precise sense of principles that played Whitey like a fiddle. In one scene, Dolemite takes a machine gun and shoots at the feet of a White redneck sheriff which illicits a high stepping act that put a whole new spin on the concept of Bojangles and Stepin Fetchit. In another scene, he beds the sheriff's White wife. *The New York Times* would later call the film, *The Citizen Kane of Blaxploitation films* and Quentin Tarantino would regularly mention it as one of the films that influenced him the most.

After a few months in business, I'd talked to so many people at both the wholesale and retail level that had confirmed the consumer demand for *Dolemite* that I set out to find it. But where was it? Dimension Pictures (not to be confused with the current version of Dimension Pictures) had gone bankrupt. The trail was cold.

One day, I got a call from a guy named Nicholas Mercer. He'd been my main contact at Beech Video, a company Xenon was selling to. Mercer had left Beech and was now an independent film broker. "*I got you Dolemite.*" He'd arranged a deal with Rudy Ray Moore and now had the rights. We executed a deal which also involved another Rudy movie, *The Human Tornado* and a concert film, *Rude*. Later, we did a photo shot with Rudy and began selling the *Dolemite* videocassette.

The reaction in the U.S. marketplace was instantaneous. We began selling thousands of copies of the VHS cassette to video stores and small regional wholesalers. Many of the wholesalers, like Universal in Philadelphia, and Select O Hits in Memphis, were record distributors who had sold Rudy's party records (as well as *N.W.A. and The Posse* from Macola) and recognized that *Dolemite* and films like it would work in record stores.

Dolemite was Xenon's first exclusive license, and opened the door to more content and better distribution. Suddenly, the video market and the independent supplier community started viewing Xenon as a Black label. From a company called Fox Lorber, we picked up a film called *Welcome Back, Brother Charles*, which had been the UCLA thesis project of filmmaker, Jamaa Fanaka, who had been one of the most important Black film-makers from the 70s and early 80s. Later, we got two other films Jamaa owned, *Penitentiary I* and *Penitentiary II*. We acquired the first two films of director Tim Story, who would later direct *Barbershop* (in fact, Xenon's Chief Operating Officer Steve Housden recommended Tim for the *Barbershop* job, his first Hollywood film), *Fantastic Four*, and the *Ride Along* films. Through producer, Michael Jaffe, we got *A Woman Called Moses* with Cicely Tyson, which was about Harriet Tubman and the Underground Railroad. Consumers were asking for gospel titles and through producer, Rueben Cannon, we got a live concert with one of gospel's biggest groups at the time, The Winans. From producer, Shep Morgan we got *Half Slave, Half Free: Solomon Northup Odyssey,* which would later be remade into the Oscar winning film, *12 Years a Slave.*

For the very first time, consumers were recognizing a video label that solely carried Black content.

As we started licensing more titles, we were able to step up the quality of our distribution infrastructure. I hired a sales force, and then went on the road and talked to key people in virtually every major city in the U.S. We established vendor relationships with the major wholesalers, like Ingram Video and Baker and Taylor. Through Amarillo-based Anderson Merchandisers, we put the first Black video initiative into Wal-Mart. Drawing a page from the music industry, we put the video industry's first corrugate displays of Black film content in places like Woolworths. The country's major video chains like Blockbuster, and Family Video, started buying from us, and the country's biggest record retailers like Trans World Music, Camelot Music, Music Plus and The Wherehouse all came on.

By our third year, we were doing $3 million dollars a year and sub-licensing studio owned films like *Three The Hard Way* from Fox.

Our next big step was to hire a team to finance and produce the first full biography of Martin Luther King, *Dr. Martin Luther King Jr: A Historical Perspective.*

Later, amid a climate where CBS and other major broadcast entities were in litigation with the King Foundation over copyright issues relating to Dr. King's speeches, I worked out an arrangement with the foundation's lawyer, Philip Jones and

Xenon became the first company to have a fully authorized biography on MLK. The major broadcasters had spent millions fighting the King Foundation because they felt Dr. King's speeches were in the public domain. Philip Jones and I had worked out a deal over the phone in 15 minutes. A biography of Mahalia Jackson soon followed.

One day in 1989, Rudy Ray Moore walked into my office and told me that Nicholas Mercer wasn't paying him what he was owed. I called Mercer and found out it was true. Very quickly, I made a decision I'd never regret. I breached my contract with Mercer and began paying the royalties that were owed to him directly to Rudy.

Later, I was sued by Mercer and settled with him. After that we worked with Rudy to restore the copyrights of his films in his name. The business relationship between Xenon and Rudy would last nearly two decades until Rudy's death in 2007.

****

There were three pioneering, Black film-makers in the 70s era, and all three owned their own copyrights. I called them *The Big Three*. With Rudy and Jamaa Fanaka, I was in business with two of them, and I wanted to be in business with the third guy as well.

His name was Melvin Van Peebles.

His life would later be immortalized in the film *Baadasssss,* but there was a lot more to Melvin than his pioneering film, *Sweet Sweetback's Baadasssss Song*. He was fluent in several languages including French and Dutch. He'd produced Broadway plays, including *Don't Play Us Cheap*, which was one of the first to feature an all-Black cast. He was the first Black man on the trading floor of the American Stock Exchange. He had a recording contract with Capitol Records, and performed in the clubs in New York City. He got interested in Astronomy and became an expert.

As I got to know him, I'd ask myself, *where does it stop with this guy?* His accomplishments were just off the charts. I thought about his son Mario, who'd attended Columbia University, and had become a successful actor/director in his own right. I tried to imagine what it must have been like to have a guy like this as your father.

Business with Melvin didn't happen quickly. He did things that no one we'd done business with had ever done before. He spoke to many people we were in business with including Jamaa Fanaka and Rudy Ray Moore. He came to our office and started talking to the people that worked for me to see if he liked them. He examined the films we'd acquired. We did many drafts of his contract, and on the day he signed with us he took the final draft and the previous draft, put them together and held them up to a light and examined them. This was his way of verifying if the changes we discussed had been implemented, and if we'd added any language that hadn't been agreed upon.

Later on, something else happened with Melvin. He became a Xenon shareholder.

Bullets in the Studio

As Dr. Dre worked on the tracks that would become the basis for the Deep Cover soundtrack, the third floor of the Solar building became a hub of activity where a number of aspiring artists compete for Dre's attention. A phone line was established for Michael Harris to communicate with Suge, Dre and others from prison. Suge ruled the roost with an iron fist. As he and Dre felt the pressure to deliver great music, tensions rise and there were frequent episodes that involved violence. In July of 1992, there was a now infamous incident involving aspiring rappers, George, and Lynwood Stanley.

VIRGIL ROBERTS: When Death Row was in the Solar offices, we pretty much gave over the third floor. There were a lot of young, street folks hanging out. But it wasn't what it became.

MICHAEL HARRIS: When they had the offices at Solar, Lydia set that office up. (Suge's) office -- he wanted it to be red. That was the first sign. The walls were black. The rug was red. And he started using the word *blood* a lot. I started seeing it. He might say to me joking, *"All right, blood."* I might fool and joke with him. But when I'd see him face to face, I'd tell him, *"That ain't cool. If you keep doing that, you're gonna separate yourself in this city."*

DICK GRIFFEY: There was a lot of tension. An element showed up that my people were not accustomed to. I'd show up and guys would be sitting on the steps eating chicken, throwing chicken bones in the driveway. I said, *"Man, you act like you're at your Grandma's house. Get up off my steps!"*

S. LEIGH SAVIDGE: During the entire three-year process of making *Welcome to Death Row*, Michael Harris seemed to have near constant access to a cell phone. He had an insider at Lancaster that was making one available to him. And when his cell access became restricted, which it did from time to time, he would call collect from a prison pay phone. There were periods where, every day, my receptionist, Sandre Wiley, would pick up the phone and hear, *"You are receiving a call from an inmate at a California State Prison."*

MICHAEL HARRIS: There was a phone in the studio that was reserved for me to call on. Suge made it clear that phone should not be tied up. Because of my situation, the phone could not be busy.

LYDIA HARRIS: Mike would call collect. Everyone at the studio knew to answer the phone and accept the call.

JEWELL: I knew him as 'Mike'. He used to call from jail. And I'd answer the phone, because in the beginning, we didn't have a lot of people.

JOHN PAYNE: Those calls would last an hour, an hour and a half.

SNOOP DOGG: I was aware of Michael Harris. I talked to him a few times when he called.

MICHAEL HARRIS: I talked to Dr. Dre on a number of occasions. I would give him the street level. (Afterward) Suge would say that he'd be hyped up after talking to me. There was a lot of content associated with me that they could use that had the reality they needed.

DICK GRIFFEY: So, Dre had invited these guys (the Stanley Brothers) over to the studio. When Suge came, they were using the phone. So Suge gets off the elevator and sees these strangers using the phone.

THE DOC a.k.a. TRACY CURRY: They Dre's homeboys. They wanted to be rappers. You know, rapping ain't for every fucking-body. Everybody wants to be a rapper. And they'd come around and be so serious about their shit.

DICK GRIFFEY: They tell him, *"Hey we were invited up here by Dre. Dre told us we could use the phone."* Suge says, *"I don't give a fuck what Dre says. Dre ain't payin' no bills."* An argument ensued.

MICHAEL HARRIS: At the time, Suge did not affiliate with a lot of gang members. He came across as a strong, forceful individual. Kind of like an enforcer.

THE DOC a.k.a. TRACY CURRY: And (one of them, presumably Lynwood Stanley) the dude says (to Suge), *"Hey man, don't be coming at me with that gang bang shit. I'm from Philadelphia."*

MICHAEL HARRIS: By challenging Suge about the phone, and also challenging Suge about his authority, they just found themselves in an awkward position.

THE DOC a.k.a. TRACY CURRY: Suge said, *"Okay."* There wasn't no arguing, none of that shit. And I was thinking to myself, *"Man, he (Lynwood Stanley) shouldn't have done that."* And then I seen (Suge) go down the elevator.

MICHAEL HARRIS: That was Suge's domain. And no one would talk back to him, and no one would go against him. And for somebody to be visiting, and taking a stance against him, well, he had to clear that up.

THE DOC a.k.a. TRACY CURRY: (Suge) said to me, *"I'm about to give those niggas the blues."*

MICHAEL HARRIS: In dealing with this music and these artists, there has to be a strong presence. Or you will be run over.

DICK GRIFFEY: Suge went down to his car, and got a gun. And hey, he beat these guys up in the studio.

S. LEIGH SAVIDGE: According to an article in 1997 by Chuck Phillips of *The Los Angeles Times,* a search warrant affidavit filed subsequent to the episode said that the Stanley Brothers were ordered to strip and fall to their knees at gunpoint as Knight fired a shot near their heads. Then he pistol whipped Lynwood Stanley.

DICK GRIFFEY: He shot through the wall to scare 'em -- the hole is still there. The cops came and dug the bullet out.

THE DOC a.k.a. TRACY CURRY: Later, (Suge) said to me, *"Didn't I tell those niggas, Doc?"* I said, *"Yeah, you told their asses. You told their asses good."* Me, Suge and Jewell and them two niggas rode down the elevator together. We was all dressed and they was in their drawers.

CHRIS BLATCHFORD / NEWS REPORTER: (FOX TV archive) George and Lynwood Stanley later sued Suge. He agreed to a million dollar settlement, but only paid a third of it.

S. LEIGH SAVIDGE: Subsequent coverage by Chuck Phillips in the *Los Angeles Times* suggested that the 1995 *settlement* was actually done in the form of a record contract for the Stanley Brothers. The settlement required the Stanley Brothers to provide testimonials that any claims that they had in a potential criminal action against Knight and Death Row had been resolved. When Knight defaulted on the contractual terms, the Stanley Brothers sued and tried to reopen the criminal case. The case came before prosecutor Lawrence Longo, whose daughter had been signed as the first White artist on Death Row Records. Longo dropped the case, saying that the Stanley Brothers had compromised their rights and the case by signing the record deal.

LYNWOOD STANLEY: (12) (Longo) is acting like we ruined the case. But that is the exact opposite of what he told us when we accepted the offer. If he had told us that our settlement was going to ruin the criminal case, we would have never taken it.

S. LEIGH SAVIDGE: Others we spoke to said that the favorable result for Suge and Death Row was largely due to the handiwork of David Kenner, who had maneuvered behind the scenes and pulled favors to get Suge out of hot water.

DAN O'DOWD: The business end was falling into Kenner's lap.

S. LEIGH SAVIDGE: Mark Friedman, an associate of both Michael Harris and David Kenner, told me that it was in the wake of this settlement that Kenner's star within Death Row really began to rise.

GEORGE STANLEY: (12) Larry Longo used his position for his own benefit. We trusted the guy. He told us justice would be served.

S. LEIGH SAVIDGE: The *Los Angeles Times* later reported that subsequent to the settlement, Longo had rented a Malibu beach house he owned to Suge Knight for $30,000 a month. The arrangement was done through David Kenner. Kenner's name was on the lease agreement.

"Our Stories Are Not Being Told"

Rudy Ray Moore knew I'd once been affiliated with Jay Leno, and for years would ask me, *"When are you gonna get me on The Tonight Show?"* One day, after deflecting this question for several years, I finally told him there two reasons why a Tonight Show appearance was never going to happen. *"Number one, Jay will hate your act. Number two, he hates my guts."*

The Leno project had evolved into a whole theater of the bizarre situation. We'd sued Leno, then settled in a deal where he paid a small judgment and Xenon retained the rights to the show on a royalty free basis. But when Xenon released the videocassette of the show that became *The 1984 Los Angeles Comedy Competition with Jay Leno*, Leno's lawyers went in for a temporary restraining order, claiming that, among other infractions Xenon had used marketing materials that made his face appear *"frightening to small children."* It would be two decades later before Leno would finally acknowledge that he no longer had an issue with the show.

****

By the mid-90s, I could see clear signs that the winds were changing in my chosen market segment. Spike Lee had become the most important Black director in America by following *She's Gotta Have It* with *School Daze, Do the Right Thing, Mo Better Blues, Jungle Fever,* and *Malcolm X*. Will Smith had done *Bad Boys* and *Independence Day*, back to back. Ice Cube had starred in John Singleton's, *Boyz in the Hood* and had followed it up with *Friday*, which had been helmed by an up-and-coming director named F. Gary Gray. Wesley Snipes was starting to break with *White Men Can't Jump*.

But all these films had been financed and / or distributed by the major studios. I was in the independent space, so my business was really dependent on the next breed of filmmaker making his first or second low budget film. So I began trawling the new breed of film festivals that the Spike Lee generation had spawned. There was Urbanworld in New York, run by Stacy Spikes, whose roots were in video like mine. There were others like the American Black Film Festival in Miami, and the Pan Pacific Film Festival in Los Angeles.

I began wrestling with a crisis of confidence about what I was seeing and what I was doing. Almost 90% of the films I was seeing dealt with life in inner city America. For every rapper that might be pressing a record that Dr. Dre thought sucked, there were three people making a Black, or so called urban film, that in my view was unwatchable. Suddenly, we'd gone from a marketplace with virtually no new content to one where there were literally thousands of films that were being produced. And the vast majority of them, that I was seeing, had bad writing, bad acting and poor production values. I couldn't imagine that these films would appeal to a wider Black audience.

But the reality was that these films, which I had made a value judgment on and passed on, were getting picked up by other small labels and finding their way into Blockbuster and Wal-Mart. My COO, Steve Housden and I would have these long circular arguments. We wanted to be seen as a label of premium independent Black content. We were picking up older films like early 80s mini-series, *The Sophisticated Gents* and *The Women of Brewster Place* with Oprah Winfrey. But the video market suddenly was very enamored with these *hood films,* and by passing on them, we were assisting the rise of new competitors. And the numbers didn't lie. Significant numbers of Black consumers were buying and renting these films.

Were we just being stupid?

I would grow to understand that what I was seeing was the direct result of the growing influence of hip hop culture. *Boyz in the Hood* and *Barbershop,* and albums like *The Chronic* and *Doggystyle,* had inspired a lot of quasi-talented people to create thousands of films that examined the same themes over and over again. Even so, this *transitional cinema* was signaling a sea change where Black artists were recognizing that they could control their destiny and their portrayals on film. And it was running concurrently with the activities of Sean *Puffy* Combs and Jay Z in New York, Death Row Records in Los Angeles and Master P's No Limit Records, based in New Orleans.

I started hearing some things that gave me a lot of pause. In meeting after meeting after watching a film that I was sure would disappoint any audience, I would be told the same thing, *"You don't understand Black people. You don't understand the Black experience."* No less than 15 different films were presented to me that I was advised represented the Black male response to the film, *Waiting to Exhale*. One of them featured two men at a dining table, free-associating back and forth for 90 minutes, about how awful Black women were. At some point, I asked the filmmaker to turn off the tape. When I told him I didn't want to sell the film, he went ballistic on me. *"You don't get this because you're a White guy who doesn't understand Black women."* I told him, *"Maybe you're right. But this is not a good film and I don't understand you, either."*

I wrestled with was this idea that I was starting to be viewed as a White gatekeeper for Black filmmakers. *"Was I really the right guy to do this? Is my judgment correct for this?"* I picked up films like, *A Day in Black and White,* with Harold Perrineau, and *The Other Brother*, with Mekhi Phifer, and their rental revenues had paled in comparison to a film like *I'm Bout it* from Master P's new No Limit Films label. I felt in my bones that one of my real skill sets was evaluating whether audiences of any ethnicity would like a film. But guys like Jeff Clanagan at No Limit were starting to eat Xenon's lunch. The success of *I'm Bout It* suggested that he knew how to reach his audience better than I did.

The other chorus I heard from Black filmmakers, especially those who had a project they wanted to make was *"Our stories are not being told."* They weren't seeing stories that reflected the larger dimensions of life in Black America and didn't recognize themselves or anyone they knew in most of the films that Hollywood was making. They felt that White directors and producers were presenting Black characters from an image they had, and those images did not reflect reality.

This made sense to me. I also understood that the key to changing this situation was rooted in these filmmakers getting access to Black capital. A coterie of Black professional athletes would finance Harry Davis's *MVP,* which premiered at the Sundance Film Festival, and Xenon later released as *Joy Road.* Whether you liked the film or not you had to acknowledge that you were seeing portrayals of Black characters that you hadn't seen on film or television before. I'd seen hundreds of this new generation of films, probably more than anyone in the country at that point. And some of them did have portrayals that seemed new and different from what I'd seen before. *They simply did.*

The U.S. home entertainment industry had recently embraced the term *urban,* a moniker they'd borrowed from the music industry to suggest a catch-all category that a Black audience and / or the multi-cultural audience that were fans of the hip hop music movement would embrace. With rappers like the Wu Tang Clan becoming popular, I started to examine the area of Hong Kong-produced martial arts films. We did an output deal with an entity called *Eastern Heroes* which was run by Toby Russell, the son of British film director, Sir Ken Russell. The Eastern Heroes library had titles that featured performers like Jackie Chan, Samo Hung and Quentin Tarantino favorite, Gordon Lui. The new Eastern Heroes label worked right away with all fans of hip hop culture.

By mid-1997, Xenon had released more than 200 martial arts titles.

Shortly, thereafter, Eastern Heroes delivered Xenon a title outside of the martial arts genre. It was a hastily conceived and assembled documentary called *Thug Immortal* on rapper, Tupac Shakur, who'd just been shot and killed in Las Vegas. When I watched it, I thought it was terrible. *"This will be our waterloo."*

I was wrong. *Thug Immortal* would sell over a million units. For a short time, it was the top selling video in the country.

In June of 1998, *The Los Angeles Times* published an article about me and my company that appeared on the front page of the business section. It proclaimed that Xenon, a company run by *a "blonde-haired, blue-eyed white guy from Seattle"* was now the leading distributor of independent films targeting young Black Americans. Soon I was having meetings with people like Robert Johnson, the CEO of BET Networks, and Island Records founder, Chris Blackwell. But I also heard from many people that the article had rubbed a lot of people, both Black and White, the wrong way. At one meeting, a White executive had remarked, *"I was hoping you were Black."*

I wasn't blind to the often, emotional, knee-jerk reaction that some people had about what I was doing. But I also knew that the perception of Xenon's business was much greater than the reality.

In the wake of the *Times* article, I began engaging people like Karen Gordy who was connected to the famous Gordy music family to help me find capital for the business. But there wasn't a lot of interest. The question I was asked most frequently was, *"How are you going to grow this thing?"* I was only doing $8 million a year and my success had been limited to lower-budgeted Black films and a bunch of Hong Kong cinema. I wasn't an impresario in the vein of a Sean Combs, who was a magnet for Black talent. Would new filmmakers follow me just because I was in business with The Big Three? My story didn't make sense or even interest White investors and the Black capital groups I spoke to listened and seemed intrigued. But nothing came to pass.

In time, I started to see the forest through the trees. There was no real need for an independent distributor of Black film content, because the next generation of Black talent and the better independently produced films would coalesce around deals at the major studios. In the face of that, why would anyone try to set up their own infrastructure and carry the kind of overhead that I was now carrying? Just to get the titles the studios didn't want?

The new Black film culture had arrived and the train for what I was doing had already left the station. I had met or was hearing about the new breed of player that was coming up from the independent ranks and they were already in bed with the major studios. *Selma* director, Ava Duvernay, had done some publicity work for Xenon. Will Packer, who would go on to produce *Takers,* the *Ride Along* films, and executive produce *Straight Outta Compton,* was developing films like *Trois* and was in business with Sony Screen Gems. Packer told me that Screen Gems was giving *him* the funds to spend the prints and ad dollars on *Trois's* theatrical release because he understood how to reach his audience better than Sony's own distribution guys. Tyler Perry and the huge fan base he'd developed through his Black plays was something I'd heard about for years. His strategy was right out of the Rudy Ray Moore playbook. But it was much, much, bigger. Perry was talking to Lionsgate, who was getting very aggressive in embracing the Black film space.

There was another big issue: Being a film distributor was a very capital intensive business, with a high level of risk associated with it. I knew Xenon had to try and step up to small theatrical releases. But that was like throwing money off a cliff. I'd lost track of all the distributors I'd seen get flayed like a trout in the theatrical arena. I'd heard or read all the stories about men I admired like the Weinsteins and Bob Shaye at New Line Cinema - how long it had taken them to build their companies and how close to bankruptcy they'd come. Everyone saw Lionsgate as the next big thing. But they were a money raising machine that, at that juncture, was losing money hand over fist.

No way could I start with $17,000 now.

I wasn't sure how, minus equity investors, I could continue to grow Xenon on its own internally generated cash.

Things were definitely going to change and I knew it. I might have been the first guy through the door for Black film distribution in the home entertainment space. I might have laid the first independent track. But the new Black film movement wasn't anything I created and it wasn't anything I could control or even wanted to try to control. *The Times* article had landed during a window of time when Xenon's name was in lights. But I definitely needed to be thinking about new lines of business. And if I was going to stay in the Black content space, I needed to deliver something really big.

In the meantime, there was a story unfolding in the local papers that I just couldn't get out of my head.

Deep Cover

In early 1992, Suge arranged for Dr. Dre to produce the soundtrack for Deep Cover, a feature film starring Lawrence Fishbourne. The soundtrack album was released by Solar Records, and introduced Snoop Dogg's unique vocal style to a national audience. The Deep Cover soundtrack was released in spring of 1992.

DICK GRIFFEY: The soundtrack for *Deep Cover* was on Solar Records. *187 On an Undercover Cop* -- it's what made Snoop famous. We broke Snoop.

MICHAEL HARRIS*: Deep Cover* was the first time we could gauge the reaction of consumers.

VIRGIL ROBERTS: *Deep Cover* was a critical success. It was not a multi-platinum record but it established Snoop Dogg as an artist.

KEVIN POWELL: *Deep Cover* was the official break of Dr. Dre from Eazy E and Ruthless Records. It was the introduction of Dre as a solo artist. It was the introduction of Dre as a mentor to other artists, in this case Snoop Doggy Dogg.

JOHN PAYNE: The (artists) got the right exposure on the *Deep Cover* soundtrack. Until then, Snoop was basically sitting around the studio, wanting to do something. Nobody had heard of him.

JOHN KING: Snoop had this voice. It sounded like he was singin' but he was rappin'. It was something new and it took the world over.

DOUG YOUNG: So I go down to the Solar studio to listen to (Deep Cover) and thought it was dopest thing I heard in years.

MATT MCDANIEL: Snoop was just starting to get recognized. He had the *Deep Cover* single out. I go to New York. All that anyone's talking about is Snoop. I met Snoop and said, *"Oh yeah. You're really hot in New York."* And this was all new to him.

DOUG YOUNG: Some time passed and I went to New York. I was still very busy as a promoter. And the three biggest records in the clubs out there were *Deep Cover*, *Poppa Large*, and *Show Biz MJD*. I was in this club one night and Clark Kent was the DJ. He put on *Deep Cover* and them New York fools lost their minds. I mean lost their minds. I remember comin' back the next day from the airport -- didn't even drive home -- drove straight to the Solar building to tell Dre. And I remember tellin' Snoop, *"Man you're about to be huge."* And maybe an hour after I had told them about that, Snoop walks to Jack in the Box on Sunset and Cahuenga, and saw the guys from Tribe Called Quest. And they said, *"Man let's take a picture!"* and asked him for his autograph just like girls. Because of *Deep Cover*.

VIRGIL ROBERTS: *187 On An Undercover Cop* became like a national anthem.

KEVIN POWELL: That single is so significant because it shows these two different worlds that Dre was leaving, and where he was going to.

NATE DOGG: When Snoop blew up on *Deep Cover*, it looked like we were all blowing up. It pumped me up - I can't wait till it's my turn.

GEORGE PRYCE: (At that juncture) the artists at Death Row didn't understand the necessity for (publicity). Anything that was a deterrent to getting a track done was an interference. Then they began to understand.

DICK GRIFFEY: Dre and Snoop did the *Deep Cover* (video), which, by the way, I had to make them do. I had to make them put it out. They didn't want to make a video. Everybody was afraid to put it out. I told Epic to put it out and I'll deal with Suge if it becomes a problem.

As Snoop's star began to rise within Death Row, he became a mentor to two key artists, Daz Dillinger and Kurupt, whom he had brought into the Death Row fold. The duo would later be put into a group that he sponsored called Tha Dogg Pound.

SNOOP DOGG: Daz was like little Snoop Dogg in the beginning. I was his big cousin who he looked up to. I was money hustling. He was young and didn't know what money was yet. So I would break him off a few a few dollars and show him love, because he was my little cousin. When I started rapping, he started scratchin' and DJ-ing. When he found out I had hooked up with Dr. Dre, he was calling me every day, asking to stay with me. So he came out -- started wearing my clothes. Started getting on my nerves. I tried to kick him out 7 or 8 times. Then he started coming to the studio. I was writing *Deez Nuts* at the time, and I wrote him in. Then he started going in the studio on his own. His mom was a church singer. Beautiful gospel voice. She taught me how to sing in church. Warren G was teaching him producing.

VIRGIL ROBERTS: After Solar did a soundtrack for the *Deep Cover* film, there were rumblings from Ruthless that they might file a lawsuit. So when Solar arranged to do the soundtrack, we decided we'd put some songs from Death Row artists on the record, as way of testing whether or not Ruthless would file a lawsuit. I think we took four cuts from Death Row artists that we were recording at the time.

The Ruthless RICO lawsuit would be filed a few months later in the fall of 1992.

The success of Deep Cover caused a change both in Suge and the atmosphere at Death Row Records. Success seemed imminent, but money remained very tight during this period.

LYDIA HARRIS: I seen a change in Suge. He was handlin' things different. Gonna be a gang banger.

DICK GRIFFEY: Suge was somewhat playful, and kind of a bully. He'd threaten people from time to time, and they'd take him seriously. Have an argument with the engineer and tell him they were gonna shoot him if he didn't get stuff right on the board. Lots of unnecessary drama.

LYDIA HARRIS: When we first started, it wasn't violent. Because we kept it a business. But when Suge got successful, he got a whole new crew of people. And David had to keep 'em all out of jail.

JEWELL: Dick was a great man. I met him a couple of times. Laughed with him in his office. Later, I told him Suge owed us money -- our *Deep Cover* check. Dick said he paid Suge all his money. Suge said he didn't.

MICHAEL HARRIS: Griffey took the majority of the money from when they did the publishing deal and left crumbs for everyone else. (He) was able to manipulate most of the money for his own purposes.

LAMONT BRUMFIELD: Suge was rollin' up in a Benz all day. He had a Benz and a Lexus. Snoop was getting evicted when *Deep Cover* came out -- something ain't right. We helped him move his stuff from a little bitty, one bedroom apartment, in Hollywood. That's how they treat us producers and artists. If they think you need money badly enough, they're gonna offer you so little. They're just gonna play you.

JEWELL: We did the *Deep Cover* soundtrack, and once it was done, I hadn't received any money. So I go to Suge, *"Well, what's up with my check?"* and he's like, *"You guys are gonna get your check."* But it never happened.

LYDIA HARRIS: Mike said, *"Did we get the check for Deep Cover?"* And Kenner told Mike that Suge took the check cause they needed it to do something. So Mike said, *"Okay, I'm not gonna trip it."*

JOHN PAYNE: They're lots of ways to justify expenses without paying anybody. *"We got too many people on the label right now."* Harry O would say, *"You're right. Take care of them."*

S. LEIGH SAVIDGE: Michael told me that during this period, Suge came at him looking for more money. He refused to give him any more.

SNOOP DOGG: Money was hard to come by then. Because there wasn't no structure. There was no label. And Suge Knight did all he could do at that time, as far as go into his pocket, his bank account, to get us money and pull whatever deals he tried to pull together to get us money. Dre didn't have no money; he was leaving N.W.A.

JEWELL: Snoop wasn't getting money back then either. Suge told us after we put out *The Chronic* album, he was gonna give us all a hundred thousand dollars. I never saw it.

SONSHINE: DOC kept saying (to Dre), *"You need to do your own album."* One day it was like, *"Hey, we did this song called G Thang."* And bam, (Dre) said, *"I'm gonna do my own album,"* and DOC said it should be called *The Chronic.* Then DOC wrote *Dre Day.*

Friends and Family

In my senior year in high school, after many years in Seattle's Public School system -- during a time when voters never wanted to pass legislation that would allocate badly needed funding -- I was admitted into Seattle's version of New England's elite Phillips Exeter Academy: Lakeside School.

In the Seattle area, a Lakeside diploma often means more to many people than receiving a degree from Oxford. It is the alma mater of Microsoft co-founders Bill Gates and Paul Allen and people like cellular mogul Craig McCaw. Progeny from Seattle's founding families with names like Black, Pigott and Nordstrom sent their kids there. Much of Seattle's power structure has connectivity to the school.

At Lakeside, academic prowess was what defined who was cool and who wasn't. Athletic skill was viewed as secondary unless your sport was crew. In the Lakeside ecosystem, I wasn't easily pegged. My family was well-off enough to pay the tuition. Academically, my grades were sufficient but I wasn't an elite level student by any stretch. Athletically, I'd joined the football team and also signed up for basketball, tennis and rugby. Compared with the people I was about to meet, there was nothing special about me. In the Lakeside food chain, I was somewhere near the bottom.

But there is an egalitarian aspect to Lakeside as well. Every year, any number of mostly brilliant kids from modest backgrounds are granted scholarships there. Soon rumors began floating that the Lakeside admissions board had somehow jumped the shark - that of all the people they could have picked, they'd pulled some dumb-ass jock out of the public school system.

Fortunately, everywhere I looked someone wanted to help me.

My advisor was a man named Paul Thomas. Prior to Lakeside, he'd taught at Punahou, President Obama's alma mater. He'd opted out of the family's giant apple business and as an educator had once provided a forum for the Black Panthers to speak. Thomas knew I was new and out of my depth and would chase me down hallways asking what he could do to help me.

Chris Larson, who would be one of the future owners of the Seattle Mariners, decided to take pity on me and tutored me in physics. Larson used to call me "Queen Anne" – referring to the high school I'd previously attended. He did this in an affectionate way. But it was also a moniker that had an element of derision to it - suggesting that I was someone who'd been belched into the Lakeside jet stream from what he considered to be a substandard public school. When I couldn't wrap my brain around a concept he would always say *"But Queen Anne, it's so blatantly obvious."* That was easy for him to say. Larson was a stone-cold genius. A short time later, he would team up with Gates and Allen to get Microsoft started.

Lakeside was full of these kinds of people. In place of the crowded classrooms I'd left, I found myself in classes with 12 to 15 people, half of whom were National Merit Scholars. I had classes with people like Robert Fulghum who would later write the acclaimed book, *Everything I Need to Know I Learned in Kindergarten*. My class included John Bigelow, who would later be featured in David Halberstam's book, *The Amateurs* -- an Olympian who is considered the greatest oarsman in Yale's history. On the tennis team, the guys wedged on either side of me on the ladder would invest the original seed capital in Amazon.com. Next to me in the rugby scrum was a guy named Keith Grinstein. He'd become another early Amazon.com investor and advisor to Amazon CEO, Jeff Bezos.

But perhaps most importantly, at that time in Lakeside's history, the fall of 1975, the headmaster was a man named Dan Ayrault. My father's assessment of Ayrault was simply *"He's a very fine man."* Ayrault was Ivy-educated, had rowed crew in the 1960 Olympics, was a brilliant speaker and was scrupulously prudent and fair-minded. He was also very progressive. His message to students was that the single most important thing that a Lakeside graduate could do was to participate in activities that would improve society as a whole. He emphasized using the privilege of the elite education that one received at the school to help others who were less fortunate and further, that students needed to learn to sublimate their own financial needs in service of the community and society they lived in.

Dan Ayrault walked the walk and talked the talk. He interfaced with Lakeside's board of trustees with a deftness and acuity that few at the school could ever remember. He wasn't in the job for the money and wasn't necessarily impressed by people who had it. He'd granted admission to a promising Black student from a somewhat troubled background named Robert Taylor and moved him into his on-campus home. In the Lakeside environment, Taylor would flourish as a student-athlete and prove Ayrault proud. He would go onto Harvard and then Columbia for graduate school, make a small fortune on Wall Street and then retire to become a teacher. The story arc of Robert Taylor would symbolize what Lakeside School was all about.

All of this coalesced for me in a class called Myths and Heroes. The instructor was Dr. Judith Brown, the type of teacher who would invite the entire class to come to her home occasionally. One of the assignments was to pick who you thought was the world's biggest hero. You then had to persuade both Dr. Brown and your class members as to why. My hero was Dr. Martin Luther King Jr. I won hands down. By the time I got to King's words *"Be ashamed to die until you have won some victory for humanity"*, a room full of Seattle's best and brightest were hanging their heads in silence.

It was at Lakeside where I developed my first real curiosity about the ways of the world I lived in. But as I grappled with the story of Death Row Records, I found myself wondering if the general American public, including the progressive folks at Lakeside were ready to deal with a much more vexing story arc: inner city kids with limited options like Dr. Dre, Tupac Shakur and Snoop Dogg who don't have access to an environment where academics are king and passionate intellectuals give a shit about them. In Robert Taylor, Dan Ayrault had seen a diamond in the rough. Throughout the Lakeside community, for both progressives and conservatives alike, Robert Taylor was the guy that they could point to and say "See? We do good things here. America works." But the reality was that in Dan Ayrault, Robert had had a winning lottery ticket. 99 percent of the other people in the inner city in America would never be as lucky. Minus the nurturing and protective cover that an environment like Lakeside provided, their problems and issues would most likely remain the same.

In my view, the Death Row Records story offered a significant forum for the examination of, and the problems attached to, the transition of inner city kids into positions of economic power in American society.

But this was a discussion that virtually no one I knew wanted to hear or see.

When I tried to make the connection between Dr. King and the Death Row Records story, people just couldn't make the leap. I'd remind them that Dr. King's whole message was about assisting the progress of poor Blacks. Kevin Powell would reinforce this in my interview with him. This story was about poor Blacks with exceptional talent fighting to take their place at America's financial table sans the guidance you might get in a normalized corporate structure. What I'd get back from a lot of people both White and Black was that Dr. King would be mortified by the idea of a Tupac Shakur -- the underlying implication being that Black progress could only be measured by the number of Black people who took regular jobs and played by society's rules -- by what polite society viewed as appropriate accomplishments.

Most of the people we were interviewing had an edge to them. They were angry. The music they were talking about was angry. In their daily lives, they lived in fear. Violence was simply a fact of their lives. They existed in corridors of America where, unless you lived there, you never went there. They lived in a society where great wealthy surrounded them and none if it was coming their way. And part of the reason was that there was simply no Steve Jobs overseeing a well-funded infrastructure whose mandate was to help inner city kids elevate their economic station. The job of employing people in the inner city had been left to guys like Harry O who was using proceeds from a drug business to employ Black people in his legitimate businesses. Too many people with wealth, power and influence simply didn't give a shit. It was axiomatic that if you never went into America's ghettos, you could never be in position to grasp the issues there. If you didn't have to look at it, it was an out-of-sight, out-of-mind situation. You didn't have to see the pain and suffering and the pathology in your own backyard that Dr. King wanted to eradicate.

With the Death Row story, you had to look at all of this. You had to look at inner city America in all its raw, jagged glory.

I was in a silo by myself. Many of my White friends thought I'd lost my mind and too many Black people viewed me as part of some creepy, Orwellian conspiracy -- that I was a 90s version of Malcolm X's *"blue-eyed devil"*.

There was one person who *was* encouraging me. His name was Andrew Sal Hoffmann.

Andy was simply the smartest, toughest and most important friend I had. We'd met at Boston University when I was an undergraduate and he was in law school there. He'd been a wrestler during his undergraduate days at George Washington

University and came from three generations of the rough and tumble world of Philadelphia-based labor law. Within Andy there lay what I recognized as an unusual dialectic -- a man with a giant heart who hailed from the very toughest of Italian and Jewish stock. In the legal arena, Andy was simply world class. He could bring even the most vexing conflicts to resolution when mere mortals had long given up. Over a number of years, I'd lost track of the number of times he'd come to my rescue in the many legal issues relating to Xenon's business -- most of it on a pro bono basis.

As a lawyer, Andy had spent years defending criminals. He understood criminals and how they behaved. He had also spent many years defending what he referred to as *wrong place, wrong time defendants* -- innocent people who, in a number of cases, law enforcement seemed to have an agenda to convict. He was very familiar with both sides of this often difficult and complicated equation.

When I told Andy I was doing the Death Row project, his first words were *"I'm in."* He grasped the importance of the story on all levels immediately. The next day he fed ex-ed me a check for $150,000. No contract. No nothing. Just a check. Short of Andy, there was no one I knew in the world who believed in me enough to do something like that.

Andy had been my principal advisor in the construction of the Xenon label. He had a way of speaking to me in the third person as a way of emphasizing, in his view, who I was and what I represented. It was his way of calibrating my brain, helping me establish the correctness and moral consequences of anything I was contemplating. He'd say *"Leigh Savidge would do this"* or *"Leigh Savidge would have no business doing that."*

In Andy's estimation, the Death Row project was something Leigh Savidge would do.

Even so, once it became clear to me that Michael Harris and I were at cross purposes, I'd Fed-exed Andy his money back. I knew that getting through this project would be the supreme test of my life. There was the distinct possibility that all this could end very badly. Andy was not a rich man and I didn't want him to be hurt financially if something happened to me. In terms of cash-flowing this project, I was now totally on my own.

****

It was mid-production and I was facing a new battle with the Harrises. Word had trickled back from Jeff and Darryl that Michael's birthday was coming up and that Lydia had demanded the funds to fly their daughter and other family members in from Houston. I'd gone toe to toe with her over this and a flurry of brutal calls with Michael had followed. This had led to another of my many face to face battles with him at Lancaster. The core issue for me was financial survival. I needed to drive home the point that Xenon was not a money train - that our resources had to be allocated to cover the costs directly related to capturing the story. His position was "*I am the fucking story. This is part of the cost to make this film, mutherfucker.*" He kept emphasizing that I was the lucky person he had chosen to capture this amazing story - that anything connected with Death Row was going to make a fortune. Was I was so trifling an individual that I couldn't front dough so he could see his daughter? On his birthday?

I sure as hell didn't feel lucky.

This drama had come amid a long scheduled and long delayed visit from my sister, Sarah, who was flying in from our hometown of Seattle. My get-togethers with my sister were very infrequent and for both of us represented sacred ground. In the clutter of our increasingly complex lives, we utilized these often short, 48 hour intervals to laugh, tell stories that only we cared about and calibrate our current thinking as to the ways of the world. There was an unwritten rule here -- demands from our professional lives would never interfere with these visits. *Never.*

Aside from my mother, Sarah was one of the few people in my life that felt I walked on water. And I took a certain degree of responsibility in helping her justify that belief.

When I picked her up at the airport, the issue with Michael and Lydia was spinning out of control and I knew I had to go see Michael and fight this out. If he did not view me as someone who had the capacity to fight him face-to-face, I was certain that the film would soon devolve into chaos. After Sarah got in the car I told her *"I'm doing this new project. I have to go see this guy in prison."* Her happy disposition left her almost immediately. *"How long will it take?"* I told her I didn't know.

But I did know. Between the two plus hour drive, the butt check for the baggie of crack, the 2-4 hour wait in the waiting room, the multiple additional security checks, the multi-hour battle with Michael and the two plus hour drive back, it was at a minimum, a ten-hour block of time.

As could be expected, my sister viewed this as her too-busy older brother not assigning enough significance to her and her visit. We'd had a solemn dinner and the next morning I'd left her in my condo. It would be 9pm that night before I got back from Lancaster.

Our time together had effectively been hijacked by the drama at hand.

After I made a token attempt to explain the dynamics of my day, Sarah's first question was *"Why would you do something for these people that you wouldn't even consider doing for your own family?"*

Nobody can give it to you like a sibling. I knew there was no satisfactory answer to this. I tried to say that in the situation with

157

Michael and Lydia, there was a greater need. But that wasn't true. There simply was no greater need than to give to my family. That was, and always would be, number one.

Sarah was mad at me but that didn't preclude her from discussing the Death Row story with me. She was an artist and the only family member I had who could possibly understand what I was doing and why. I told her that I didn't want the rest of the family to know about this. I knew that my mother in particular would be absolutely mortified. She'd be calling me every day to get out of Los Angeles, which she referred to frequently as "*that awful city.*"

With the Death Row project, I'd gone into a silo where I demanded quiet. I was sick of talking to detractors about what I was doing professionally. Somewhat ironically, the process had started with the recognition I was starting to get as this guy who was supposedly the nation's leading distributor of independent Black film content. The upshot was that the sudden attention had created more problems for me than anything else. Many of my more liberal-leaning White friends began telling me that I was exploiting Black people. I'd get angry and say "*How does offering a financial deal to a Black filmmaker in either a competitive bidding process or in the absence of another deal at all constitute exploitation?*" The flip side of this was a steady chorus from Black filmmakers and producers who saw it as a badge of courage not to do business with me. Many of them felt that my success as a White guy doing what I was doing simply exemplified what they saw as the sorry state of financial empowerment for Black people.

With the Death Row project, I'd pushed my White / Black detractor issue even wider. The chorus from nearly everyone I knew was that I'd gone off the deep end.

I'd entered the Black content space because I recognized an untapped business opportunity there. There was never a burning predisposition or grand plan there. I just identified a niche, saw that there was a demand and recognized that this was a pathway into a highly competitive business. But I also felt like I'd had formative experiences early in my life that could help me with some of the socio-political aspects that would inevitably emanate out of it.

Sarah and I talked about the concept and meaning of courage. The discussion focused on the often fine line between someone who is viewed as courageous and brilliant and someone who is viewed as misguided, stupid and a failure. I presented the story of Fred Smith, the co-founder of Federal Express who, as the legend had it, had gone to Las Vegas, gambled everything he had and won big and then had used those winnings to make a critical payroll during the company's start-up phase. But what if Smith had lost it all? Then the story might have read that some idiot went to Vegas with some foolhardy scheme to save his company, lost all his money and had bankrupted his promising new transport company in the process.

Our discussion would end with the notion of one of life's absolute imperatives: that apart from birth, death and taxes, only history lets us know if we are right or wrong.

At the airport, when I said goodbye to her, Sarah said *"You know, you don't have to do this."* And I told her, *"That's correct. But I'm doing it anyway."*

The Chronic

By the end of 1992, Dr. Dre and Death Row Records had finished The Chronic, the album which would help define the new West Coast rap movement. But Solar's distributor, Sony Music, balked at distributing the album due to its violent lyrics and the unclear contractual status of Dr Dre. Griffey, then explored distributing The Chronic independently before finally presenting the album to Interscope Records, a then fledgling record label, led by Jimmy Iovine and Ted Field.

JEFFREY JOLSON COLBURN: The *Chronic* was a big hit out of the box. They it used to break Snoop Dogg.

DICK GRIFFEY: Part of the marketing strategy was to piggyback off of the success of each other along with the whole gangster aura. (With *Deep Cover*) I had to make Dre do a video. So that made that deal hot. *The Chronic* had all those same people - Dre, Snoop, RBX, Jewell….

NATE DOGG: I think it was a classic because everyone on it was hungry. Everybody put their all into *The Chronic* album. Because we were seeing that, not only was this going to build a record company that we were all on, but this was the first album of the record company we were going to be on. This would build all of our careers.

SNOOP DOGG: And we were vibein' straight with Dre, whatever Dre wants, it's all about Dre. Whatever you want. You want this? It's all about Compton and Dre. Dre. Dre. Dre. Dre. Boom.

JOHN PAYNE: *The Chronic* was a very good album - it showcased all the artists very well, but it took rapping to another level. It wasn't heavy samples. Technically, the quality was a lot better. But also people were happy at that time.

NATE DOGG: You just heard that whole new style from the West Coast as far as rapping and singing, and people loved it. I think it was the music - when people heard that music. The best promotion about *The Chronic* album was, *"Wow, did you hear that?"* From somebody who sat down and listened to it.

KEVIN POWELL: When you look at the period that *The Chronic* came out in 1993, this is on the heels of Kurt Cobain committing suicide, and grunge music, the latest form of good rock and roll, dying. So hip hop was the last thing that was left -- the only thing standing. It gave an introduction to Black America that most White kids don't get in the school system. In school, you learned that Black people were slaves. You learned about Dr. King having a dream. Hip hop gives you Compton.

ALLEN GORDON: *The Chronic* had major help from MTV. You couldn't turn on MTV without seeing Dr. Dre. The hip hop audience caps off at two million people. Anything after that are White kids in the suburbs, mothers, fathers, grandpas, whatever.

LAMONT BRUMFIELD: First of all, you had so many hungry, starving individuals that wanted to be superstars, who put their talent together and it came out a classic.

JAY KING: You had Snoop Dogg, who just brought a whole 'nother style to rap music.

ALLEN GORDON: It's all about presentation. If your lyrics are good, your delivery's good, and you have an engaging personality, that's the thing that sells records. Snoop was not the best rapper, but he was definitely the most charismatic rapper at the time.

NATE DOGG: He has a voice where he can rap over beats, and just rip a beat to pieces.

SNOOP DOGG: A lot of that shit was on the spot, spontaneous, right there.

DOUG YOUNG: The camaraderie in the early days over there, man. All those cats used to show up at the studio. You can feel the fun that's in there. You can feel the fun that's in *The Chronic*.

JEWELL: It wasn't like we had money to hang with our friends, so we just hung together. And we created a masterpiece.

JOHN PAYNE: They were poor as hell, but they were still a family, still havin' fun.

NATE DOGG: Before *The Chronic* album, we made records. We made records and we were hungry. I think that's when the best records come out. We were starving.

MICHAEL HARRIS: There was an ideology that if you made the cat too fat, he wasn't going to produce.

JEWELL: We were all starving. All starving. Dre included. We'd be up there eatin' Popeye's chicken, five days a week

SNOOP DOGG: I was just happy to be workin' with Dre. I had my own apartment. I was getting a thousand dollars a month, had all the best weed I wanted. My girl was lovin' me, I was lovin' her. It was all just crackin'.

JEWELL: Snoop wasn't getting any money back then either. He had a little S on his chest, and a little swap meet ring. But we still kept going. Death Row. Death Row. Death Row. Everybody Death Row.

NATE DOGG: I think it was a lot of collaboration on *The Chronic* album, as far as names like Daz, Kurupt, Snoop, Warren G, DOC, RBX, and myself, Rage, Jewell.

JEWELL: Sometimes we was just in there drinking or elevating our minds, to another level. Dre would be like working with the beats at the time. And he'd come up with something. And he'd pin it on whoever was in the studio at that particular time.

SNOOP DOGG: We had weed -- the best weed -- you know what I'm sayin'? That's why we made *The Chronic*, because we *had* the Chronic.

JEWELL: It all worked. My singin' over their hard rap lyrics. Rap had never accepted that before. I put my soft, sultry, R&B singing, on their records. Now every rapper has to have a female on their songs.

SNOOP DOGG: (2) We just putting the weed together like this, breaking it down, putting it in a zig zag. Once we twist that shit up and blaze it, if it's the chronic, we gonna keep it. If not, we'll unroll that motherfucker and throw it out.

NATE DOGG: Dr. Dre had just left N.W.A. and he wanted to make a statement that he was a solo artist, a good artist on his own, and a good producer.

SNOOP DOGG: When I did *Nuthin' But A G Thang* on *The Chronic*, I think we did fifteen takes. I did (another) song fifteen times before I got it right. I had a toothache at the time, and couldn't spit it out. (Dre) was, *"Do it the next time. I don't like how it sounds. Do it again. You had too much energy."* I'm like, this motherfucker is a *precisionist*.

MICHAEL HARRIS: Dre does what he does and, at the same time, those rappers do what they do. It's a collaboration. To say that Dre is the total orchestrator of the albums isn't true. It depends a lot on what those rappers are feeling at the time.

JOHN KING: There were people all over the world waiting for that album to drop.

GARY JACKSON: Dre is an amazing producer. He is able to put so many disparate elements together and just bring them into a real nice groove.

SNOOP DOGG: (Dre) listened to it off the board in the studio. He'd cut it together, cut the reels, splice it in. He actually had to put it together, piece by piece, by hand. Every song connected to the next song, to the next song, to the next song.

ALLEN GORDON: Dre is a great embellisher. Not to take away from his production style, but he can hear somebody else's music and enhance it. A perfect example would be Donny Hathaway's, *Little Ghetto Boy*, which he used later, on *The Chronic*, by adding a heavier drum track, and adding a flute to the album. And that enhanced the dynamic of that music. I can imagine Donny Hathaway singing over that song, and actually liking that more than the original. Which is incredible. He did it before on The DOC's album with *The Formula*, taking Marvin Gaye's *Inner City Blues*, and again adding a flute to the track. And just having that talent, to hear music and know, *"This needs a flute or you need harp strings here, you need a heavier drum track there."* That's incredible talent. Even if he can't read music himself.

SNOOP DOGG: When we worked on *The Chronic*, two or three songs, he probably gave me a cassette, and said take the beat home and write it. *G Thang, Let Me Ride, Deep Cover*, that kind of shit. And then, a lot of that shit was spontaneous, right there. Or he would give me a beat, and by the time we'd do the shit in the studio and then change the beats, so I had to spit over it a different flow.

MARIO JOHNSON a.k.a. CHOCOLATE: Production, man. The writers, all that youth, Daz, Kurupt. Niggas just coming with it. Dre and them recruited an army.

MATT MCDANIEL: When Dre was making *The Chronic*, I went

up to see Dre and he played a few songs. And he played a song that was about the riots. I explained to him about some of the footage I had from my riot documentary, and he ended up using it to open two of the songs. One was, *The Day the Niggers Took Over*, and another was *Little Ghetto Boy.*

SNOOP DOGG: I think *The Chronic* was perfect, but a lot of songs could have been on it that would have destroyed the vibe. If they didn't come out, Dre did it for a reason.

JEFFREY JOLSON COLBURN: With a superstar producer like Dre, you could sell it to almost any label. Everyone knew rap labels were going platinum, and they don't cost a lot to record. And they cost virtually nothing to market, since there's no place to market *to*. They get no radio play, there's no band to put on the road, its nearly all guerilla marketing, free marketing.

VIRGIL ROBERTS: *The Chronic* was finished. We had originally thought we'd be able to distribute the record with Sony.

DICK GRIFFEY: This would have been the first time in history that young guys would have actually had the opportunity to have a distribution deal, what they call a P & D deal, with a major and get all of the money. I usually don't mention figures, but it was like a 70 / 30 (split) with Death Row getting the 70. So if they had a record selling for 15.98, sixteen dollars, they would have gotten eleven. That didn't exist in the industry. That's the kind of deal I put together for Suge.

SAM GIDEON ANSON: In the spring of that year (1992), David Kenner, under the auspices of GF Entertainment, tries to get a label deal at Sony Records in New York. Kenner couldn't get that deal done.

VIRGIL ROBERTS: Sony refused to distribute *The Chronic.*

SAM GIDEON ANSON: Because of their fearfulness of some of

the crazy things going on around Death Row, and their wariness of the contractual status of Dr. Dre, (Sony) didn't want to get the deal done.

JOHN KING: I had a party at this hotel by LAX. Me, and Dre, and Jewel, and some other girl, went downstairs, and we were in the valet area, waiting for the cars to come. Two guys were pulling on the two girls, and Dre and the guy got into an altercation. Dre hit the guy, and the guy turned around and shot Dre in the leg. We took Dre to the hospital. But the next couple of days, Dre had to pretend like he had never been shot. Their record deal was in jeopardy.

DICK GRIFFEY: When I went to Sony with the finished product, they refused to put it out because the entire industry was shying away from so-called gangsta rap because of the *Cop Killer* (Ice-T) song. The Police union had a big stake in Warner Communications -- their retirement fund. So they're talking about selling off their stock.

JEFFREY JOLSON COLBURN: Sony has had some problems in the past with the feds, and like any label, they are under constant scrutiny. Part of their fears in dealing with rap bands is that some of these gangster rappers might be real gangsters. Indeed many of them are. There's any number of guys that go to jail every year. They go platinum and go to jail.

VIRGIL ROBERTS: Tupac Shakur had a record out on Interscope and it talked about killing the police. And a highway patrolman in Texas had gotten killed by a kid, and that tape was in the kid's car. Peace officers began demonstrating against rap music. Members of the Big Six record companies were afraid of putting out explicit lyrics about killing cops. And one of the big songs DOC and Dre had done was *187 on a Mutherfuckin' (radio version Undercover) Cop*.

JEFFREY JOLSON COLBURN: You had Eric Wright and an East

Coast attorney basically claiming Sony Music was using strong arm tactics to gain an advantage in the music industry, which is something that Sony's bosses in Japan did not like hearing. Nor did Sony's shareholders. So they gave Death Row to Interscope without much fuss. Even though it had great potential.

MICHAEL HARRIS: Because of Eazy E's insistence that he had been wronged, and robbed of his artists, Sony chose not to be part of the lawsuits.

David Kenner would fight the RICO case on Death Row's behalf.

MICHAEL HARRIS: Eazy E filed it here (in Los Angeles). Kenner goes up in front of the judge in the federal courthouse and fights the case. If he had been in New York, he would have been a fish out of water. But he was here. He knows the L.A. courthouses. He knows the courtroom. He is at his best here. This is where David gets his power.

JEFFREY JOLSON COLBURN: This violence was something the music industry hadn't seen before. They were used to distribution operations in the past, where there would be allegations of someone saying *"Take these record cutouts or we'll break your arm,"* that sort of thing. But not this level of alleged coercion.

MICHAEL HARRIS: Sony is shook up. They don't want nothing to do with this. They don't know how to deal with this.

DICK GRIFFEY: It was really politically motivated more than anything else. I mean these guys are not afraid. They just say, *"Well it doesn't look good, at this particular time."* And it was kind of ironic, because that the same gentleman that gave me my break in the music business - that gave me $5,000 for that first *Soul Train* record, was now the head of business affairs at Sony - was the one that quashed the deal.

167

VIRGIL ROBERTS: Dick and I then negotiated a deal with BMG to put out the record.

DICK GRIFFEY: (BMG) started censoring the material. Every day, we had to fax the lyrics back and forth. I said, "*Okay, Snoop. You gotta change this and that.*"

VIRGIL ROBERTS: (BMG) heard the lyrics, and they said, "*We're not going to put the record out.*" Everybody got afraid of putting out any kind of rap records with explicit lyrics that talked about killing cops and stuff.

SUGE KNIGHT: (5) There wasn't nobody out there for us. I mean, it was a time when we were shopping a deal. We had the album done.

MICHAEL HARRIS: (Griffey) felt that the challenge to get Death Row out of the hole was just too enormous.

VIRGIL ROBERTS: And so we decided to distribute *The Chronic* independently. But to put a record out independently, you need a video. Griffey said to Suge, "*I don't have the money, let's raise the money.*" Well, one of the first people that Dick talked to was Norm Nixon. And Norm Nixon brought with him his music expert, who was John McClain Jr. John was working at Interscope as their A & R guy.

DICK GRIFFEY: John McClain Jr came along. When he heard the record he went crazy. He said, "*Griff, Griff, you gotta give me this. You gotta give me this record.*"

VIRGIL ROBERTS: John said, "*I love the record. Why don't you let me take it to Interscope?*"

John McClain Sr. owned a jazz club in Los Angeles in the 1960s called the It Club.

DICK GRIFFEY: The It Club was where Miles Davis and John Coltrane and all of the great musicians played. (John McClain Sr.) was married to Dorothy Donegan.

VIRGIL ROBERTS: John McClain Sr. and Dick have a relationship that goes back many years. John McClain Sr. was really like Dick Griffey's godfather when Dick first started in the business. John's father had loaned Dick money to do concerts.

MICHAEL HARRIS: His father was like me, but 30 years ago. He was the guy that helped Don Cornelius and Dick Griffey get into business. He wanted his son to be a big entertainment guy. (John Jr.) played like 25 instruments. He used to work at A & M Records. He brought them Janet Jackson.

VIRGIL ROBERTS: So John's father, John McClain Sr. called up Dick and said, "As a favor to my son, would you go have a meeting with his bosses?"

DICK GRIFFEY: (John Jr.) had his daddy call me. I went over and had a meeting with his father. I said, "Okay, I'll take a meeting."

Snipe

Lining up interviews for the film became increasingly difficult. Nearly every day either Steve Housden or I would get a call from Jeff Scheftel letting us know that someone else had said "No." Over and over, it was the same thing. *"I don't know what to say. This project already has stink on it. Nobody wants to talk. Everyone is scared to death."*

The truth of it was more complex. There were many critical interviews that probably only happened because of Michael Harris' involvement. Virgil Roberts had supposedly spoken to Michael before agreeing to be interviewed. Doug Young had made it clear he was there for Harry O. Dick Griffey gave us a great interview, but apparently didn't know that Lydia Harris was an Executive Producer. When he found out, he stormed out of the building.

The fact was that in attempting to get the film to attract a significant audience, we had a number of things going against us. First off, we'd be short on proprietary footage of some of the story's iconic figures. It soon became clear that we weren't going to get Suge, Dre or Ice Cube, so we'd be beholden to third party footage of them. Artists like Ice-T said *"No."* Any artist or executive, connected in any way with Interscope wouldn't touch us. Plus, short of Death Row being purchased by another entity, with no association with Suge Knight, we'd never get the label's music. I'd sit in my office some days and just be paralyzed by our situation. We were going to tell the story of a music label and we wouldn't be able to use their music. The die was cast. We couldn't really examine the label's music per se. Suge Knight was never going to let us use it.

We had to capture the story in all of this. It was all we had.

Another complication for us production-wise was the early

decision to tell the story we would capture entirely in the words of the mostly Black interviewees and journalists that were eyewitnesses to, or very familiar with, the story. This was not a story that would be filtered through a third party. If you were there, and you were willing to speak, you got to speak your mind, and the audience would hear your words as you chose them. Because the story was so multi-faceted and complicated, this meant interviewing a lot of people, which in turn meant keeping a production staff at the ready, while we spent many months casting around for people willing to talk. This was a brutally inefficient and brutally expensive way to capture the story. But after many discussions, we determined that this was the way we had to go.

One of Lydia's bodyguards was a guy named Snipe. Snipe was a large, physically imposing man who looked like the Michael Duncan Clark character from the film, *The Green Mile*. Snipe had the most dangerous job on the production. His basic job description was to take the lead in safeguarding the set and production staff, and defuse any problems that might happen. Suge Knight's long time, *modus operandi*, when he wanted something or wanted to send a message to someone, was to show up unannounced with a gang of thugs and scare the shit out of people. Even though Suge was in prison, we knew he had a long hand. Harry O had made it clear to me, "*You're gonna need protection.*"

On more than a few occasions, Jeff Scheftel would call me and say, "*Well, we lost our interviewee today because some thugs showed up and pulled some guns. Snipe got in their face and they left.*" Harry O had told us that Snipe, whose real name was Mark McNabb, was one of the toughest people he had ever known. He had the gunshot wounds to prove it. One day on the set, he lifted up his shirt and showed me his chest. Ten or more gunshot wounds formed a large U shape across his breast.

The irony with Snipe was that he had a nice, gentle side to him.

In calmer times, he bore a shy, sweet smile. He told our associate producer, Ian Haufrect, that guarding our set was the best job he'd ever had. He was proud to be there, and it showed in his attitude. He was also a great chess player, having learned the game during a previous prison stint. Haufrect, who would later get an MBA from UCLA, played him numerous times and was never able to beat him.

Later on, the production team heard rumors that things had not ended well for Snipe. Snipe had told Haufrect on more than one occasion, *"I will never go back to prison."* After we'd shot our initial group of interviews and shut down our base of operation, we'd heard that Snipe had gotten himself into trouble again. The story went that rather than submit to police arrest, he chose to turn his own gun on himself.

But those rumors turned out to be incorrect. The man who had shot himself was another man who'd been hired to guard our set: John Frazier.

Interscope

When Griffey offered The Chronic to Jimmy Iovine, and his partner, Ted Field, Interscope was on the verge of closing the business. In spite of this, Iovine and Field stalled in making a final deal with Griffey, and secretly contacted Suge, offering him a contract that would essentially cut out Griffey and Solar. Suge agreed to their terms, and The Chronic went on to sell five million copies. And with it, Interscope's legacy as one of most successful labels in the history of the music business would begin.

JEFFREY JOLSON COLBURN: An opportunity appeared for a young aggressive label to distribute Death Row. Interscope had two established industry people - Jimmy Iovine, a superstar producer of rock records and Ted Fields, a movie producer who had produced some hit music. They had some controversial rock acts of their own, like Nine Inch Nails. Later, they signed Tupac Shakur, the other hottest rapper in the business. These two owners believed in the artist being able to say whatever they wanted. And the more controversial, the better.

DOUG YOUNG: Interscope was dibbin' and dabbin' in rap, and they was hittin' and missin'. Most of their other stuff, with the exception of Tupac, didn't do too well.

VIRGIL ROBERTS: At that point in history, Interscope had no product. The Tupac record had been taken off the market and they had no records.

DICK GRIFFEY: Interscope was out of business. They were getting ready to close the doors. Warner Atlantic was dropping the deal and Ted Field was tired of pouring his personal money in there. So here comes Dick Griffey, with *The Chronic*.

VIRGIL ROBERTS: In the meantime, there was no money - no

cash flow at Death Row. Some of the guy's houses were going into foreclosure, their pagers had been cut off. They needed money.

DICK GRIFFEY: And I was tired of paying them out of my pocket.

JEFFREY JOLSON COLBURN: You can't go independent in this day and age. You need distribution partners - there're too many stores and too many computers.

VIRGIL ROBERTS: Dick and I met with Jimmy Iovine and David Cohen. We played them *The Chronic,* and they said they were interested.

DICK GRIFFEY: I took a meeting with Ted Field, Jimmy Iovine and Cohen. I said if you want to make a deal with us, you have to advance the guys some money -- just a good faith payment to talk to us. So these guys told me, "*Dick, we're going to advance you $200,000.*" This was on a Thursday. I said, "*Okay.*" Friday, no money. Saturday, no money. Sunday, no money. Monday, no money. Tuesday -- they advanced *100* thousand dollars for which we had to sign as a loan. Now Interscope didn't give the money to Dre or Suge. They made me sign for it. They specifically said, "*We don't give Dre and Suge no money because they don't have no assets.*" And Suge and Dre hadn't heard from us. Suge was hiding out so he couldn't be found. He could only be beeped. He had the case with the incident in the studio with the (Stanley) brothers.

VIRGIL ROBERTS: After the meeting, Jimmy and David told Suge, "*Griffey was here. He won't make a deal. But if you bring us the record, we'll give you a million dollars.*"

DICK GRIFFEY: By Wednesday, Suge and Dre are up at Interscope, and they're calling Virgil cursing him out. Talking about, we stole their money. Iovine got a hold of Dre, and (told him), *"See Dre? They're doin' it to you again. These guys are taking advantage of you."* The Man, once again, had done the old *divide and conquer.*

JEFFREY JOLSON COLBURN: Interscope stepped up to the plate. They were very aggressive, very pro-artists rights. But Interscope also doesn't distribute independently. Interscope distributes through its agreement with Time Warner.

SUGE KNIGHT: (Stephanie Frederic archive) There's a lot of prejudice in this business. People think it's so much Black and White. But a lot of it is young and old.

DICK GRIFFEY: Most of our young people don't really know what's available for them out there. That's how they get taken advantage of.

MICHAEL HARRIS: (On Griffey) He was a powerful guy in his day. Dick was like a father figure to Suge. Dick has that kind of demeanor. He's a strong individual. And for Suge to be up under that, he had to be strong.

SUGE KNIGHT: (5) Older guys, all they want to do is sit you down and say, *"Suge, you say you're a young entrepreneur. This is what we gonna do. Give me all the stuff you got. Give me your tapes, give me your masters, give me your groups and I'm gonna go over there and make you a deal."*

DICK GRIFFEY: Suge didn't know contracts. He didn't know manufacturing. He didn't know publishing. And like most of our young people that don't know what's available, they get taken advantage of.

SUGE KNIGHT: (5) But you know what my opinion was, I ain't no punk. You don't gotta talk for us. We gonna go over there and speak for ourselves. Instead of getting a dollar, we want five. You know? And our masters. And our own shit.

MICHAEL HARRIS: Basically, Griffey laid in the cut. If it blows up, I'll be part of it. If it doesn't, I won't.

VIRGIL ROBERTS: Everyone didn't get rich and go home happy, unfortunately. Suge and Dre ended up making a deal with Interscope. They got a million dollar advance for *The Chronic*. And that became the rupture of the relationship between Dick Griffey and Suge, and Doc and Dre. And that ultimately ended up in litigation that was filed by Dick to be compensated for his interest in the partnership in Death Row.

DICK GRIFFEY: They ended up getting one of those regular slave deals. We got crossed by Iovine and Fields. And so did Suge. Iovine and Field are responsible for a lot of the tragedies that took place. If Suge had been over here with Virgil and I, none of this stuff would have gone down. They took the kids away from the nest too soon.

HANK CALDWELL: You had a whole distribution and marketing department at their disposal through Interscope. You had more guidance as far as distribution was concerned.

ALLEN GORDON: It was really Dick Griffey who was cut out of the deal. Interscope could offer Death Row more than Solar could because Solar doesn't have the MTV and BET connections that Interscope would have, as a subsidiary of Time Warner. And even though *The Chronic* was an incredible album, it got major help from MTV.

DOUG YOUNG: I think the deal that Jimmy was gonna cut with Suge was, "*Okay you can have Tupac. All of our real hard-core streety style rap, we'll let you have it and let you do it cause you seem to be doin' a really good job.*" Interscope actually does well with that Nine Inch Nails and all of that other stuff -- all that alternative stuff.

VIRGIL ROBERTS: At least initially, Suge said to Dick, *"Don't worry. I'm only making a deal to give them this one record cause we all need money. The rest of the product we have, we'll put that out independently. We'll take this advance we're gonna get from Interscope and we'll use that to continue to fund our company, so we can do the other product."*

JAY KING: Interscope clearly saw the money. And this is the record business. I think they were smart enough to see, whoever this guy Suge Knight is, and knowing the track record of this producer, Dr. Dre -- and you had the legal mind of David Kenner there. They've got all the tools in place. Everything we need is right here. We don't really have to do anything. All we have to do is fund these guys, and do what we do, which is promote records, market records, advertise records.

KEVIN POWELL: A lot of people don't know that Dick Griffey was connected to Death Row Records. Just like folks didn't know Michael Harris was connected. It's interesting how Griffey fell away from it and Michael Harris fell away from it. Griffey was a savvy businessman. Griffey never imagined he'd get screwed by a company where his mentor's son was working.

DICK GRIFFEY: I never really felt that Suge screwed me. A lot of people don't understand that. A lot of people came out, even family members and some friends, *"Why ain't you mad at this guy?"* You know. Because he was loyal. He stayed there (at Solar) a long time. It was the industry that screwed us. Those deals got bogged down. Sony should have been sued for not putting the record out. They were obligated.

MICHAEL HARRIS: (Suge) felt he was in a position to renege on his deal with Dick because he felt Dick reneged on him.

KEVIN POWELL: Jimmy Iovine had to pay off Ruthless Records, Eazy E, Jerry Heller and have *The Chronic* distributed through Priority Records.

S. LEIGH SAVIDGE: Jerry Heller's role in this transaction was critical. He understood that it made better business sense to get a piece of what Dre and some of the other artists who'd been ripped from Ruthless would create going forward, than spend a small fortune pursuing the RICO action. At this juncture, both Suge and Dre had little in terms of personal assets. So a deal that would settle the Ruthless / Death Row dispute from future earnings, made the most sense. Heller told me he took the lead in negotiating the deal with Jimmy Iovine.

MICHAEL HARRIS: (Griffey) never thought in his wildest dreams that Death Row could fix that (the RICO) situation. Me and Kenner believed we could fix the Eazy E situation and we did through Jimmy.

DOUG YOUNG: Eazy was getting like twenty-five or fifty cents a copy for Dre's *Chronic* album. That's why on Eazy's album, *187 Killer*, on that song, *Dre Day is My Payday*, that's what he's talking about -- meaning he had *Dre Day*, he talking shit about me. But every time *Dre Day* sell a record, I get 25 a copy.

VIRGIL ROBERTS: After (Death Row) signed the agreement, they realized they needed to leave Solar. All of a sudden, they disappeared.

JEWELL: Suge cut off all ties with the people from the beginning, and we got a whole new office and a whole new crew.

SNOOP DOGG: The first time I remember seeing *Nuthin But a G-Thang*, I was at my cousin Tammy's house in Pacoima. I was having trouble paying my rent in Hollywood, and I was trying to shake the landlord cause she was always knocking on my door, "*Where's the rent money?*" And I was trying to shake the bitch, so I shook her, and went and stayed at my cousin's house. And she had this channel called *The Box*. And man, that mutherfucker came on, *G Thang* came on, about thirty times in like two hours. I swear to God it kept on coming on, back and forth. And she was like man, *"That shit is tight"* and *"Woah, Woah."* And I'm like, *"Damn."* I was happy on the inside. But I was like *"Damn."* It was like fucking me up that it was coming on so much.

DICK GRIFFEY: *The Chronic* rolls out and sells five million copies. Generates fifty million dollars. It saved Interscope. *Made* Interscope. So the work that Suge, and myself, and those young people had done saved Interscope.

VIRGIL ROBERTS: Dick ended up suing Dre and Suge for his share of the ownership of (Death Row Records). That lawsuit got resolved earlier this year (1998). There's a confidentiality agreement that prevents me from discussing the terms of the settlement.

ALONZO WILLIAMS: *The Chronic* was a great record. I'm surprised he did something that good. Dre has lots of help when he's in the studio. He is not the genius that everybody makes him out to be.

JEWELL: Me and Rage were living in an apartment in La Mirada. I was the only one holding up the deal with Interscope. 'Cause I didn't agree with the contract. *The Chronic* sold four million. I hadn't gotten any money from *Deep Cover* yet, so I wanted my chips. I cussed that nigger, *"I want my money!"* He has this $15,000 check. And (Suge) said, *"Sign this. It's the only way you're gonna get your check."* So I did. Me and Rage were being evicted. I was a single parent. I had to eat.

SNOOP DOGG: The first family member I called when I heard my shit being played was my Pops. Because he'd seen me go to jail for selling dope, and I started writing raps with him when I stayed in Detroit with him in the summer of '84. So when I went through the transformation, from going to jail and selling dope to trying to become a rapper and getting with Dre, he was happy for me.

FREDDIE RHONE: The impact from *The Chronic* was awesome. When the video first hit The Box, it was playing back to back. I thought it was the only video on.

SNOOP DOGG: When *The Chronic* came out, I was sought out for interviews. I was very shy and I'd hold my head down, and didn't want to look at the camera. I didn't know what to expect. I had to learn how to conduct myself and not explode on every question I didn't like. Just take my time and listen. If I just be me, it'll be alright.

CPO: The money started comin' in right after *The Chronic*. That's when the money started getting' made.

MATT MCDANIEL: After *The Chronic* was done, they did this show, I call it a secret show, in South Central at a place called La Casa. I think they were just kind of testing out their show for a live audience. And they did all their cuts from *Dre Day, The Day the Niggers Took Over, Let Me Ride, Little Ghetto Boy*. It was one of the best shows I've seen them do.

SNOOP DOGG: The first time I performed songs from *The Chronic* was with Dre in a small concert in Compton. And man, these motherfuckers were singing every word of the songs. And that made me feel "*Damn, this is my life is right here.*"

TONE DEF: To me it wasn't like, "*Okay, Dre is advocating everybody smoke weed.*" He wasn't saying that. He was saying, "*My album is dope.*" Do you understand what I'm saying? "*My album is dope. Buy it.*"

ALONZO WILLIAMS: It was a good record. I know a lot of cats that was pissed off because they say they haven't been paid, or didn't get credit for it. I was surprised by it. I was happy with it. I play it from time to time. I don't like to listen to his (Dre's) voice on the shit, but I still listen to it.

The Crab Pot Syndrome

I felt lucky to have secured Darryl Roberts as the film's director. Since he was living with me, we got to know each other fairly well. He'd attended a historically Black college and had a fairly charmed life in Chicago. He lived in a loft downtown and suggested to me that he ran in Black celebrity circles that included Dennis Rodman and Michael Jordan. He talked about how competitive Jordan was. I'd say, "*Tell me something I don't know*" and he'd say, "*No. He's competitive with me.*" He told me a story about how they had been on a basketball court, and Jordan had challenged him to a duel where one would buy the other dinner, depending on which of them sunk a shot from 35 feet. Darryl had taken the first shot and sunk it and Jordan had missed. "*He went crazy, Leigh. He was so mad, he wouldn't talk to me.*" It was amusing to hear this stuff, particularly since Darryl was this soft spoken, teddy bear, type guy.

But I knew Darryl was very conflicted about *Welcome to Death Row*. He felt, as I did, that this was an important story and that there was something in the footage we were collecting that contained insights into the human condition in America. But he was scared to death of Lydia Harris who had showed him the gun in her purse, and was bullying and threatening him on a near constant basis. He'd say, "*Are we really going to glorify her and her husband?*" We'd go round and round on this issue. I'd say things like, "*We had to do it this way. We had to figure out how to work with them, and get their side of the story*" and, "*People will draw their own conclusions about Michael and Lydia.*" And he'd come back with "*A lot of Black people will hate this story. We are risking our lives. If we live, we'll deliver this film and we'll be reviled for it.*"

These discussions would nearly always evolve into discussions about race.

People who know me well know that I'd rather have a root canal than talk about race relations in America. But with this kind of project and what I was doing professionally, it was hard not to. Darryl was particularly interested in intra-race relations. He liked to discuss what he saw as *the crab pot syndrome* in Black America, where people who had left ghetto environments and transitioned into middle and upper class lives were embarrassed by, and would distance themselves from, their less fortunate brethren who remained in the inner city. With their new status, they were no longer willing to pull their old acquaintances out of *the crab pot.*

In these discussions, I would argue back that same condition existed in the rest of society as well. I told him I'd grown up with people who had gone into the technology and finance fields who were now worth hundreds of millions of dollars -- that financing our project would be lunch money for them, but if I ever called them for help, they'd tell me to get lost. Darryl thought that that response would represent a window into their racial leanings, and my position was that the issue was more complex than that -- that a lot of people just hate people who try to do things that are different from the norm. That there was simply a class of people across all ethnicities that wanted mavericks or disrupters to fail.

Darryl would hold firm that I couldn't place the crab pot syndrome into some kind of all-inclusive issue that cut across all ethnicities. *"Leigh, you didn't grow up in the fucking ghetto. Okay? Don't try to put some kind of reasoned, academic spin on this. No White person is ever going to fully understand the complexities involved in transitioning from a Black ghetto environment to the middle-class and beyond."*

On that point, Darryl was right.

Darryl and I also discussed the issue of have-nots that suddenly have unreasonable expectations of, and grow to resent people they knew from less prosperous times, who had entered a higher financial station. In *Welcome to Death Row*, the crab pot syndrome was best expressed in Suge Knight's epicly bad judgment in bringing members of rival gangs into the office atmosphere under the pretext of keeping the music *real*. The people we had spoken to were all pointing to the same dialectic: The gang members loved being there, but didn't want to see Suge have what he had. Michael Harris had a slightly different take. He felt it was a user / use situation where Suge could get these guys to do things, often bad things, when he wanted to send a message to someone - a message he didn't want traced back to him.

For hours into the night, Darryl and I debated whether we were doing something that America needed to see and examine. I kept coming back the notion of *Our Stories Are Not Being Told,* and that getting stories right often meant delving into information a lot of people didn't want to know about. Darryl was haunted by the notion that, in his view, a significant percentage of Black America wanted Suge Knight and everything he represented to go away. This assumption appeared to be confirmed by comedian, D.L. Hughley, in a discussion the three of us had one night in the Foundation Room at the House of Blues in West Hollywood. When the subject of the film came up, Hughley did a mock recoil and took a step back. "*I really don't think I want to see that.*" He had a smile on his face when he said it, but I thought his reaction represented a lot of the conflict Darryl was feeling about the correctness of what we were doing.

Darryl argued that the visceral nature of the way the story had played out in the media had created a huge divide, and I saw that. But I argued that it was in the basic nature of man to resist or be threatened by sweeping changes in the success, social class, and the financial lives of people they once knew.

There were a lot of issues that the two of us could not agree on. But we could agree on one thing: The Death Row Records story was part of a sea change in the way all Americans perceived economic opportunity for Blacks in entertainment.

It was also a story about the ruthless nature of man, and those who end up making it in American business and those who don't.

****

We needed at least one marquis name, and it needed to be someone who had a front row seat to what had happened, who would speak with confidence and without fear. At one of my many low ebbs on the project, I called Allen Gordon, who was the editor-in-chief for *Rap Pages* magazine. I explained the interview situation and he said, *"I think I can get you Snoop."*

By the time our filming had begun, Snoop had left Death Row, and was on Master P's No Limit Records. One day, Gordon called me with the news that Snoop would talk as would Master P. It was one of the brightest days in the entire production. Snoop's interview, conducted by Allen Gordon, was magnificent. Snoop spelled out what happened in a way that no one else could. It would be a major step in getting us credibility.

"A Black Man with a Lot of Power"

With the amazing success of The Chronic, Death Row Records was suddenly in the spotlight. Suge Knight took over management of the label, recklessly spending money on cars, entertainment, and jewelry for himself, and to a lesser extent, the artists. But to the outside world, it didn't seem to matter. Death Row's astonishing success spoke for itself. The Chronic was followed by Snoop Dogg's album, Doggystyle, the soundtracks for the films, Above the Rim, and, Murder Was the Case, the Dogg Pound album, Dogg Food, featuring Daz Dillinger and Kurupt and later, the Tupac albums. In the face this out-sized success, Suge Knight became the public face of Death Row Records.

HANK CALDWELL: If you understand what was going on in the street at the time, and even now, word of mouth is everything, and Death Row became really hip on the street. Every young, Black entertainer wanted to be part of it. So there was no problem finding talent. There was an understanding at Death Row that (the artists) weren't getting at the major companies.

ALLEN GORDON: I can't really think of a major label that has broken a major (rap) superstar that we didn't already know about. The streets dictate where the next superstar comes from. Then, the major labels just blow it up bigger.

HANK CALDWELL: Once Suge, Jimmy Iovine, and myself came to an agreement as far as my involvement with Death Row was concerned, I came into the Company as President. And in theory, my day to day operations were just that -- running the company as President of Death Row.

DOUG YOUNG: One of the things about these major labels,

186

they'll never understand street music. They'll never understand the stuff that starts right here in the neighborhood. They'll never understand it, never will, never will, never will. That's why you'll always have some young entrepreneur who will come along, who really knows how to do that and make a killing.

ALLEN GORDON: Hip hop gravitates around the measuring stick of manhood. And Death Row had it.

HANK CALDWELL: I came along at a time when the music industry was a 180 degree departure from where it is today. And a lot of guys who came along in my particular time, just don't get it. They haven't been able to adjust. They haven't been able to accept the fact that it is the time of these youngsters, and what they're doing musically.

LAMONT BRUMFIELD: First of all, they had Dre. They had Kurupt, who was the lyrical assassin at the time. They had Snoop, with the laid back lyrics. They had Rage who was serving a lot of the females. And you had Daz, and Warren G, doing all these beats and helping Dre out. So you had an accumulation of talented people working together to make songs.

HANK CALDWELL: By having hits, we were able to come out looking like geniuses at that particular time. I have a philosophy in this industry, that hit records cure cancer.

MASTER P: Suge Knight motivated a lot of kids on the street. Just to see a Black man with that type of money, and be able to control a company, and control his own destiny. He opened up a lot of eyes to people that wanted to have their own business.

SUGE KNIGHT: (Stephanie Frederic archive) I'm not Hollywood. You know, if you see me out somewhere, I don't care who you is, I'm gonna come over here, hear your hook, talk to you, "*How you doing?*" Whatever. You're gonna speak to me. I ain't gonna throw you, "*Let's do lunch.*" I ain't with all that. I'm

187

still from the ghetto. I still got a house in Compton. I may not be there every night, but I still got a house there. I go there and hang out and feel it. That's where the talent's at. 'Cause when people stay away too long, they get scared of it. There's no goin' back. How am I gonna run from something I'm part of?

HANK CALDWELL: It was a very good time for young kids looking for a break. There was an opportunity there. There were people there who understood them, understood what they were about. Kids would come in and audition right off the street.

ALLEN GORDON: Rap is, and always will be, street music no matter how mainstream it gets. Because that's where your next superstar is going to come from.

GARY JACKSON: Suge Knight was definitely the Berry Gordy of the early 90s.

JONATHAN CLARK: Basically, it's the same thing Motown did. They took the mindset, spirit, dreams, hopes, wishes, and thoughts of the people of a time period, and they set it to music.

MASTER P: Nobody in his wildest imagination ever thought they'd hear this type of stuff on mainstream radio, until these records broke like they broke with Death Row. The streets were screaming for them - calling the radio stations, putting pressure on the radio stations.

HANK CALDWELL: We constantly had people coming into the offices. I couldn't begin to tell you how many tapes we received on a daily basis. Kids would come in and want to audition right off the street. But that was the kind of energy that we never tried to negate or discourage. We really wanted that to happen.

DOREADOR: On every Death Row album you can play the first song and listen to it all the way to the end. And there ain't a lot of record companies puttin' out an all bomb album. The whole album just bein' a bomb. Where you don't want to fast forward one song. So you gotta give Suge and Dre respect. I bought every album Death Row put out.

ALLEN GORDON: The appeal of Death Row records was that Suge Knight was a Black man with a lot of power. And, he was a fearsome individual. That's the type of person you want on your team.

MATT MCDANIEL: I was there. It was all good times. Everybody was hungry. Everybody was seeing their dreams come true. Dre had a birthday around the time *The Chronic* went platinum. And, I'm glad I caught a lot of that footage. It was a great thing -- one of the best things to happen in L.A.

HANK CALDWELL: If anyone would stop and analyze what happened at Death Row, it's really a miracle. You have a small company, run by a Black entrepreneur, and he releases five or six LP's. And, all of them went at least double platinum. It's a known fact in our industry, if you're working at a major, and you release ten LP's, and you have three or four hits out of the ten, you're considered a genius.

KEVIN POWELL: They create this album and you get Snoop on there. And the next thing you know, he's got an album out. You've got Daz and Kurupt on there and the next thing you know, you've got *Tha Dogg Pound*.

DOVE C: To see a powerhouse headed by a cat that came out of the hood -- that had business sense. That was inspirational.

MASTER P: Suge Knight is the person that probably introduced gangsta rap and wasn't scared to stand out in the forefront and represent it.

DICK GRIFFEY: I was talking to an ambassador from South Africa and his daughter. Very eloquent, articulate, people. Very educated. And these people had bought into it. Suge was a cult hero around the world.

SUGE KNIGHT: (5) I think the most important thing in my situation is, that I wasn't coached. I think if a person is coached about the business, they tend to make the same mistakes that other entrepreneurs been making all along.

ALLEN GORDON: Everything said *Executive Producer, Suge Knight*. Suge let you know who he was.

SUGE KNIGHT: (5) My thing is look, you sit out in that meeting, you should know what you want, and go get it. And, at the end of the meeting, you should say, *"Okay, now how much is the check for, and when do I get it?"* Once that part is done, we can sit up there and talk all day.

JEFFREY JOLSON COLBURN: There's one thing I've learned working in the Hollywood trades -- once you've got the money, you want the power. And that's true if you're a Michael Ovitz or a Michael Eisner or a Suge Knight. Once you've got the money, you want the power.

HANK CALDWELL: Loved him. Vibrant, charismatic, quick study, very bright young man. He had a talent. Suge had the knack about him of being able to bring a young artist into the fold -- convince them to believe in him and believe in his dream.

MICHAEL HARRIS: Suge can charm the pants off a bear. He can also put a bear to sleep.

MARIO JOHNSON a.k.a. CHOCOLATE: Suge and I kept up our relationship. One time I was on a freeway. My nigga Porsche broke down. Suge paid the tow for it. He just happened to be comin' by, saw me and pulled over. *"What's wrong?"* He was like, *"Fuck it"* and paid the tow.

HANK CALDWELL: Like any other young entrepreneur, Suge Knight ran the business out of a briefcase. He was on 24 / 7. He was involved in every aspect of the business. He would be running things from his car, cell phone, studio, or whatever. But all decisions really began and ended with Suge.

George Pryce had worked at Hill & Knowlton, a large public relations firm, and later, had founded a magazine called Modern Black Men. After the magazine folded, a friend who was a publicist for Michael Jackson advised him that Suge Knight had been through a lot of people and was looking for a publicist.

GEORGE PRYCE: Well, I always got a big kick out of Suge Knight. The day that I met him he said, *"Look I'm gonna interview you when I can. But it may take a while."* So I sat for seven days in the lobby, between all of these huge, hip hop types. The only awareness I had of hip hop was on the east coast with a group called Run DMC. And I knew Heavy D. I sat for seven days - a solid week. Suge may have been somewhere, looking through a peephole. I may have been scrutinized in a way I'm still not aware of. On the last day, I finally saw Suge. He came down the aisle and said, *"Hello, how are you? I'm gonna see you in a few minutes. But first I've got to have a staff meeting. As a matter of fact, come on in to the staff meeting."* So when the meeting was called to order, the first words out of his mouth were, *"Everybody, I'd like you to meet George Pryce. He's the new publicist, the Head of Communications and Media Relations for Death Row Records."* No contract. No conversation about salary. Nothing. But I knew it was gonna be okay. That's just the way Suge is.

GEORGE PRYCE: One of my first jobs at Death Row was to set up a communications and media relations department, which they did not have in-house. I'd heard that Suge Knight wasn't happy with how the publicity was going for the company. He wanted more. He'd been told by members of the Black press that they weren't getting the cooperation they needed. So, he added his own publicity department.

FRANK ALEXANDER: Because of Suge's size and his stature and who he was and what he was representing, there was an automatic fear factor. And once you receive a reputation, it's hard to live it down.

HANK CALDWELL: Suge's tremendous size intimidated people. When you got a 300 pound guy saying something, it means a lot more than if you have Mickey Rooney saying it. Suge was bright enough to use his size, like Don King uses his hair.

DIANE FRANK: I don't think size has anything to do with making you successful. Even the smallest person, can be dangerous. I don't think size had anything to do with him getting an Interscope deal.

GEORGE PRYCE: Suge Knight is an intimidating individual. When he enters a room, you notice him. You can't help it. I think he would be considered a handsome man.

BILLY MOSS: The hype got so big that people started fearing it.

VIRGIL ROBERTS: I have friends at Sony, and one of them called and said, "*Gee, you know. We really want to get a track. Will you do me a favor? Will you talk to Suge?*" And, I said, "*Yeah, I'll go talk to him.*" So I went over to talk to Suge and said, "*Suge, What are you doing? You got people out there that are afraid to talk to you*". And he was the same ole Suge. To him it was all a game.

ANGELA WALLACE: For most people who really knew Suge - he had a nice side to him - a warm heart. Obviously there was a street side and as his popularity escalated it was as if he was put in a position where he had to maintain a certain image. Perhaps he went beyond what was really necessary.

HANK CALDWELL: Suge became a folk hero after a while.

These stories just developed a life of their own. You got Suge doing everything from throwing people off of a 30 story building to, you know, putting rocks and buying them in cement.

GEORGE PRYCE: Out of the ghetto, you have what you call *ghetto buzz* or *street buzz*.
There are certain members (of the press) that would go along with whatever they heard. Some journalists would just take that at face value and print it.

KOMACAUZY: The media, they put bad names on people and try and drag your name through the mud. But as an individual, you have to do what you got to do to get paid.

JEWELL: He was a very brilliant businessman. Whatever his tactics might have been, whoever he had to step on to get there, his main objective was just to get there. At any cost.

GEORGE PRYCE: Suge just had certain innate qualities. There was a genius there. There's a genius that's part of him and you know what they say about geniuses? They're not far from being insane.

JEWELL: When Death Row first started blowing up, you'd see Dre on covers and Snoop started being on covers. And all of sudden, it got to a point where you'd see Suge Knight on the cover of magazines. It was almost as if he became more important than the artists he represented.

ALLEN GORDON: Suge pretty much blew his cover by appearing on the front of magazines. You're no longer a figure behind the scenes. You're a celebrity.

JEWELL: It's almost like taking a drug. If you keep taking it, it's gonna overtake you.

MICHAEL HARRIS: Originally, I told him he should never put

himself on the front of magazines. Always stay in the cut, stay in the background. That's how you have more power. But as the social thing started to grow, and people started to recognize him, he lost or forgot that teaching.

ALLEN GORDON: Clive Davis is not on the cover of *Rolling Stone*. Tommy Mottola's not on the cover of *Rolling Stone*.

ALONZO WILLIAMS: You look at guys like Russell Simmons. Laid back, low profile, makes a ton of money. You don't see him all over a bunch of magazines flashing and flossing. Puff Daddy gets away with it 'cause his music is so harmless. He's not advocating anything. He's selling a pipe dream. *Money Ain't a Thing*......

ALLEN GORDON: This has been the problem with hip hop journalism. The best stories that have come out on Death Row have been either in the weekly newspaper, *Vanity Fair*, *GQ*, or the *New York Times Magazine*. They're a little more observant. They're not scared like most hip hop writers are. So, once you put yourself out there in the celebrity status, like Suge did, that's when the research begins - that he was a (football) player at University of Las Vegas - but also had a fairly long rap sheet for abusive and violent behavior. That stuff is easy to find. It's public record.

SNOOP DOGG: After *The Chronic* came out, we did a 7-day tour. (Then) Dre wanted to work on my album. So we went into the studio with nothing, no concept. All we knew was that the title was going to be *Doggystyle*. Dre would come pick me up. We would do our thing at the same time every day. No girls. No nothing. I heard Atomic Dog on the radio and got the idea to change (my name) to *Snoop Doggy Dogg*. From there, I was busting out songs in one take. *Tha Shiznit*. He made the beat. I just went in there and just bust. One take.

DICK GRIFFEY: When Snoop's album comes out, this is the most anticipated rap album in history.

SNOOP DOGG: Doggystyle was, *"We're through with The Chronic. It's all about you, Snoop. LBC. Eastside. You're the hottest thing coming up on the West Coast in a long time. You're the big dog. George Clinton on your album. All your homeboys from the DPG on your album."* And, Dre's gonna produce it, and when Dre produces an album, you can't lose.

SNOOP DOGG: (2) (The new album will be) gangsta shit. Smooth, gangsta shit.

JEFFREY JOLSON COLBURN: Nobody in the modern era had ever had their first album go to number one. This guy had such incredible street cred and such a buzz behind him from *The Chronic.*

ALLEN GORDON: Dr. Dre's first album sold four million copies. Snoop came right behind him and sold 4.5 which became five million. Then you had the two million selling album, *Above the Rim.*

JEFFREY JOLSON COLBURN: Interscope took over the label, had an instant hit with *The Chronic,* and drew instant attacks. Interscope distributes through its agreement with Time-Warner. Interscope became so hot because of Nine Inch Nails, Tupac, and the Death Row acts, that it became the hottest independent record label in the world, doing about 2% of the entire record industry income which at the time was $12 billion dollars a year. With 40 or 50 employees. So this tiny label with a few guys is doing one-fifth of the business of whole label groups, with ten labels, and a thousand lawyers.

SNOOP DOGG: We started Tha Dogg Pound from my apartment, because my apartment was called *Tha Dogg Pound.* Kurupt and Daz were not *Tha Dogg Pound* on *The Chronic* album.

They became the *Tha Dogg Pound* on my album, *Doggystyle*.

LAMONT BRUMFIELD: It was like a plan that Suge must have had, because he couldn't put everybody out at the same time. Dr. Dre introduced Snoop. Snoop had to introduce something, so I guess he introduced *Tha Dogg Pound* after he was blowing up on his record. So Kurupt and Daz was like, *"Okay. We gonna be Tha Dogg Pound."*

SNOOP DOGG: (With) *Murder Was the Case*, me and Daz, we sat there and thoroughly concepted that shit. Daz was telling me, *"You need to talk to the devil in this song."* He gave me that concept. Dre put the beat around it, and made it scarier than a mutherfucker.

DOUG YOUNG: I heard that Death Row was actually in debt during the Snoop album. After the Snoop's album came out, it was all gravy. 'Cause Death Row was flyin' high then.

Jimmy Iovine's Voice

As the interviews unfolded, a multitude of story threads began emanating, clearly challenging us to make the big decisions as to how much space should be allocated to each story piece. There were six major pieces to consider:

> There was the Ruthless Records piece which would later provide the foundation for the initial drafts of the screenplay for *Straight Outta Compton*.
>
> There was the Solar Records piece.
>
> The Harry O piece.
>
> The making of the soundtrack for *Deep Cover*.
>
> And *The Chronic*. And later, the arrival of Tupac, the various controversies and the collapse of the label.

And then there was the Interscope piece.

Prior to its association with Suge Knight and Death Row Records, Interscope had been a fledging, money losing label, with a billionaire backer in Ted Field, and a superstar producer/leader in Jimmy Iovine. The business deal that Iovine had worked out with Jerry Heller and Eazy E at Ruthless that allowed *The Chronic* to become an Interscope product, had set the stage for Interscope to secure six consecutive multi-platinum releases from Death Row, and had provided the foundation for what would become the most powerful label group in the music industry.

Many of the people we spoke to wanted us to delve deeply into the Interscope piece of the puzzle and illuminate the extent to which Interscope understood, and potentially enabled the craziness that transpired at Death Row. Interscope's offices were adjoined to Death Row's. Jimmy Iovine and Suge Knight were very close at one time. Serious money was coming into both companies. I wanted to know what Interscope knew about what went on. Iovine had claimed he didn't know anything about Harry O's involvement until the Harrises' claim had hit the press. But he'd handed Lydia $500,000 to make a record years before. There was a time with he communicated almost daily with David Kenner. Kenner had never mentioned to him that he had set up Harry O's partnership in Godfather Entertainment? It seemed inconceivable. There were other issues as well. In the face of all this success, did Interscope just do what they needed to do and look the other way as Death Row blew up and then imploded?

And yet, in nearly all of our interviews, no one would say a word about Interscope Records on camera.

I'd been aware of Jimmy Iovine since my college days at Boston University. I'd seen his name on Tom Petty's album, *Damn the Torpedos*, which I probably listened to every single day of my senior year. Later, I became obsessed with other Iovine-produced tracks like the Stevie Nicks and Tom Petty duet, *Stop Draggin My Heart Around*. And the list of Iovine-produced music that I admired, only got bigger from there. By the time we started *Welcome to Death Row*, Interscope was in full bloom and Jimmy Iovine, the son of a Brooklyn longshoreman, was one of the most powerful people in the music industry. From the people we spoke to it was clear that he inspired loyalty and fear in equal measure. He understood and used power to his advantage every day. Additionally, he appeared to have the unique sensibility required to work with the personalities attached to Death Row's music. An article in *The New Yorker*, written by Connie Bruck, entitled *The Takedown of Tupac*, quoted a rival music executive saying about Iovine, "*Jimmy is comfortable with gangsters. He can deal with them. It doesn't bother him. He's a street guy himself.*"

At some point after the interviews with Griffey and Virgil

Roberts, news about the existence of our project had apparently gotten his attention.

One day, an unsolicited call came in from a lawyer at Interscope named Rand Hoffman. He was heavy of breath and jonesing for a fight. *"I need to see a copy of your film. I need you to send it over to me today."* I told him I didn't have a showable copy of the film, which at that point was true. Hoffman continued to come after me like a tiger shark, his voice rising with each passing second. *"Is Jimmy Iovine's voice in the film? Is Jimmy's voice in the film? Jimmy Iovine's voice better not be in that fucking film."* Hoffman was completely unhinged.

"So, I guess an interview with Jimmy is out of the question."

I have a longstanding policy of hanging up when someone goes ballistic on me. So that's what I did. Immediately, Hoffman called back, and asked for Steve Housden. *"I need that fuckin' film sent over today. Don't you want a relationship with Interscope?"* At that point, Steve replied, *"Is this what a relationship with Interscope is like?"* I was pretty sure I knew where a relationship with Interscope would lead, and I didn't want to go there.

When I was able to speak to Michael Harris again, I told him about the incident and he got very energized. He told me that Suge had put him on calls with Iovine. *"He probably thinks somebody recorded it. He doesn't want anyone to know that he ever spoke with me."* I said, *"Are you sure Suge wasn't fucking with you? Just playing games?"* Michael explained that Iovine had a very distinct Brooklyn accent. *"Unless Suge hired a magician, it was him."*

Michael's other thought was that Suge Knight might have recorded private conversations with Iovine and Iovine or his people might have thought that those recordings had been made available to us. Michael said *"Suge's sneaky like that. His whole thing is to have something to hang over your head so you have to play ball with him."*

Regardless of what was going on in Interscope's head, I certainly didn't need to see another demonstration of power by another bigwig in show business. I'd already had my Leno experience. That had been a legal bloodbath which had hurt me financially for years and I didn't want a repeat of it. But what were we going to do? Interscope was an integral part of the story. I called Scheftel and relayed what happened. His response was roughly the following:

"Look at it from Interscope's perspective. You have a federal investigation going on with Death Row and you have the feds up at there at Interscope's offices sticking a catheter into their dicks. Iovine's probably telling the feds he's never heard of Harry O. You've got Griffey and Virgil talking about how Griffey got fucked on The Chronic. But wait! There's more. Interscope gave Lydia a $500,000 advance for a record and it got pissed away. Then, they paid her more money when she threatened to go public with the story of the Harry O connection. This is the story you're telling. Why are they gonna like you? They want you to die in a warehouse fire!"

With that tirade I let go of my hope that someone from Interscope would speak to us. Jeff was right. That was never going to happen. It would be up to someone else to fully examine the relationship between Interscope and Death Row Records.

The other guy we wanted to speak to was Suge Knight's former Death Row consigliere, David Kenner. In a story featuring a rogue's gallery of fascinating characters, Kenner was near the apex. A graduate of USC Law School, Kenner met Michael Harris after establishing a very lucrative career representing a storied group of criminals in the drug trade, including Mario Villabona, who had been Harry O's main drug connection. Under the auspices of handling his appeal for attempted murder, Kenner had established a friendship with Michael Harris, who had then introduced him to Suge Knight. Subsequently, Kenner established a partnership with Michael and Lydia, and became the funnel that put Harry O's funds into Death Row.

Kenner's first order of business had been to neutralize a series of battery cases that Suge had that stemmed from when he was a bodyguard. It was a brilliant scheme. In the criminal defense business, many clients pay in cash. So most of Harry O's cash went through Kenner's law office to help fight Suge Knight's cases and cases involving the other artists. This was why the government was never going to be able to pin Death Row's foundation on drug money. Kenner could claim that cash was used to pay him for legitimate business purposes and the source of the cash could never be traced. Later, Kenner would become essential to the Death Row enterprise, beating down the RICO action from Ruthless, providing a successful defense for Snoop Dogg in his murder case, and becoming the key conduit between Death Row and Interscope CEO, Jimmy Iovine.

During this time, David Kenner's loyalty to Michael Harris would fade.

Jeff Scheftel felt that there was no way Kenner would talk to us. *"Not gonna happen."*

However, in a rare moment of agreement between us on any issue, both Lydia and I thought it was possible. Kenner was a brilliant lawyer -- a brilliant defender of people. Why wouldn't he see this as an intellectual challenge? Could our questions be so difficult for him to respond to? He'd made a career out of turning smart people into mush. He was a master of verbal Aikido. Why wouldn't he perceive speaking to us as something akin to child's play? Both Lydia and I wrote letters to Kenner's lawyer, Don Re, who would later become part of the so-called *Dream Team* that would defend Suge Knight in the wake of the kicking episode at the MGM Grand Hotel in Las Vegas (and the death of Tupac Shakur).

Eventually, Kenner agreed to speak to me on the phone. I don't ever recall preparing for a phone call more assiduously in my whole life. My message to him was *"Just give us your side. Say what you want to say. There are plenty of voices in this film that support Suge Knight and what he accomplished."* I enumerated specific things that had been said that I thought he would appreciate, and emphasized how critical his role had been in Death Row's success. People say that world class bullshitters are the hardest people to persuade of anything - but in Kenner's case, his personal conflict came through very clearly on the phone. In his heart of hearts, he had something to say. He wanted to say *yes*. I felt like I had him on the one-yard line. But in the final analysis, his legal instincts were warding him off this case. He told me he'd think it over. But I knew the answer was *no*.

I would replay the calls from Rand Hoffman at Interscope, and David Kenner in my mind many times over the years. These were two men whose livelihoods depended on the sanctity of free speech. Hoffman had shown me Interscope's hand. There was no room for interpretation there. And Kenner couldn't reconcile that he'd made a fortune off of Death Row and sold Harry O, his former partner, down the river.

In my view, they were punting. They were denying themselves and the companies they represented a voice in one of America's great stories and, in doing so, opened themselves up for much deeper examination down the line.

Crazy Money

DOUG YOUNG: Suge always come into the office late. But when Snoop started really happening, he *really* started comin' in late, and you might see him one day a week. And we just had stupid money. I mean crazy money. There's some stuff I can't say on tape that I was doing.

JEFFREY JOLSON COLBURN: Until Death Row, you had (occasional) million sellers. You hadn't had triple platinum, which is three million. Death Row upped the ante for everybody. In other words, a triple platinum album is 30 million dollars to the record label. It's more like 45 million dollars on the retail level. You're talkin' some serious money here. And then you had some of the later Death Row records selling six million, so you're talking nearly a 100 million dollar album.

HANK CALDWELL: We had to beat the vendors off the doorsteps who wanted to do business with Death Row. When you have a fatted cash cow the likes of Death Row -- at any given time, in the lobby, there were guys looking to pitch us -- computers, you name it. Every businessman wanted to do business with us.

JEFFREY JOLSON COLBURN: Death Row became the core of Interscope, which became the core of the Warner Brothers Music, money machine for a while. That was the lowest cost, highest return, product on anything on the whole Warner Music label group. This is Prince's label, Madonna's label, Eric Clapton. There's nothing that you could make a $50,000 record for, and have it sell three million copies within a month with virtually no marketing.

ALLEN GORDON: They were going to start a magazine at Death Row called *Death Row Uncut*. That probably would have sold three million copies. Everybody wanted to leave their

203

contracts and move to Death Row.

JEFFREY JOLSON COLBURN: They can buy anything they want. They can buy anybody they want. That made it all very, very serious business.

DOUG YOUNG: We were getting pretty crazy. We either stayed at the Ritz, or some five star hotel. We had DJ parties in our hotel rooms. We'd rent the President's suite for that. There was so much money floating around Death Row for anything. I used to run through thousands of dollars a day. I hear stories about how Death Row didn't pay people. On the Snoop project alone, I made a quarter of a million bucks. And I'm just a lowly promoter. That was just my salary, not perks.

JONATHAN CLARK: Any young person, if you give them 25 million dollars and you don't have some older people around them to guide them and teach them respect -- go give the average 18 year old person $10 million and what they gonna do with it? They gonna fuck it off.

DOUG YOUNG: Suge was *The Man*. He had a couple of penthouse apartments on Wilshire, a house out in Malibu, one in Woodland Hills and some Rancho Cucamonga ranch-style houses. Those were the five or six houses I knew about. Imagine the ones I didn't know about?

S. LEIGH SAVIDGE: One the many homes that Suge Knight owned was directly across the street from a friend of mine. It was neighborhood of multi-million homes on the Los Angeles side of Mulholland Dr. Over a period of many years, the home, which had been relatively modest given the neighborhood morphed into a mega-mansion featuring a giant Jacuzzi, tennis courts and a giant carousel. The home was a perennial construction site that featured 24 hour security. My friend told me that in the 14 years that he owned the house, she never saw him once.

JEFFREY JOLSON COLBURN: They should have been thrilled with this kind of revenue and been able to build a long-term record label. One hundred and fifty million dollars -- put that into perspective -- all of Motown sold for less than 60 million dollars, with that catalog and all those great artists. The first time it sold it was only 18 million. So these guys are makin' many times what Motown was ever worth, and, and did it from scratch in two years.

JONATHAN CLARK: (Berry Gordy) sold Motown for 69 million dollars. Does anybody around here have $69 million dollars? He still owned Stone Diamond and Jobete Publishing. Which means, *"Let me give you this for 69 million dollars, so you guys can get happy about this thing I paid $600 to start and made hundreds of millions of dollars on for 20 years. I still own the publishing. Which means every time you sell a record, I make a nickel."*

DOUG YOUNG: I would have checks piling up at my house like for 20 thousand bucks, 30 thousand dollar checks. I'd sometimes look at the checks to make sure I cash 'em before the expiration date. I'd have a car full of records and if I needed some money, I'd go to a record store, get me a quick 200 bucks. I never cashed all of my checks. Never cashed 'em. Built 'em up to maybe 200 thousand -- gave my mom a 150 thousand, *"Here, you go buy a house."* That's when times was gravy.

ATRON GREGORY: Death Row didn't put out a whole lotta records. They just sold a lot of the ones that they did put out.

DOUG YOUNG: When Snoop did *Above the Rim*, we were down in Atlanta.   We was in a mall down there, doin' the free thing, and I thought we was gonna get killed from all of them groupies chasin' Snoop. It was like the Beatles.

FRANK ALEXANDER: Wherever we went, there was drama. You had a bunch of kids with a lot of money. And it's like giving someone an uncontrollable amount of money and saying, *"Here, go on a shopping spree."*

ALLEN GORDON: David Kenner was walking around with gold bracelets and a Rolex and all this finery. And the artists have celebrity status and their goin' there too. And it goes to everybody's head.

GEORGE PRYCE: This was overwhelming success. People didn't have time to adjust.

ALLEN GORDON: There was no control (over spending) at Death Row. *Rap Pages* printed a story in the September 1997 issue about BL Diamonds, where Death Row got all their jewelry. And we have the invoices of all the jewelry that was purchased there on credit. And you go down the list and its *bracelet for wife number one, earrings for Michel'le, cut gold, diamond cuff links for Casey and Jo Jo's Grandfather.* And after a while the artists started going there and ordering their own jewelry without the consent of Kenner, Knight or George Pryce or any figure of authority. Suge Knight probably doesn't even know that all these artists went down there and started purchasing this jewelry. I was there with these artists and they just had on the regular chain, maybe a ring, you know, maybe a bracelet. Or whatever gold they had. But you see 'em later, on the street, talking to females or at different parties and there's more jewelry on. It only made sense after you found out that they owed a million dollars to one jewelry store.

KEVIN POWELL: One thing I remember from the interviews I did with the cats from Death Row for Vibe Magazine, they all said, *"Suge takes care of us."* If you're coming from a single parent household, where you haven't had any money, and this person is giving you stuff, you're gonna feel like, *"This person has my back."* A lot of people outside of urban America don't realize -- for you to be given a car when you've been riding a bus your whole life -- that's a big deal.

WILLIE MOSS: There's a lot of people out there with platinum albums that don't have a dime in their pocket. Mainly because of mismanagement or else they just got fucked.   Some people aren't smart enough to read a contract. You got kids that want to be in this business so bad they're willing to sign any piece of paper or just do anything to be the next Tupac. It's real hard when kids never had nothing -- you got kids out of the projects -- there's more honor in the streets than there is in the music business. I don't know any artist that's debt free.

SUGE KNIGHT: (5) There's a lot of jealous people out there that feel cheated. They feel that they went to college and they became a lawyer or a doctor, and then some guys who never graduated from high school -- they make more money than them and they're upset about it.

DOUG YOUNG: Death Row was bombin' out of control. All you had to do was tell a girl you worked at Death Row Records -- anything you want. Any shop you go into -- *"I work for Death Row"* -- anything you want. Any record store you go into -- *"I work for Death Row"* -- you come back with some promo goods. There was no club, no guest list you weren't on. *"We'll fly you here, we'll do this for you, that for you. We'll give you clothes."*

JEFFREY JOLSON COLBURN: Death Row at its peak was making about $150 million dollars a year. For a tiny label, that was a shocking amount.

JEWELL: Suge kinda pacified everybody, you know. He'd give you a Benz or a car, some money in the bank. Snoop got a nice house and all that. But I'd rather have my own money so I can get my own things, hang with my own people.

LAMONT BRUMFIELD: All that glitter and glamour you seein' in the videos? Believe me, them artists is livin' at home with mommy and pops. It ain't like that. The record company is supplying them with all the assets, renting houses for 'em -- the cars -- everything to make 'em have that life.

In 1997, Chuck Phillips of The Los Angeles Times began covering the story of Steven Cantrock, a partner in the firm of Gelfant, Rennert & Feldman which Death Row had begun using to pay some of its bills and reconcile its royalty statements to its artists. Cantrock had been accused of stealing $4.5 million from Death Row's accounts. Sources close to close to Cantrock said that Knight forced him to get down on his knees and sign a two-page confession which included an IOU for $4.5 million. Subsequently, Cantrock was fired by his firm, a unit of Coopers & Lybrand and went into hiding. Later, he began working with the Justice Department in its investigation into Death Row.

PAUL PALLADINO: Unfortunately, (Suge) gave them a lot of power, which was to say Cantrock could write checks without any counter signature or anything else. There were a lot of problems compounded by the way they handled the Death Row account. I'd hear things like a number of artists would say they hadn't gotten accountings from Death Row. How can Death Row give you an accounting as to what's happened with your royalties if they can't get an accounting from Gelfant themselves?

SNOOP DOGG: A lot of people mismanaged my career early on. And I want to thank them for that because they showed me how not to go through that again. Now, I'm aware and can educate new rappers. A word of advice - If your friend, girlfriend, wife or company CEO is your manager -- get rid of them! Get people that believe in you.

DICK GRIFFEY: One of the most important lessons is to get a good lawyer. This is such an incestuous industry. You have a few guys out there representing everybody. I've talked to all of these young guys and they would have a guy making a deal for them, and this very same lawyer was representing the company or the CEO of the company. You better find somebody that is knowledgeable that can take care of you.

Death Row Records allocated significant funds for both national promotion and inner city street teams, for its marketing. This spending was critical in building Death Row's national profile.

JOE ISGRO: Death Row was very knowledgeable and very on the cutting edge of street promotion.

BILLY MOSS: Suge wasn't scared to spend money. He spent money on promotion. Whatever it took to make Death Row large -- to make his artists large -- he did it. Kevin Black -- the promotion people -- were out there promoting. They did whatever it took to get their artists out there. That's why Death Row worked.

SIMONE GREEN: Suge was a marketing master. A guy came to us and said he does statues of artists. Suge said, "*Do me one.*" He did a six-foot one of (Suge). Then he did Snoop. Then he went right down the line. They cost a lot. But Suge started putting those things all over the country. He had Snoop standing on Tower Records when they dropped his record. They were real, live statues of their actual height.

DICK GRIFFEY: That whole gangster aura was the marketing plan. And the way they carried it out, they became cult heroes. They had good street people who really knew how to get out there and get things happening on the street.

BILLY MOSS: We'd give away snippet tapes and posters in the neighborhood and communities. Instead of going to Wherehouse Records in Beverly Hills, I'm gonna go down to VIP in Long Beach, in the ghetto, or whatever they want to call it in the neighborhood, and let the kids shake hands -- meet and greet. People don't realize how much it means to some of these kids, in these communities, to see a artist and to see their face on a CD, with that person right in front of them. They like the record and, whether they buy it the next day, or just copy it off a tape, they're still into the song. And it's the same thing with clothes. You give away free starter t-shirts or free Adidas t-shirts. For every free one you give out, there are ten kids on that block that's gonna want that same shirt or those sneaks or that tape. So you flood the neighborhoods and the streets with tapes, samples, and goods and it pays off. That's proven -- the streets don't lie.

MASTER P: The promotion they did opened the eyes of the industry. They started doing a bunch of big billboards. Hitting big cities. Plastering it with a lot of posters and stuff. Just letting people know. This is it, you gotta have this here.

ALLEN GORDON: Death Row's street teams were the best. There wasn't a major urban community where they didn't have *Doggystyle* or *Dogg Food* stickers posted up or even *Chronic* stickers when this was going on. I remember being in Omaha, Nebraska and seeing a *Chronic* sticker on the lamppost. 'Cause I didn't think anybody in Nebraska listened to hip hop. And same thing with Oklahoma. But a lot of these guys that played football were from Los Angeles, Oakland and Texas. So they probably passed it on.

Changing of the Guards

The film that Interscope was so worried about was going nowhere fast. Darryl was living with me, so I saw him at the end of every day. Fear had absolutely consumed him. There is a place where many documentary filmmakers get in a project, where the finish line seems too far away and the roadblocks to telling the story seem too imposing to overcome. With Darryl, a kind of paralysis had set in.

Darryl continued to be scared to death of Mike and Lydia. He'd grown up on the south side of Chicago, but all the techniques he'd learned about diffusing or neutralizing bullies didn't seem to work in our situation. In his early youth, one of Darryl's tricks had been to lend a bully a small amount of money and then use the debt as a pretext not to lend more. *"I can't lend you more until you pay back the old debt."* If only that had worked with Michael and Lydia. Later, Darryl would grow into a filmmaker with a strong personality and a very strong point of view. But in this situation, the near constant mind games and fear mongering from the people I had chosen as partners, made it nearly impossible for him to concentrate.

There were other external challenges that had all of us frightened. Even more than the Harrises, we feared the prospect of a random act of violence on either one us that might be perpetrated by a gang member looking to curry favor with Suge Knight or otherwise earn his *bona fides* in a gang hierarchy. Periodically, calls would come into Xenon where the voice on the other line would hint at this. For a time, both Darryl and I and Xenon's COO, Steve Housden, took different routes going back and forth between our homes and our work environment.

Equally as troubling was the fact that the iterations of the film that Darryl kept bringing me in his collaboration with Karl Slater lacked a coherent story flow. Darryl would always tell me that the next cut was going to be a breakthrough. But the next cut always looked like the previous one - like a music video with a lot of free associative dialogue from the interviews.

By the summer of 1999, I'd paid Darryl nearly $90,000, which when combined with what the Harrises had extracted from us put us at nearly $650,000 all in. I was beside myself with misery. I had been in film distribution long enough to know that most documentaries with budgets north of $500,000 never made any money unless the director was named Michael Moore or Ken Burns.

I'd put this project into motion and everyone around me felt that my need to get it completed exceeded the value I put on the lives of the people around me. I'd installed a security guard from the Wackenhut Security Agency in the reception area of our office. But I knew that was a fool's journey. The guy they gave us looked like jowly comedian, Louie Anderson. I knew that the minute Suge Knight sent a posse to the office, this guy would go down like a bowling pin. The people at my company were scared to death, questioning me daily about whether it was safe to work there.

I knew Darryl would never be able to complete this film and I knew he knew it. I also knew he would never quit. So I let him know he could leave if he needed to. And he did.

When we parted ways, he looked relieved, like the air had come back to his body. A few months later, I got a short letter from him requesting that his name be taken off the film. The film had become my curse to bear.

The target was fully on my back. I was now the director.

America vs. Death Row

By 1995, the violent and misogynist lyrics of gangsta rap had become a national political issue. Time Warner and Interscope were being pressured to drop Death Row by politicians on both sides of the political aisle. Anti-rap activist C. Delores Tucker led the attack, and quickly became a media sensation, reportedly demanding her own sanitized rap label at Time Warner. Finally, Time Warner bowed to governmental pressure and sold Interscope to MCA, which due to its lack of cable television subsidiaries, was free to distribute controversial materials without risking government retaliation.

JEFFREY JOLSON COLBURN: There is an old adage that any press is good press. And, that's true to an extent. Especially if you're doing something controversial.

HANK CALDWELL: I can remember when The Beatles wanted to put out an album cover that had body parts cut up and the industry stopped them from doing it.

MILLER LONDON: Rappers didn't give gangsta rap its name. The music industry gave gangsta rap its name. They said, *"This music has cussing in it. They're calling women bitches. So it's gangsta rap because it comes from the gangs and the gangstas."*

KEVIN POWELL: I don't know what gangsta rap is. This is something the media put on it. I remember Eazy E saying to me, *"It's reality rap, just rap about what's real in the community."*

GARY JACKSON: Gangsta rap isn't something that was born and invented in the quote-unquote *ghetto*. It's something you see in American movies, the glorification of Al Capone and Lucky Luciano. And that's kind of glamorous in any American's eyes.

ALLEN GORDON: Gangsta rap is, by definition, anything that involves some type of criminal activity being told over and over again, be it a drug sale, gun play, solicitation of firearms or genocide.

MASTER P: Gangster rap takes you on a journey, where it takes you through different neighborhoods, different communities, through different people's lives. It takes you to a whole 'nuther level where you could feel the realness of it. I call it *reality rap* because most of these guys are really going through it.

MICHAEL HARRIS: My life and people like myself in the early 1980s created the atmosphere for gangsta rap to have a life.

MASTER P: What makes gangsta rap so appealing is that the people could feel the realism in it. People could feel the anger, the pain, the whole nine that people go through.

GARY JACKSON: It really puts the truth of society in front of America. And America not used to that is obviously going to be shocked about it.

DICK GRIFFEY: I guess I'm kind of a guy from the old school. You don't carry the fiction past the fiction. If you're a gunfighter in a film, you can't come out and be a gunfighter on the street.

ALLEN GORDON: Even if your story is based on truth, once you add a rhyme to it, you've already fictionalized it.

JEFFREY JOLSON COLBURN: My own personal philosophy is that the motive to create art to improve your situation doesn't lessen the art that's created.

MICHAEL HARRIS: The essence of the whole genre is that (gangsta rap) is our CNN, our 60 Minutes, our Dateline. Most artists try to be as factual as possible in depicting the actual experiences in our community.

GEORGE PRYCE: They are from the television generation, and their role models were people like Al Pacino, the *Godfather* series, *Scarface*. Most of these kids are God fearing and most African Americans who are into any form of music, have their roots in church, in gospel (music). Most of the artists on the Death Row label were from church families, had sung in choirs, that sort of thing. But they weren't getting in church what was going on in the streets. This is what they wanted to talk about. On one hand, rap is a plea.

HANK CALDWELL: Suppose they started rapping about the six o'clock news? Would it be gangsta rap?

LIONEL RANDOLPH: Gangsta rap is like the movies. Drama sells.

ALLEN GORDON: A big aspect of hip hop is hypocrisy. You don't want anyone to get harmed. But you still love the bad guy. You like the guy with the power.

GEORGE PRYCE: The *New York Times* Magazine. My finest hour. I did it for Suge. Because I felt he wasn't getting the recognition that he and Dre deserved. It was all my doing.

ALONZO WILLIAMS: When you got brothers perpetuating gang violence or gang affiliation, that's a problem. No Black man should get on the front of a magazine with a 12 inch cigar, (standing) in front of two Rolls Royces, wearing what could be considered gang colors in America. That sends a bad message.

DR DRE: (2) We write about the stuff going on in our neighborhood and if people don't like it, fuck em.

TONE DEF: I take it for what it is. It's a record, CD or tape. I'm not gonna live my life by it and other people shouldn't either. It's entertainment. You don't go buy a Scarface movie, or an Al

Pacino movie, or an Arnold Schwarzenegger movie, then go buy a big old submachine and start shooting up all of L.A..

JEFFREY JOLSON COLBURN: Women's relationship to rap is a tenuous one. There aren't many female rappers and there aren't many female rap fans. Everyone likes the beat, (but) the lyrics aren't terribly appealing to girls.

GEORGE PRYCE: Regardless of what people say about the bitches and hoe's syndrome, all the artists will tell you when they speak of bitches and hoes, they weren't speaking of women in general, and especially, not Black women. Just that particular category.

SONSHINE: It basically boils down to what kind of woman you are. If you're a respectable woman, those kinds of lyrics won't bother you.

MICHAEL HARRIS: We had become the new rock and rollers in the eyes of young people and in America, that means White suburban children. They were attracted to the rebelliousness. They could listen to the music, and experience what we were going through, without having to go through it themselves.

JAY KING: Young people are united in ways that America doesn't understand. Young people start to look at themselves and to the voices like theirs. And that's what Dre touched.

MICHAEL HARRIS: They could take on this façade through the dress wear and the information that they could obtain from watching the stories and the videos.

JEFFREY JOLSON COLBURN: There's a profit motive for rappers singing this real hardcore gangsta stuff. There's one-upsmanship being played. Who can be more lyrically radical? Who can describe a more gory scene? Who can sound like the toughest hombre in the corral?

GEORGE PRYCE: Publicity, when it was negative, played a role also, because it was part of this role that Suge Knight had chosen for the company. I mean these kids were not gangsters, real gangsters. Many people there were not, as a matter of fact, gang members as it has been portrayed in the press.

JEFFREY JOLSON COLBURN: Time Warner loved Interscope's income and figured Interscope would keep all its little rappers in line. But soon Death Row blossomed out of anything anybody could have expected in terms of income and controversy.

HANK CALDWELL: It wasn't just Death Row perpetuating the violence, it was the media. I mean let's face it - the coverage was just awesome. And all of a sudden, Death Row and gangsta rap was the reason that every youngster in America was going bad.

JEFFREY JOLSON COLBURN: It spun out of control and became a topic for national politics and for debates on late night TV and radio talk shows. And, it all focused on Warner distributing Death Row.

ALLEN GORDON: Nobody in the hip hop media was really interested in doing these stories on (Death Row) at the time cause nobody really knew what to do. In hip hop media, most of us were still learning to be journalists. We were fans, too much in awe of the industry, so stories of magnitude weren't being done. Had that been Time or Newsweek, they'd have been on it in a minute.

JEFFREY JOLSON COLBURN: They couldn't be seen as giving in to the right wing. Here you have Charlton Heston standing up at a Time-Warner shareholders meeting attacking the Chairman of Time Warner for distributing gangsta rap. When you have that kind of publicity working against you, what do you do?

HANK CALDWELL: It's very easy to focus on a company that

by that time had done over a hundred million dollars and talk about violence -- as opposed to talk about the violence that was happening every day. I don't think Death Row cornered the market on that.

JEFFREY JOLSON COLBURN: The record industry likes to sell records. But it likes to keep a low profile. A lot of records have political content and you want to be able to balance your free speech with a minimum of interference from the government. Doug Morris, who was head of the Warner Music Group, had fights with the incoming administration which was Michael Fuchs, who'd been moved over from HBO to run the music group. They had a big fight over what to do with Interscope. What do we do? It's making money but they're too much trouble.

Much of the media attention was focused on the impending release of the Dogg Food album from Tha Dogg Pound, a duo which featured rappers, Kurupt and Daz Dillinger.

JEFFREY JOLSON COLBURN: Everyone was afraid of what would come out in the Dogg Pound record. All these front page stories that say, *"What Will Happen at Time Warner? It'll all come to a head when Tha Dogg Pound comes out."* Michael Fuchs, the head of the Warner Music Group said, *"This is not the most opportune time to distribute Tha Dogg Pound album."* And yet, if they didn't distribute it, they'd be in breach of contract with Interscope. Did that help it in the opening week? Sure.

ATRON GREGORY: Interscope, I give them credit, because they are very artist-oriented. But there was nothing they could do because they were distributed by Time Warner at the time.

JEFFREY JOLSON COLBURN: So they blamed the old administration who was Doug Morris (for) allowing this to happen and the new administration gained political currency by accusing (him) of causing the company all this trouble. And so eventually, he was out. And the incoming group tried to play a game, where they would silence or tame Death Row and still keep the income.

Presidential candidate Senator Joe Lieberman denounced Time Warner citing "lyrics that promote rape, murder, racism, drug abuse and violence."

SUGE KNIGHT: (5)   I think a lot of entrepreneurs should understand that sometimes they get too personal with the people they do business with. I have a great relationship with Jimmy and Ted at Interscope. But if you don't have a relationship like that, you should keep it on the table.

JEFFREY JOLSON COLBURN: Remember who was bankrolling Suge -- Ted. Ted loved a controversial act. Ted Field had no problem putting money out for these acts. He was a free speech advocate and a political activist. The more the conservatives started reacting to Interscope, the more he supported these acts.

DELORES TUCKER: (CNN archive) Time Warner's music division promotes music that celebrates the rape, and torture, and murder, of women.

KEVIN POWELL: C. Delores Tucker is symbolic of this split between the civil rights generation and the hip hop generation. A lot of people from the civil rights generation think Black America won. We didn't. We lost.

JEFFREY JOLSON COLBURN: C. Delores Tucker (was) a political activist that embodies herself in matters of African American decency questions. She involved herself in Time Warner politics along with an odd bedfellow for her, (former Drug Czar) William Bennett.

GEORGE PRYCE: She'd seen me in the background with my artists on television. She took an instant dislike to me without knowing me.

GARY JACKSON: In the beginning, she was trying to protect America from the threat of gangsta rap. But by that point, the cat was out of the bag, and there was very little she could have done.

C. DELORES TUCKER: (8) You can see words that you can't even repeat in a locker room. "Doggystyle"-- Do it from the back. We African-American women particularly, are tired of being called hoes, bitches and sluts, by our children, who are being paid to do this by Time Warner.

KEVIN POWELL: C. Delores Tucker is a house negro, brother. Just like the plantation master had to make sure the field negroes stayed in check, you had the house negroes. Like Malcolm X said, you dress them better, give them a little bit of education, you feed them a little better and they become mouthpieces for the master. C. Delores Tucker and her husband were slumlords in Philadelphia. Philadelphia is peopled by a lot of Black folks. That means you're a slumlord for a lot of Black people. How can you flip it and say you're concerned about what's coming out of the lyrics of young America when you don't give a damn about young Black America?

MICHAEL HARRIS: She was used as a tool because she was a Black woman that could come out and make a statement and say it was wrong.

JAY KING: We're forgetting that this is entertainment. Arnold Schwarzenegger never goes home and kills 142 people.

KEVIN POWELL: Older White folks are like, "Why are kids even into this thing?" Ice-T said it best, "It's home invasion." You can't walk through New York City or Los Angeles without seeing White kids that have been shaped. The Godfather series -- American classics -- which basically promoted violence and sexism. There's a classic scene in The Godfather where they talk about dropping the drugs in Harlem. That's a classic. Why isn't *The Chronic* a classic? There's a hypocrisy there.

WILLIAM BENNETT: (8) We don't understand the moral obtuseness of Time Warner. We don't understand why they don't get it.

JEFFREY JOLSON COLBURN: These are right wing conservatives, both of them. They are would-be censors. Both were attacking Time Warner along with Dole.

BOB DOLE: (8) A line has been crossed. Not just of taste. But of human dignity and decency. The mainstreaming of deviancy must come to an end.

JEFFREY JOLSON COLBURN: You've got a presidential candidate (Bob Dole) accusing Time Warner of debasing a nation for handling Death Row product.

MICHAEL FUCHS: (8) I do think we have problems with the social fabric of this country right now. I do have trouble believing that it is caused by song lyrics or movies.

JEFFREY JOLSON COLBURN: Time Warner was also doing Ice-T. They got T off the label. But they were stuck with Death Row and the numbers were so huge, they didn't know what to do with it. They'd put a 120 million dollars into (Death Row). They're getting all that money out and then some. But here's the twist. They can't be seen by any other artists to give into political pressure whatsoever. If they do, they'll never get another act again. And no self-respecting manager would ever sign with a label who they thought could be pressured for content.

JONATHAN CLARK: What does the music industry care about children? What do Black artists in the music industry care about children? Nothing. The music business is full of chicken-shit, money-hungry motherfuckers. That's what the music industry is.

Chicken-shit, money-hungry, motherfuckers, that'll do anything - lie to you, fuck you, cut your throat, anything to try and get some cash. That's the music business. People backstabbing each other. Brothers fighting. Friends all fucked up. That's the music business.

GEORGE PRYCE: A lot of stuff was blown out of proportion. Like that song of Tupac's, that (Tucker) said affected her sex life. I don't know if you've ever seen Delores Tucker or her husband. But they were way, way beyond that before there was ever a Death Row.

KEVIN POWELL: It's not just White people not understanding. It's middle-class Black people. C. Delores Tucker made these grand proclamations about marching with Dr. King. Dr. King's last thing was a poor people's march. If you really march with Dr. King and you're really about civil rights, you need to realize that the very people you're condemning, are the people he was trying to help. Poor people.

JEFFREY JOLSON COLBURN: (Tucker) came up with an idea, which she reportedly pitched to Fuchs that, what if she started a label, a positive rap label, and got Suge to distribute Death Row through her, with her as the watchdog for the lyrical content. Michael Fuchs, reportedly desperate to try and figure out a solution to this, apparently listened to her. She got Fuchs to guarantee 80 million dollars if she could pull this off.

GEORGE PRYCE: One thing that comes out of the ghetto is a certain respect for elderly people. Suge showed Delores nothing but respect.

JEFFREY JOLSON COLBURN: C. Delores Tucker sent out a truce message to Suge Knight, "*Come to Dionne Warwick's house. We'll have a talk about making rap clean -- taking out the violence.*" Suge was probably laughing, you know, holding his hand over the mouthpiece and laughing hysterically saying, "*Sure, sure. Tell me about it."*

MICHAEL HARRIS: She was trying to solidify a position with Warner Brothers by changing the nature of gangsta rap and making it more like pop rap or children's rap. Which is somewhat impossible.

JEFFREY JOLSON COLBURN: Interscope was not about to let Death Row go without a fight. Suge Knight also protected these artists lyrically. Made sure everyone was allowed to say whatever the hell they wanted to say.

SUGE KNIGHT: (8) Whatever happens, we're gonna stand up tall and we'll be more successful. Only thing anybody's doing is making us stronger and better.

GARY JACKSON: To condemn Suge Knight and the rest of rappers as being evil and then telling people, *"If you sign with my distribution company, I'll distribute your stuff"* -- that's not cool.

JEFFREY JOLSON COLBURN: No way was he gonna let C. Delores Tucker decide the lyrical content of a Snoop Doggy Dogg album. That wasn't going to happen. But apparently they thought it was. Michael Fuchs reportedly flew to Los Angeles, in the Time Warner jet, to Dionne Warwick's house, where C. Delores Tucker is sitting there waiting for Suge Knight to come over to cut a deal that would make it a tame Death Row Records.

C. DELORES TUCKER: (8) Never. Never have I discussed $80 million dollars with them about any kind of business deal.

GEORGE PRYCE: (Suge) was not going to show up at a meeting, which really ticked her off.

JEFFREY JOLSON COLBURN: The story is they waited five hours, Michael Fuchs, C. Delores Tucker, at Dionne Warwick's house and that Suge never showed up. (Later) Suge went right back to Interscope and said, *"Do you know what these guys tried to pull?"* So Interscope sued Time Warner and C. Delores Tucker for interfering with their contractual relationship. That took her out of the game really quick, because she'd tried to make a business deal out of it. It shut her up.

GEORGE PRYCE: What (Tucker) really wanted was a record company. Or to have more involvement in that business. I mean, it's a very lucrative business. She had the wherewithal to see where this rap situation was going. How it had the nation really sort of unnerved. She was just trying to parlay it into something for herself or she had been promised it would be something for herself.

JEFFREY JOLSON COLBURN: Time Warner is a cable company. And cable companies use regulations and must be approved almost every step by regulatory bodies. They're constantly in government hearings. Their telecommunications businesses exist because of co-operation with the government. So there was more at stake here than just the Warner Music Group.

Time Warner has decided to get out of the gangsta rap business by selling its 50 percent share of Interscope back to that company (8).

JEFFREY JOLSON COLBURN: Pressure kept building for Time Warner to shed its Interscope stake. It was one thing to distribute, and it was another thing to own. This partially owned and distributed label was causing all the problems. And yet, if they didn't distribute it they'd be in breach of their contract with Interscope. That was a contract that says you must distribute any album we give you. This provided a window of opportunity for Interscope to get their stake back from Time-Warner.

WILLIAM BENNETT: (8) They made the right decision. The morally responsible decision, we think. And we believe that by their actions, by divesting themselves of Interscope at some financial loss, that they have set a standard for the entire entertainment industry.

BOB DOLE: (8) I commend them for it. I think they're being good corporate citizens.

JEFFREY JOLSON COLBURN: In other words, they sold half of Interscope for a 120 million dollars. A fraction of what it was worth. Let me put it that way. Time Warner practically gave it back to them or sold it back for the same 120 million dollars. Doug Morris, having left Warner amidst all the controversy with Death Row, moved over to MCA. He was now in position to buy the 50% stake in Interscope that Warner just sold. So Interscope ended up at MCA. MCA was not getting into the Telco market. So it did not need all the co-operation from the government that Warner did. MCA was totally willing to accept triple platinum controversial albums. It had a Canadian owner. Edgar Bronfman and the (Seagram's) Company were in there to build the number one label and they eventually ended up doing so. Death Row Records was at the center of a controversy that brought down two administrations at Warner Brothers and Time Warner. And, if the Republicans had had their way, it would have brought down a President. That's how big the controversy got.

Channeling Sandy Howard

On one of the last days before we shut down our set, I got a call from Jeff Scheftel. He said, *"Look, I'm calling you because I promised Nate Dogg I would and obviously you can say "No." Nate got in a domestic dispute and was hoping the production could float the dough to get him out of jail."*

To feed or not to feed the beast. That was the seemingly inexorable question on *Welcome to Death Row*.

During my mid-80s period as an assistant film editor, I'd ending up working on a series of films for a company called Sandy Howard Productions. The company had three films going at once, and I got bounced around between all of them. They were making last minute tweaks to *Avenging Angel*, a sequel to a film called *Angel,* where the tag line had read *"High School Honor Roll Student By Day, Hollywood Hooker By Night."* There was one of Charlie Sheen's first films, *The Boys Next Door*, directed by Penelope Spherris, and a film called *The Supernaturals* which starred Max Caulfield and actress Talia Balsam who was George Clooney's first wife and is now married to John Slattery of *Mad Men* fame.

The films were all produced by a swishy, old-school producer named Sandy Howard. Howard was a real character. He was renowned for always showing up at his film premieres with a woman that people said was a $1,000 a night hooker. Sandy's sense of humor was always kind of off. He'd come in every morning and greet me with the same line, *"How ya doin, cocksucker!"* Then he'd start yelling at all of his editors. His favorite line was, *"It's all sizzle and no steak,"* meaning it looks good but where's the story?

At Sandy Howard Productions, the editors always used to talk about the difference between legendary producer, Roger Corman, who had produced the directorial debuts of Frances Ford Coppola, Peter Bogdanovich and Ron Howard, and Sandy Howard. Everyone agreed that the reason for Corman's greater level of stature and success was because he knew when to cut and run. He'd set a budget, set imperatives for the film and that was that. If the film reached its assigned budget and wasn't finished, Corman would figure out how to finish the film without spending another cent. Or he'd figure out how to incorporate the film's footage into another film he was making. In the editing room, we came to the conclusion that the key to Corman's success that he was fairly dispassionate about the film's he produced. He never fell in love with them.

Sandy Howard had a different attitude toward his films. Every one of them was a special child and, if that child got sick, he'd find the dollars for the medicine, he reasoned, that would make it better. Howard was always trying to make a flawed film better. Or as we used to say in the editing room, he was always trying to "*polish a turd.*" Corman would never polish a turd. And that's why, we reasoned, that Corman would die a rich man and Sandy Howard would die broke.

With *Welcome to Death Row*, I was starting to think I'd become Sandy Howard. I was certain I wasn't polishing a turd, but Karl's iterations of the film continued to be of the all sizzle, and no steak, variety. I wasn't leaving anything to chance. I gave him memo after memo of what we needed to achieve in each sequence, sound bites that needed to flow together and he couldn't seem to get the instructions executed.

Even so, it was during this leg of the journey that the film's 17 chapters would become formalized. Footage that needed to be put in, finally got put in. But the story flow was still very awkward and I started to see what Darryl had been up against. Karl Slater was a great music editor. But this was a different type of project, a different animal.

I needed a hard core story guy.

One night I showed up at Karl's house to view where he was and there were cuts all over his face. He'd been beaten up. I asked him what had happened and he didn't say anything.

Oh Man. Was this another message from some unseen force telling me to stop? Was someone profiling my editor? The editing machine was in his house. All the media was on the disc drives there. If someone came in and jacked him when he was alone in the house, we'd be shit out of luck.

For what seemed like an eternity, Karl and I just sat there and starred at one another.

I'd gotten to the point where I had zero desire to speak with anyone about what was happening with the film. Zero. Discussions about it would only invite criticism of why I was doing it in the first place. *"You mean you were too stupid to understand that these were the kind of things that were going to happen?"* I'd never experienced anything like this before. There were bullies at Catherine Blaine Junior High in Seattle. One time a local thug had come after me with a knife. But that was child's play compared to this stuff. Day in and day out, I was living in fear of my life, not knowing who the potential assailant might be or where it might happen. These are the kinds of thoughts that would race through my mind: *Will it happen in restaurant like in the mob movies? In a meeting in someone's office where I was lured under false pretense? During my nightly run on San Vicente Boulevard? When was someone going to emerge from the nightly shadows and slit my throat?*

Tom Petty once wrote *"The waiting is the hardest part."* I had reached a very irrational state of mind where I was playing out the potential attack in my head, *"Just bring it the fuck on and let's get this over with."*

I wasn't going to press Karl on what happened. I didn't need to. I had an 'Executive Producer' with a gun demanding more money in the face of all my reserves drying up. I was doing a film on a record label where I couldn't use their music. Death threats were my every day bedfellow. My employees were ready to mutiny. And now my editor had just gotten the shit kicked out of him. I didn't need a search party to do the math. I'd really fucked up.

I asked Karl to show me where he was and he half-heartedly suggested that significant improvements had been made. But when he pressed *play,* I saw that the cut was virtually the same as before. It was like I was dealing with a zombie from the film, *The Invasion of the Body Snatchers.* I'd now spent almost a year with Karl and the relationship wasn't working. We were spinning our wheels.

He had to go -- both for his sake and the film's.

The decision to remove Karl caused relations with the Harrises to go straight into the toilet. They framed the decision in racial terms which didn't come as a surprise to me. The Harrises had seen Karl as *their guy* and took my decision to fire him as a shot across their collective breast. And Karl wasn't going quietly. There was a very arduous process to get the Avid drives that held the current cut back.

At this juncture, things would get really bad with Michael and Lydia. We had no new editor in place and I was not going to spend another dime until I was sure we had a plan that would really get us to the finish line. Lydia called constantly to argue, fight, and threaten me. When she couldn't get me on the phone, she screamed at my employees, most of whom thought I'd lost my mind. I was pulled aside constantly and told, *"This woman is crazy."* They continued to ask, *"Are we safe? Is something bad going to happen?"* It was a situation that was beyond any skill set I had in my psychological arsenal. At one point, I filed a police report and restraining order against Lydia with the Santa Monica Police. A representative in the department ended up calling her and things seemed to calm down a bit. Time passed as Steve, Jeff and I scrambled to find the guy that might help pull us out of documentary hell.

Then Lydia called with the news that O.J. Simpson prosecutor Christopher Darden was now handling Michael's latest appeal. He wanted to meet with me at the office.

"How you gonna punk me?"

After acting as the go-between for the flow of funds between Michael Harris and Death Row Records, David Kenner became the in-house attorney for the label, dividing his time between business duties and working to keep Death Row's artists out of jail. His successful defense in Snoop Dogg's murder case and the cases of other Death Row artists and his crucial interfacing with Interscope on a myriad of issues, made him indispensable to Suge. Meanwhile, Michael Harris was becoming increasingly frustrated by the growing distance between himself and Suge Knight. Though incarcerated, Harris was well aware of Death Row's success and began demanding repayment of his invested funds and his share of the label's profits. When his phone calls to Suge began to go unreturned, Harris wrote a letter to Interscope, threatening a very public lawsuit. There is a final meeting between Michael Harris and David Kenner. A day later, Michael discovers that he's been poisoned. Eventually, the Harrises receive a settlement from Interscope.

ANONYMOUS: The music business is a cruel and shallow money trench, a long plastic highway where thieves and pimps run free and good men die like dogs. There's also a negative side. *-- reworked from an original quote by Hunter S. Thompson about the television industry.*

ALLEN GORDON: The origins of Death Row, starting with David Kenner, Michael Harris and Suge Knight didn't seem out of the ordinary until all the information started   flowing, because David Kenner -- nobody knew who he was.

SAM GIDEON ANSON: When they signed with Interscope in 1992, (Death Row) had John Branca and Gary Stiffleman -- two of the top music attorneys in the business. In 1995, they were fired by Death Row, in the midst of the renegotiation with Interscope, and David Kenner became the principal attorney and the signatory on the accounts.

MICHAEL HARRIS: Kenner is a loner. He became immersed in our community when he hooked up with Death Row.

SAM GIDEON ANSON: David Kenner became the principal business attorney for the label, as well as the criminal attorney for many (artists) at the label.

S. LEIGH SAVIDGE: Michael told me that Kenner's star had fallen precipitously in Suge's eyes when he couldn't get the earlier Sony deal done. But, Suge kept Kenner around because he needed him for the artists' legal cases.

SAM GIDEON ANSON: It took David Kenner several years of working his way back into the point where he again was the main man for Suge. Dave Kenner was much more than Suge's criminal attorney. He was also signatory to Death Row Records' accounts. Death Row employees used credit cards in his name. No one else at the label had any credit.

DOUG YOUNG: He would come in with his dope suits. I didn't know he was Harry and Lydia's attorney before he was Suge's attorney.

SNOOP DOGG: (Earlier in my life) I had two public defenders and went to jail two times.

PAUL PALLADINO: I was hired to do investigative work. David Kenner hired me to do work for him. Most of what I did during two years was Snoop Doggy Dogg's case. There were other people who signed on as new artists on Death Row and had problems, either past or present. Nate Hale (Dogg) was another rapper that got involved. They were charging him with a robbery down in San Pedro. Jewell was charged with attempted murder on her boyfriend. So I handled that also.

KURT LODER-MTV NEWS: *Los Angeles Police announced that twenty-one year old Calvin Broadus, better known as rap artist, Snoop Doggy Dogg had turned himself into police Friday along with two other young Black men, all accompanied by an attorney in connection with the murder on August 25th of a man named Phillip Woldemariam, in what police believe was a gang-related shooting.*

PAUL PALLADINO: My focus is always on the justice system and how it works. It's like a chess match. I know how to play this chess game. That's the game I was hired to play.

SNOOP DOGG: The financial side of the business wasn't that important to me until my court case was over with. And the reason for that was that I felt that every dime I had was needed to beat that case -- to prove my innocence.

RICK JAMES a.k.a. PRETTY RICKY: Snoop's bodyguards were with him. It wasn't like Snoop went out looking for trouble and went to find somebody to shoot at. Some Blacks see Snoop, knew he was getting famous and said, "*F you. You ain't shit.*"

PAUL PALLADINO: I located a witness who confirmed what the defendants were telling me which is that the victim had a gun. The police were saying that they had been told by the victim's two associates, that they were with him that afternoon, that he had no weapon. I went through a number of instances where we were telling the D.A., "*This guy had a gun.*" Ultimately, what happened is these two witnesses confessed in front of the Grand Jury that they had hidden the gun because they were afraid if the police found the gun on his body, they wouldn't have prosecuted Snoop.

DAVID KENNER: (5) It should never have gone to trial. The alleged victim in this case had a gun, and was reaching to his waistband to pull out that gun, at the time Snoop's bodyguard fired a shot. That what we've said from the beginning, and the testimony makes it clear. This is a case of self-defense.

SNOOP DOGG: The D.A. was a pain in the ass. He just tried to do everything in the world to make me seem like the most negative, gang-bangingest, criminal minded motherfucker, he could just imagine, and tried to paint a picture of me that just wasn't happening. It was crazy, knowing that that's his job was to get me locked up for life. You know what I'm saying? I just want to say, *"Fuck you, bitch."*

JAY KING: Dave Kenner was the guy who made Suge feel legally secure.

MICHAEL HARRIS: Suge had five or six pending cases that Dave Kenner was able to control and get rid of.

SAM GIDEON ANSON: Death Row artists and the people around them were getting in criminal trouble quite frequently.

PAUL PALLADINO: One of the benefits that Suge Knight gave people to join Death Row was to say that, *"I have a legal team, people that have a lot of experience in the criminal area that can help you."* Whereas in the past, coming from a Black community, where you go into a White justice system, where all the cards are stacked against you, here, for the first time in most of their lives, they were given a lawyer that was very capable and an investigator on top of it. And the results spoke for themselves most of the time. They got to see instances where they were acquitted on cases where they normally would have been convicted. In the rap industry, the problems happen at one or two in the morning. So it's not a nine to five job. David was the rare lawyer who would be available to his clients at that hour.

SAM GIDEON ANSON: Of the eighty million dollars that Interscope paid them between 1995 and 1997, about 13 million dollars went to the law offices of Dave Kenner or to Dave Kenner (directly). Certainly this company was his bread and butter for some time.

MICHAEL HARRIS: Interscope wouldn't have been able to deal with the Death Row problems if it hadn't been for Kenner. Kenner was the mediator. He would go to them and tell Jimmy (Iovine) how much money he needs to fix the situation and let him handle it his way.

KEVIN POWELL: I met David Kenner a few years back and it was clear to me that he had all the skills necessary to help the multi-faceted life and career of Suge Knight -- be it the business stuff, the legal, or the criminal stuff. His job was basically to make sure this ship was taken care of on all fronts -- no matter what those fronts were.

NORMAN WINTER: I was quite surprised because you would expect a music business attorney. But he wasn't. He was a criminal attorney.

JAY KING: (Kenner) had entertainment attorney qualities. He's flamboyant and he's sharp and kinda mafia-ish, you know. His whole persona.

JOHN PAYNE: After a while, David might have got so caught up in his lifestyle that he might have become somewhat confused because, the thing is, he was supposed to be working on getting Mike out (of jail).

MICHAEL HARRIS: The (music) business became dominant and the legal situation got put on the back burner.

JEWELL: I sit back and watch people - watch what they do. (Kenner) wasn't on the up and up.

After tirelessly hounding Suge and David Kenner on money issues, Jewell would leave the label for two years in 1993.

JEWELL: I'm trying to talk to Suge and he's telling me, *"Let's not worry about what happened in the past. Let's start from right now."* And I'm like, *"No. Heal my wound. Sew it up."* So I ended up cussing out David Kenner, and that made Suge not want to deal with me anymore.

SAM GIDEON ANSON: David was handling Michael's appeal and was very much involved in Lydia's life. He was friends with Lydia. This was a person that was very trustworthy to him.

Lydia's relationship with Kenner began to unravel while she was still living at his house, a supersized mansion in Encino.

LYDIA HARRIS: My house was broken into, so David said, *"You can come over here until you find a place."* I see something is funny when David said, *"Hey Lyd, Suge's coming over. You might need to leave for a minute."* Kenner didn't want him to know that I was staying there. I'm like, *"What difference does it make?"* Kenner told me Suge (had) a problem with a woman handling the business.

Eventually, Lydia moved out. Later, when Lydia was in Las Vegas for a boxing event, she was told that she couldn't enter Suge's club, 662.

LYDIA HARRIS: Me and Suge got into it. But he never threatened me or called me a bitch. He never did because he knew Michael. He knows who Harry O is. David knows and Suge knows.

PAUL PALLADINO: Suge ran the company from everything I saw. He was a hands on guy - wanted to have control over a lot of things. Even though David would consult with him and give him advice, the decisions were always up to Suge.

JAY KING: I'm thinking, *"Man, Mike is making a ton of money."* Then you see David Kenner there, so you say if David is there, then Mike is there, and then the stories start flashing, and then you know that there's a war going on.

RICK JAMES a.k.a. PRETTY RICKY: Suge is one of my homeboys. We grew up in the same neighborhood in Compton. He started (Death Row) about the time I got outta jail. So I hooked up with him, doing music, doing tracks for him.

MICHAEL HARRIS: I read a lot. I read *Billboard* every day. *Variety, The Hollywood Reporter*. I read all the entertainment magazines. I (keep) abreast of what's going on.

SAM GIDEON ANSON: (Suge) tried an avenue with Dick Griffey and he tried another with Michael Harris and when the Interscope deal is the one that finally goes through, that's the one he went with. And he left several people who thought they were his partners, in the wake.

LYDIA HARRIS: There were rumors that Suge was over there trying to get a deal at Interscope. But when he would go down to visit Mike, Kenner would say it wasn't true. But Mike would say, *"Hey, what's this here in the newspaper?"*   And Suge would say, *"Oh, you know how the newspaper just prints up a lot of articles."* So Mike says, *"Well, they're not just gonna print up anything."*   So (Mike) started asking David, *"What's going on?"* Then David came and said, *"Suge did this behind my back."*

MICHAEL HARRIS: People would say, *"That's Harry O's boy, that's Harry O's company."* (Suge) could not stand tall if I was in the picture. At first it was okay because it needed to be connected to the street element. Then things changed.

SAM GIDEON ANSON: That started to cause Michael concern about what exactly was going on. Michael started getting word that Suge was telling people, *"Michael Harris is nobody. He's not my partner."* And the word on the street was that Michael Harris is really pissed off with Suge. *"It's on."*

LYDIA HARRIS: (Suge) wanted to get all the credit. Mike don't trip the credit. The world thinks Suge did this all on his own.

MICHAEL HARRIS: Once Suge got a taste of the spotlight, he wanted it all by himself. If Suge didn't want to be my partner, I didn't have a problem with that. But at least compensate me for my time and the monies I invested.

SAM GIDEON ANSON: In 1994, as a way to placate Michael Harris, David Kenner helped Lydia set up her own record label (Lifestyle Records) which had offices in Westwood right down the street from Death Row.

S. LEIGH SAVIDGE: *The Los Angeles Times* reported that Interscope had financed a $500,000 recording session for Dana Dane, a rapper affiliated with Lifestyle. Later, Interscope passed on signing Lifestyle to a broader deal.

JAY KING: Mike's in jail. But he's got a wife. He's got a kid. He's got family out here. He's got people he's taking care of. So, you know, his reaction is, he's stunned. And he's kind of mad about it, you know? *"How you gonna punk me?"*

MICHAEL HARRIS: The nature of the beast with Suge is that once he has used you to the point where he doesn't need you anymore, he moves on.

SAM GIDEON ANSON: He didn't need Michael Harris. He didn't need his money. He was getting money from Interscope. He was getting advice from Interscope. And he had the number one record in the country.

MICHAEL HARRIS: A baby can get anything from me. But a gorilla can't take nothing. And that's what this is about. It's about respect.

In deference to Harry O and Lydia, John Payne who'd worked with Dre as a studio engineer on both Deep Cover and The Chronic, decided to leave the label.

JOHN PAYNE: I saw the way things were going to go. I saw the greed that was about to take place. I can't take advantage of someone who saved everybody's life.

DOUG YOUNG: The phone (at Death Row) was never blocked because it always had cats calling from the pen. Harry O wasn't the only one. But after a while, and I even remember, I think it was because of Harry, that they then blocked the phone where it couldn't take no more calls.

LYDIA HARRIS: When Michael would call Kenner's office, they would always say that Kenner was in court. David had a private number, where Mike was able to call an answering service and they would hook David up whenever Mike called. Then all that stopped.

Battlecat was a producer that Harry O had a business relationship with.

DOUG YOUNG: I was told, *Man, they didn't accept Harry-O's call today.* And I was kinda nervous, cause I knew who Harry O was. Battlecat was a soldier for Harry O. And he said, *"You still workin' there, Doug? You better get out of there."*

JAY KING: Mike started saying, *"Okay. There's another game being played here."*

MARK FRIEDMAN: Kenner was basically general counsel. Obviously he was in very close contact with Suge on a day to day basis. I'm not saying David ran the record label. I don't think he had the experience or the knowledge to do so. But he certainly knew the day-to-day logistics. Any decision that was made, his input was involved and rightfully so, because he is a lawyer. I think he was a wise man. But even wise men make bad decisions.

Kevin DJ Black and Doug Young formulated the core of Death Row's promotion team. Black would later transition from Death Row to Interscope and become one of the most respected promotion men in the music industry.

DOUG YOUNG: Black used to say, *"What you gonna do when Harry O gets out? He might send somebody up here to tap this whole motherfucking office."* I told Black, *"I'm gonna monitor Battlecat so he can let me know when to get out of here before it goes down."*

JAY KING: David Kenner started off to play these guys against each other. Once the rift between Suge and Mike happened, Dave Kenner had to pledge allegiance, one way or another.

SAM GIDEON ANSON: David is a very persuasive individual. Throughout this time, even if Suge was denying his partnership with Michael or denying that Michael had any role in the company, David would still be going up to visit Michael and saying, *"Oh no, everything is okay, there's no problem. Everything's fine. We're gonna get this taken care of."*

S. LEIGH SAVIDGE: Michael told me that Kenner often used issues in his home life to displace the issues that Michael was concerned about.

MICHAEL HARRIS: David had problems with his wife. Linda is a pill. Straight up. She is real manipulative. He would buy her cars, houses, he bought her a gym, trainers -- she would be dating them -- one of them *steroid dudes*. David would come down and cry. I'm trying to get out of jail. I'm trying to work on my appeal. But David wants to come and tell me about his problems at home.

S. LEIGH SAVIDGE: According to Mark Friedman, Kenner was terrified of Suge. If Kenner did something that displeased Suge

240

or failed to comply with something he wanted, Suge would slap him around. Sometimes these incidents happened in full view of Death Row's artists and business associates. Friedman told me of in incident that was relayed to him by Marc Benesch, a former Interscope executive, where Suge slapped Kenner around at a meeting that involved Interscope executives John McClain, Jimmy Iovine, and Ted Field.

Simone Green began working for Death Row after being introduced to Dr. Dre by her ex-husband Tony, a bass player who'd worked with Dr. Dre on The Chronic. She was Death Row's in-house photographer, performed office duties, and was frequently on the road with Death Row's artists.

SIMONE GREEN: (Kenner) said *yes* whenever (Suge) said *do*. Suge was the man, and David had to follow orders. David had to do what Suge said. Later, I figured out that Kenner was the boss and Suge was just carrying everything out.

DAN O'DOWD: Mike Harris. I'm glad I played straight with him. Because he seems to be the only person in the equation that played it straight. It reminds me of Brutus and Caesar.

SAM GIDEON ANSON: At some point, Michael gets hold of the incorporation papers of Death Row Records and realized that Suge and Kenner had sit up a different company of Death Row Records, that was independent of this GF Entertainment Michael had a hand in. And I think Michael began to suspect that things were not so kosher with their partnership.

MICHAEL HARRIS: They both had their own agendas. But they had one thing in common. They had both crossed me. The person that brought them together.

SAM GIDEON ANSON: It's an interesting question how David Kenner, who is a lawyer, was able to legally rationalize starting a company with Michael Harris, and also be involved in a signatory in the accounts of another Death Row Records.

RICK JAMES a.k.a. PRETTY RICKY: (Michael is) the one who told David, "*Hey, look at this man. That guy Suge. I like him. Go talk to him. Okay. A record label? Okay. I'll give you this amount of money. You tell him to do this. Okay.*" Then it's Suge talking. Suge going to visit him. "*Suge, check it out. Put it down like this. Put it down like that.* (Mike to Kenner) *You do it today. You do this part. Keep him out of jail. You make sure you keep him out of jail.*" That's why Suge's got all them probations and stuff. They fighting like they're crazy. "*Keep him out of jail.*" Because Mike's telling him to. "*Keep him out of jail.*" But guess what? Soon as the money starts coming in, "*Who? Harry O?*" They turned all Scooby-Doo on him. "*HbhbHarry O? WhbhbhoWho's that?*"

JEWELL: It was all a bit confusing. I didn't know what happened between (Mike) and Suge or why GF Productions wasn't since around -- since they were our parent company.

SAM GIDEON ANSON: When Suge goes by himself and gets a deal outside of Michael, without Michael and David's help, at Interscope -- if we want to pin a moment when Suge said, "*This is my company, not Michael Harris'*" -- it's when he went to Interscope and got his own deal.

LYDIA HARRIS: Mike said, "*Where's the money?*" and they said, "*You know, it's gonna be 60 to 90 days, before we see a royalty check.*" So those 60 to 90 days turned into a year. Mike like kept asking, "*What's going on? Let me see an accounting.*"

JAY KING: You start hearing stories about how Suge isn't paying Mike, or Lydia and Suge have problems. My cousin, Andre -- God bless his soul -- he went to go collect some of the money from Suge that was owed to Mike.

JEWELL: I don't know too many people that give away large amounts of money to help you get started that don't want anything in return. Whether it's a regular business deal or not.

MICHAEL HARRIS: I would send my representatives to the office at Interscope to make arrangements to collect. I was paid on a number of occasions -- not what I deserved. But what they could get their hands on at the time.

RICK JAMES a.k.a. PRETTY RICKY: Harry-O helped them start the label. When Suge came to the federal joint, we sat in court talking about two or three hours. I said, *"Look at me, man. You can't tell me that dude didn't help you."* Suge said, *"Rick, he did. I gotta figure out a way to get him some money."*

S. LEIGH SAVIDGE: Rick James told us that Suge proposed using him as a middleman to get cash to Michael and Lydia Harris. But it never happened.

RICK JAMES a.k.a. PRETTY RICKY: He don't wanna give no money. Period. He coulda found a way without nobody knowing. I think he's just chicken-shit.

LYDIA HARRIS: That's when Michael typed up a letter.

MICHAEL HARRIS: I felt that Jimmy was the source and he needed to be aware of my position at the time. I wrote a motion, asking for my share of the company, which at the time I felt was about a hundred million dollars. This was a private letter. Somebody let it out to the media.

CHRIS BLATCHFORD / KTTV NEWS REPORTER: He's serving a life sentence. But he wants his share of Death Row revenue.

LYDIA HARRIS: I went over and met with David Cohen (at Interscope). He was the guy in business affairs. He said, *"What if we don't pay you?"* I told him, *"I'm not threatening you, but I'm gonna go on national TV and tell what really happened."* Then he said, *"Oh, no no. We can work this out."* So that's when he did a paper up for $300 thousand. They wanted Mike to sign off on it and get it notarized. Sam Anson, told me that somebody at Interscope gave him the paper. And that's how the paper got out in the media.

DOUG YOUNG: Everybody knew Harry O wasn't no joke. Okay? And everybody knew Harry O had chips. All you gotta do is be no joke and have chips and you can get somebody handled.

SAM GIDEON ANSON: At a certain point in 1996, Michael put his concerns on paper in the form of a lawsuit, that could have been filed, that was never filed, laying out his grievances as to how he had been a founding partner in Death Row Records and had been denied his fair share of the proceeds. The papers were shown to Interscope and Interscope paid a fairly generous settlement to make it go away before it ever got filed.

PAUL PALLADINO: The people at Interscope, Jimmy at Interscope was concerned about this letter, whether it was going to mean harm to his family. So he ends up paying off and settling.

S. LEIGH SAVIDGE: Mark Friedman told me that though the settlement was with Interscope, David Kenner was blind cc'd on each draft. Friedman told me that Kenner didn't want the settlement to mention him or to indicate a tie between Michael and him.

RICK JAMES a.k.a. PRETTY RICKY: I asked Suge about it. *"Didn't that dude start your record company? Ain't you gonna look out for him?"* But he would always say, *"There's more to it than I know."*

JOHN PAYNE: It was really wrong that Suge reaped the benefits of the seed that Michael Harris planted.

LYDIA HARRIS: Once the money started rolling in, you could never catch (Kenner). One day I called David and I said, "*Mike needs you to come down. I don't like the way he sounds.*" So David went down to visit Mike.

PAUL PALLADINO: David's saying, "*I'm owed some money for legal work. I gave him legal work and I didn't charge him or collect money for it. I don't understand how this guy could be turning on me.*"

MICHAEL HARRIS: The last meeting I had face to face with Kenner was when I was going to sue Interscope. He felt that I was right in what I was doing, but the timing was wrong.

LYDIA HARRIS: He told Mike, "*Suge keeps control on everywhere I go. If I come down here, he wants to know everything we talk about. He feels that my allegiance is with you, Mike.*"

S. LEIGH SAVIDGE: At some point in the meeting, Kenner went to a vending machine, bought two 7-Ups and returned to where Michael was sitting.

LYDIA HARRIS: The next day, I got a call. They told me that Mike was in a wheelchair. He couldn't walk. His mouth was twisted. He couldn't use his hands. I called David. I said, "*David, Mike is sick.*" He showed no remorse. I said, "*Can you give me some money to get a doctor to go to visit (Mike)?*" He said he didn't have any money. I said, "*You don't have two thousand dollars?*" He said, "*No baby, I don't.*" He didn't care if Michael died.

S. LEIGH SAVIDGE: Eventually, Beverly Hills music attorney Mickey Shapiro persuaded Kenner to send the money and a doctor was dispatched to examine Michael.

LYDIA HARRIS: The doctor said he had Guillain-Barre which (he said) comes from being poisoned. I asked Mike, "*Did Kenner give you anything?*" And he said, "*He got me two 7-Ups.*" I said,

"Did he open 'em up in front of you?" He said, *"I know when he brought 'em back in to me, they was open."* So (after that) the prison wouldn't let attorneys buy inmates food.

S. LEIGH SAVIDGE: We spent many days wrestling with the idea that Kenner might have poisoned Michael Harris in his last visit to see him. It was a strange coincidence that Michael had become afflicted with Guillian-Barre syndrome (which is a sudden weakness of the limbs due to a disorder affecting the peripheral nervous system) shortly after Kenner saw him. But there was no way to conclusively prove a connection there.

MARK FRIEDMAN: I think that David was totally overwhelmed by the legal entanglements of dealing with Death Row, the artists. And it got to a certain point where Suge basically said to David, *"You're with me. Forget about that guy (Harris)."* Now usually when somebody stops coming to see somebody it's over an argument, a fight, money or whatever. In this particular instance none of those things applied. And it's very difficult from where Michael's sitting, he's in jail, it's not like he can reach out and say, *"Hey David, why aren't you talking to me?"*

LYDIA HARRIS: Get (Mike) outta jail. That's why I'm working so hard. When we started Death Row, that was our goal. To get him home.

S. LEIGH SAVIDGE: The Harrises suggested to me that, up until this point, Kenner had continually messaged to them that he had an angle to get Mike out of prison and that when his duties with Death Row let up a little, he would pursue Mike's case. Having watched what Kenner had done on behalf of Death Row's artists, they both believed that Kenner was Mike's ticket out of jail.

LYDIA HARRIS: David played everybody against everybody. He started playing both sides against the middle. David came in real strong and never got Mike out (of jail).

MARK FRIEDMAN: I think David couldn't look Michael Harris in the eyes and say *"Look, there's nothing I can do. I don't have any control over this guy,"* referring to Suge. I ran into David one morning in 1995 at a restaurant in the valley. He was sitting with a young lady and I walked up, *"Hi Dave, how are you and what's going on?"* I said, *"Do me a favor, when you talk to Mike, please say hello for me. Wish him well."* And he said, *"Uh, you know, we're not really talkin' that much."* It shocked me. And that was really the first indication that something had happened to these two guys who were really inseparable.

PAUL PALLADINO: At that stage of the game, the lack of communication is caused because everybody's too frightened to talk because of a federal investigation. No one wants to step into this arena and find out that Michael's being an informant or that something else is going on.

DAN O'DOWD: Is it Dave Kenner's dream? Don't think so. It's Dr. Dre's dream assisted by who -- that's the question.

PAUL PALLADINO: [Do I think David Kenner wanted to be another Phil Spector?] (chuckling) Never mentioned it to me.

RICK JAMES a.k.a. PRETTY RICKY: David ain't talkin' to Harry O. He talkin' to Suge. The only thing he tellin' Suge was shit. I thought Suge was smarter than that. I didn't think Suge would let nobody pump him up like that - especially no White dude.

LYDIA HARRIS: You gotta understand, Mike had foreseen everything. He knew they needed David. Suge was a wild guy out there. He knew that you needed David on the team for the legal aspect, to keep everybody outta jail, to make the money. 'Cause the talent was there.

SAM GIDEON ANSON: One time I had the pleasure of speaking to Mr. Kenner on the phone, during which he would not answer any of my questions. One time I met him outside of a courtroom. He looked horrified to see me and was not in the mood to answer my questions on that morning either.

MICHAEL HARRIS: David is smooth as you want to be or vicious as you want to be, given the scenario.

8 p.m. with Christopher Darden

Christopher Darden had suddenly entered the lives of Michael and Lydia Harris and Michael had positioned this to me as major coup. He told me that in the wake of his high profile prosecution of O.J. Simpson, Darden had taken a lot of heat from large segments of the Black community and was very focused on legal projects that would repair what he saw as his damaged image. Handling the appeal of Michael's attempted murder conviction fit squarely into that category. Michael told me he'd finally found a credible guy to fill the hole that David Kenner had left behind. My initial reaction was *"Great. He got Darden on a pro bono basis."*

Christopher Darden had said publicly that he had listened to *Straight Outta Compton* and other N.W.A. tracks when he had driven into work every day during the O.J. Simpson trial. I'd always sympathized with his situation, as an African-American prosecuting a sports icon like Simpson, much to the consternation of much of Black America.

But I couldn't envision that his desire to meet me represented anything but more trouble.

And I was right.

When Darden came to Xenon's office, I took him into an empty office and showed him a trailer we'd made for *Welcome to Death Row*. When it was finished, I asked him what he thought and he turned to me and said, *"I think it's a great way to get your ass shot off."*

Things didn't get better from there. Darden spoke in somewhat cryptic terms about the appeal he was working on for Michael Harris. But with my basic knowledge of the details of both cases, it was hard for me to listen to him very carefully. I was pretty sure there was no way on God's green earth he could get Michael released. I'd been told by several parties that he'd exhausted his ability to appeal his attempted murder conviction. But Darden had clearly convinced the Harrises that he had an angle. He explained to me that he'd done in the neighborhood of $100,000 worth of work and could not continue unless funds were paid to him.

I wanted to go home and take a shower.

It was at this point in the conversation that Lydia suddenly appeared. It felt like the whole thing had been scripted, with Darden giving me his pitch and then Lydia suddenly showing up. I explained to Darden that I'd partnered with the Harrises to help tell the Death Row story. That we'd already paid them way more than our agreement mandated and that this was an unfair position to put me in -- to position me as the man whose funds might stand between them and Michael's prospective early release from prison. At this point, Lydia stormed out of the office and was standing on the sidewalk. Darden followed her outside, spoke to her for a while and then came back inside and sat back down. He said, "*You've got a very angry lady out there. You better go talk to her.*" Darden and I sat there and stared at each for a while. Then I went outside to speak to Lydia.

It was 8pm and the only people in the office were Steve Housden, Darden, myself with Lydia outside. Xenon's office was on a side street that didn't have streetlights, so it was very dark as Lydia and I stood toe to toe on the sidewalk. She had her purse with her which everyone on the production knew contained a gun. She gave it to me straight, "*I got nothing to lose, Leigh. I got nothing to lose.*" Lydia was one of those people with an over-actualized *id*. Her body language and moods told more of a story than the words that actually came out of her mouth. But in this instance, I heard her words loud and clear. This was a different kind of encounter than any we'd had before. She had really touched a nerve. She was completely consumed by her desperation. Her man was in prison and she'd completely ingested Christopher Darden's Kool Aid. I was her only shot and, short of funds to pay Darden, life, the film, everything, didn't fucking matter to her.

The implication in her words to me were *"If you don't help me here, **you** are the person with something to lose."*

As I studied Lydia's ice cold eyes, I felt she could snap at any second. I sensed that this was one of those moments where, if I did one thing, I'd live and if I did another thing I might die. I was not going to gamble with my life. There was no way I was going die on the sidewalk in front of my office with Steve and Chris Darden sitting inside. That was not going to be how it ended for me.

And so a few days later, I wrote Lydia Harris a check for $100,000, modifying my agreement with the Harrises for a fourth time. I never confirmed what actually made its way to Darden. But as I suspected, aside from a letter from him that suggested that he was involved in a soundtrack for *Welcome to Death Row*, I never heard from him again. Later, he would distance himself from the Harrises.

"It was like working in a prison"

By late 1995, the environment at Death Row, both in the office and in the recording studio, was said to resemble a prison yard. Suge became unapproachable, instilling fear in everyone who worked there. Even though they were housed in an office adjacent to the offices of Interscope Records, in a high rise building in West Los Angeles, the label seemed to exist in a separate and often violent world.

VIRGIL ROBERTS: When you get money and you get success and you're doing gangsta rap, you're going to attract a whole different kind of people. You're going to attract a lot of hangers on.

JOHN KING: We were at the BRE (music convention) in New Orleans at some hotel. *Harlem Nights* had just come out and there was a guy in the movie that said, *"I'm gonna knock you the fuck out."* And Dre was reciting the line, and we were laughing about it. And some kid heard Dre say it and came up to Dre and said, *"I bet you can't knock me out."* Just out of the blue. The guy puts his hands on me, and the next thing you know, one of his buddies had jumped on my back. And Dre jumped on his back. Next thing you know, they had seven or eight guys fighting me and Dr. Dre. And at that point, Rage came, and DOC helped us fight these guys. And the police came to the hotel on horses and charged us with inciting a riot.

HANK CALDWELL: I've met guys who were big guys that were really brutal and wanted to carry that out every minute of the day. Now Suge could get angry. He could snap like everyone else. But for the most part, we called him *Sugar Bear.*

JEWELL: Suge started out a big old teddy bear. I'd see him comin' and my face would light up when he walked into the room. He turned into a monster.

FRANK ALEXANDER: (Suge) had the world at his fingertips. And to be involved with the artists to the extent that he was -- he carried the neighborhood and the block into work. And you can't do that.

DOUG YOUNG: I started thinking that Suge was getting himself caught up into too many situations that were unhealthy. This gang-banging style mentality of the label is about to get out of hand.

VIRGIL ROBERTS: He had created an image that was working for him and sometimes that image merged with reality, and I'm not sure that, as time went on, that Suge didn't draw the line between when there was the image and when there was the reality.

DICK GRIFFEY: Suge wasn't a gangster. Suge came from a family -- his mother and father are still together. He was a college football player. The whole thing was an act and the world bought it.

MICHAEL HARRIS: I was raised in a Blood and Crip neighborhood. I never joined a gang. But I understood them. It was a form of recreation.

SUGE KNIGHT: (5) I feel I've got a whole lot of street credibility. Street smarts. And at the same time, I graduated from college. I hit the books. And I put both of them together.

DOUG YOUNG: (Suge) didn't realize how petrified he was making everyone around him.

MICHAEL HARRIS: I didn't understand how a person could achieve something and want to become something that everyone that is in a gang is trying to get out of. He was dealing with a multi-million dollar situation -- and you're wasting your time with things that other people try to grow up out of and leave in the past.

KEVIN POWELL: One of the things that made me mad when I interviewed Suge was that he was so wrapped into his version of the world, that he never stopped to ask where you're from. He assumed, because I was a journalist, that I must be, as Allen Gordon puts it, "*Backpacker, college-educated, kind of middle-class Negroes.*" Prejudiced. He had no idea that I came from the same world he came from. That's very dangerous because you don't realize that you're shutting off people who might be able to help you.

CPO: L.A.'s ghettos. Compton's ghettos. It's a warfare thing all the time. Even if you're not in it, you're aware of it, and you keep yourself at bay.

VIRGIL ROBERTS: It's almost a reversal of what happens in real life. Somebody who is a gangster wants to be legitimate and so they try to move away from the streets and those contacts. In the case of what happened at Death Row, you had somebody move from the suites to the streets, rather than the streets to the suites. I don't think that Suge had the knowledge and understanding of what street life really is -- what he was getting involved with. Somebody from the streets would have been better able to control the other guys from the streets that got involved in your business, and with Suge, it was the reverse.

MICHAEL HARRIS: The problem with individuals who come from the streets who are not truly entrenched in that world, they don't understand the rules. And they think that money puts them in a situation where they can control the rules and change the rules.

RICK JAMES a.k.a. PRETTY RICKY: The reason that Death Row started getting a bad reputation is because it's that thing that goes back to Blacks that can't stand to see each other with nothing. The fight stuff went down because people just see another Black person making money and feel like they going to start some problems.

KEVIN POWELL: I don't think we can ever underestimate the level of self-hatred and confusion and hating, player hating, in the Black community. We are oppressed communities and these are the sort of manifestations of it. Suge Knight made some mistakes in terms of the people he surrounded himself with. I've seen it happen with so many hip hop figures throughout the years. You've got cats around who don't care about anything else except getting drunk, screwing women, starting fights and pulling out pieces on people. Some of that definitely played itself into what happened at Death Row Records.

DOUG YOUNG: I'm not gonna even lie to you right now. I used to try to stay out of that office. I would come up with any drama I needed to stay out of that office. 'Cause it was like being in a penitentiary cell.

JOHN KING: They had cliques. Suge had his clique; Dre had his; Snoop had his. Everybody did their own thing. Suge's people weren't his artists, they were the people he grew up with. His homeboys.

SIMONE GREEN: He ran that company like it was his gang. That's his family. He may not love us. But he made us think he did.

SUGE KNIGHT: (5) Family. I got some spoiled artists. I have one problem with our artists on Death Row. Since we started together and it's a family, I never say *"No"* to anything, right?

VIRGIL ROBERTS: A lot of what followed, in part, had to do with trying to establish Death Row as the label with the most street credibility. We're doing gangsta rap and we're keeping it real and we're keeping it legitimate. So when guys get out of the joint, you can come get a job with me. That sort of thing.

JOHN KING: We called ourselves a family. Yet your clique is over here -- our clique is over there and (there's) animosity between the two. The loyalty factor wasn't there.

THUG LIFE GROUP MEMBER: You think if you go over there, you're gonna be in a better position because you're all the same culture. But it's not. You don't know until you're in that position.

LAMONT BRUMFIELD: You put a piranha in a tank and you starve him for three weeks -- you throw anything in there, he's gonna eat that bone up.

MICHAEL HARRIS: (Gangs) have their own codes, rules and regulations and, as crazy as you think it is, they are consistent. So for you to try and control somebody when you haven't put in the work, they would never respect you as an original gang member.

HEROIN: (10) I never had a job in my life until I started working for Suge. You know, in and out of jail, you know what I'm sayin? Did a little bit of everything. You know what I'm saying?

DOUG YOUNG: We had a lot of them cats that was fresh from the penitentiary, with the penitentiary mentality. It was like working at a prison with no guns, no knives, no nothing. You just had to be in there on your own and handle it. How many companies you know that have Crips and Bloods (working) there? Crips and Bloods!

MICHAEL HARRIS: I don't think that was a good idea. When Suge started to participate in gang activity, I was very adamant with him about that. I told him it would be his demise.

The street parlance for Bloods is "Blood". For the Crips it's "Cuz".

JEWELL: I ain't gonna lie. I done said *"Blood"* a few times, hangin with them. *"What's up, Blood?"*

DOUG YOUNG: You go to the right side of the office and get *Cuzzed* to death. Go to the left side and get *Blood* to death. You gotta remember, *"Don't say Cuz or Blood."* I remember when I would get out of the elevator, *"Okay, Man, Man, Man. No Cuz. No Blood."* You don't want to get on nobody's side 'cause you don't wanna get caught in no Catch-22 when the other person's gone.

MICHAEL HARRIS: (Suge) called it *"keeping it real."* I called it the keys to his destruction.

JEWELL: (Suge) had me riled up. I used to think I could knock it out. I'll be quick to grab a bat, too, and knock somebody over the head. Because that was the realm I was in. And I didn't even come from that type of background.

DOUG YOUNG: I seen a lot of fools go up there and be *Cuz* and *Cuz*, and then be on the other side, and be *Blood* and *Blood*. And as soon as *Blood* came out of their mouth, they just ratpacked 'em. Pow!

MICHAEL HARRIS: Me and my brother -- we grew up in Crip and Blood neighborhoods. So we could never choose. We did business with everybody.

GEORGE PRYCE: Whatever was happening or whatever the real deal was, I always brought it forward when nobody else would. (Often) people were frightened to say what really happened. I would always say, *"Suge, this is what happened. You take it from there."*

JAY KING: People say Suge was a bully and a bad guy. I've seen some of these guys. You had to treat them the way Suge treated them. One thing I will say in Suge's defense, Suge will run over you if you let him. But if you stand up to Suge -- I don't care how big or small you are -- Suge is gonna respect that.

THUG LIFE GROUP MEMBER: Everybody talk on the streets. Everybody's hearin' that Suge's beating on people and slapping people and *Cuz* and *Blood*. Sometimes talk is cheap. But sometimes talk make you think.

DOUG YOUNG: At first, I was totally with Death Row's concept. Because it was about time we had a brother who wasn't takin' no shit from these companies, that wasn't payin' brothers their money. So I was totally with it. It was when the nonsense got too out of hand...

SIMONE GREEN: Nobody ever questioned Suge about anything. He was always right. I have a smart mouth. He didn't like that but he was like, *"That's my girl. She ain't gonna let me say anything."*

GEORGE PRYCE: We had a system of that kind of thing, sort of like a demerit system for artists and so on and for some of the office workers.

JEWELL: Anytime you're the CEO and hang out with people from certain backgrounds that don't have proper upbringing, you're gonna get situations. When your adrenaline is running and you've got all these people around you who don't want to see you with what you've got -- they're going to misguide you.

SIMONE GREEN: Suge got to a point where he just didn't know how to control some of the gang behavioral stuff either inside the office or outside on trips. How did he handle the situation? Have you ever put gasoline in some fire? You get a big fire, right? Suge kind of fed the fire.

DOUG YOUNG: A typical day working at Death Row? As long as I wasn't at the office, it was easy. You gotta realize, every record that was coming out was a good record. So, it wasn't really too much hustling. I was just uncomfortable being at that office. And it wasn't even Suge. It was Suge's homies, the different homies that would be up there. I mean some of 'em, I was cool with. But it was like pledging a fraternity. And then it turned into straight hell. I would go in like the square, just going to work. I would just sit over at Interscope, find me a room go to sleep in, play like I was in there doin' some work and then say, *"It's time to go!"*

ALLEN GORDON: Am I afraid of taking on the Death Row story as a journalist? No. I know several employees that have worked there and no longer work there. I just wish some of the stuff that I know that goes on I could substantiate in print without being sued for libel.

BILLY MOSS: (Suge) had to act that way because of the type of people he was dealing with -- the rappers. They're from the street. So you have to deal with them in the street mentality. But the hype got so big that everybody started fearin' him.

RBX: (13) If you say something, you get smacked. If you come late, you get smacked. If you do this, you get smacked. It was like pimps and hoes.

CPO: I'm not a Crip. But when I'm (surrounded) by Crips, some part of your soul gets sucked back into it. You don't even mean to. Bloods' was sittin' in the office at Death Row. They're friends of someone, friends of friends of the artist. So you know, they're stealin'. Stealin' Post-its. That's how they are.

JEFFREY JOLSON COLBURN: Some of the people in the hard core rap business did not act the way people in the record business expected them to act. Answering a grievous harm with a lawsuit. This was not the gentlemen's club any more. So that shocked some people. Live by the sword. Die by the sword.

DOUG YOUNG: I just knew how, after awhile, Suge was

unapproachable; You couldn't talk to him no more. This guy is the fucking *man*.

SIMONE GREEN: (Suge) never really liked to make eye contact. When I talked to him, I would look him directly in the eye. I could tell that would sometimes make him uncomfortable.

JOHN KING: I think it was more or less power. I gotta show everybody that I got more power, that you're under me. I don't know what it is about people that makes them think that way.

SIMONE GREEN: He knew I was gutsy. The relationship with me and Suge set me in a comfort zone, because he always made sure I was all right. Things were happening to other people, but it wasn't happening to me. So I was like, *"He wouldn't do that to me. I'm a girl. I'm a woman."*

DOUG YOUNG: That company was by no ways, forms, or fashion, Hollywood. You know how White folks like to do it. They scream at each other, *"I'm gonna get my lawyer on you!"* But the new brothers weren't doing it like that. They was coming through doors, coming through windows and doin' the whole nine on people.

MICHAEL HARRIS: I never had to use violence to make my point. But I was very forceful. If I had to put my hands on somebody, it didn't get out of hand.

JEFFREY JOLSON COLBURN: I heard someone describe them as all thinking they were in a *Godfather* movie.

SUGE KNIGHT: (5) I don't have an ego. I know who I am. I'm the man. See when you're the man, you're the man. You got males and you've got men. I happen to be a man.

HANK CALDWELL: There were some groups that we signed that came right off the street. Kids could come in right off the street and get the attention.

SIMONE GREEN: (Suge) didn't have no problem smacking the shit out of you.

NATE DOGG: Suge was famous for applying the old Mafia tactics and he would instill fear in everybody. (One day) A guy just walks in. He has no idea we're in the middle of a meeting. He wants a record deal. He walks in and says, *"I rap."* So Suge says, *"Okay, rap. If we don't like what you do, we gonna kick your ass."* He said maybe three words, and they just lit his ass up.

MICHAEL HARRIS: Real gangsters don't use weak people to make themselves who they are.

DOUG YOUNG: Suge, when he was mad, he wasn't playing. I've seen people get beat up. You understand. I've seen people get that door locked on them. The infamous door lockings; where they take you in a room and touch you up and down.

SIMONE GREEN: I wasn't the only woman who got beat up. But I was the only lady that got beat up that (Suge) held down.

S. LEIGH SAVIDGE: Simone Green told me that Suge Knight had given her a car and that Kim Hassan, another woman who worked in the office, had been jealous of the gift and had told Knight that Simone thought the car was *"a piece of junk."* Simone soon learned that she'd been demoted to office work on a full-time basis. On her first day in this new role, Suge summoned her to David Kenner's office.

SIMONE GREEN: (Suge) said, *"What's in your hand?"* I said, *"A pencil."* He took the pencil out of my hand and (Kim Hassan) cold-cocked me. (Suge) had a room adjacent to David Kenner's office called, *the roll-up room.* The doorway is on a slant, so as soon as I step back, my shoe got caught on the thing and I fell back. Suge grabbed me by my feet and everything went haywire.

He grabbed my legs. I just remember him having his arms around my legs -- with a grip that was unbelievable. He was helping her contain me where she could kick me in the head and do whatever she was going to do. She loosened up my teeth and I had two black eyes. David Kenner stood up and watched. Somebody else videotaped it. I kicked Suge in the nuts and got the hell up out of there. I ran out the back door and directly into Interscope. The receptionist at Interscope -- she panicked and ran into the ladies room. As soon as I walked out of there, they locked the door. Interscope locked their door. And then here comes Suge. He said, *"This ain't how it's supposed to be. You're my sister. I love you."* But he had it all set up.

MICHAEL HARRIS: He took a lot of joy in it. It was funny to him. It made him feel good to have that kind of power or to instill that kind of fear.

S. LEIGH SAVIDGE: Simone told me that the trauma from this event haunted her for months. Then she got angry and sued Death Row for battery.

SIMONE GREEN: You're in this office and you've got this guy who's your boss, who's been paying you, holding your legs. And the attorney for the company is watching. He not once said, *"Stop. Y'all need to stop."* He never did that. I was scared. But I said, *"To hell with it. You're not going to kick my ass for nothing, and get away with it."* (Death Row) didn't want to settle. They said I didn't work for the company. David Kenner came up with all kinds of things. But I had pay stubs. When the lawyer for the insurance company heard it was Death Row Records, they were like, *"Let's just settle this."* I have not laid eyes on Suge since that day. He won't lay eyes on me until he sees this.

S. LEIGH SAVIDGE: I asked Simone why Suge would instruct someone to videotape her beating.

SIMONE GREEN: Because *"We don't love them hoes,"* that's why.

262

They don't love us. He considers me a *hoe* too. If you ever look at Death Records and say, *"How many women became famous from Death Row?"* A big, fat zero. Rage was the hottest female rapper. Jewell was the best R & B singer to roll up out of there. They could have made millions just off of them.

DOUG YOUNG: All that drama that people knew was happening right there at Death Row on that 12th floor -- this is at the building right down there by UCLA on Wilshire. It never leaked over to the Interscope side. You see the Interscope side. It looks nice and woody, when you go into reception. Death Row was just a door. A mahogany covered door, with a camera. We were all on the same floor. People always say, *"Well, didn't Interscope know what was going on at Death Row?"* Yeah. But they didn't care. Death Row was making Interscope a whole lotta money.

SIMONE GREEN: Interscope was playing like they were Stevie Wonder -- like they couldn't see anything.

KEVIN POWELL: What people have to understand about the music industry -- there's a creative disorganization. Out of all that chaos, you get *The Chronic*, you get *Doggystyle*, you get *California Love* -- you get some great music. And so, you just let it be. Let it be across the hall. Let them do their thing. We go to the bank.

GEORGE PRYCE: I think it had to do with *Murder is the Case*. Suge said, *"I don't want any of this information disseminated."* He was out of town and I saw something coming on *Hard Copy* or one of those shows in regard to (it). So I went across the hall and asked Jimmy Iovine's assistant if I could see him. I went in and said, *"Jimmy, my name is George Pryce and I'm the director of communications at Death Row Records. I just saw this on TV tonight. My boss is telling me he did not want this out."* And he said, *"Your what? Well I'll be damned. I thought you were Suge Knight's new chauffeur."* That's how we started off.

MICHAEL HARRIS: Jimmy (Iovine) always felt he could convert Suge -- that he could make Suge into this low profile, suit-wearing, CEO. But Suge's mind don't work like that. There could be $5 million dollars sitting over there and he's trying to fix his low rider because he wanted to ride down Crenshaw Boulevard. What about the money? *"It'll be there."* That's the kind of guy he was.

SNOOP DOGG: DOC and RBX both had problems with Suge. Basically, they seen what kind of person he was on the inside. Not to say nothing bad about him. Not to say nothing good about him. But they seen the type of person he was. And through the grace of God and good attorneys, they were able to leave. Everybody else was forced in a choke hold after that.

DOUG YOUNG: I didn't want to get caught in the middle. I hadn't got beat up yet at Death Row. I hadn't got locked in one of them rooms. So I figured I better get out while my luck was still good. When I told them fools I was quitting after *Above the Rim*, they couldn't believe me.

Shakespeare's Iago

In the months when we were in between editors, I spent long hours thinking about what I had heard from the interviewees, both on and off camera. I found myself fixating on something that people had said over and over about what had happened at Death Row Records: "*It was Shakespearean.*"

I started to ask myself which of Shakespeare's plays seemed to best encapsulate what had happened there. Eventually, I settled on *Othello*, a play that finds Iago and Othello as soldiers in arms until Iago, stung with jealousy, feels the need to usurp Othello's power and spread rumors intended to destroy him. That definitely fit with what happened with Suge Knight and Dr. Dre. The jury was out whether Dr. Dre was Othello. Othello was a heart-on-his-sleeve, overtly emotional kind of person. And Dre was more the *still waters run deep* type. But I was pretty sure that the character trajectory of Iago matched that of Suge Knight.

For a while, Suge and Dre had been soldiers in arms. Dre had needed an enforcer to get him out of Ruthless Records and do what was necessary, both financially and operationally, to put him in an environment where he could create the music he wanted, and work with the artists he felt were in sync with the rapidly emerging hip hop zeitgeist. Additionally, Dre wanted to own the company for which he was creating his music. Michael Harris' assessment was that the relationship between the two was what he described as a user / use situation where each man felt that the other was necessary to achieve the individual goals they had set for themselves.

Even so, the success of Death Row Records was firmly rooted in Dr. Dre's skill as an artist / producer and his ability to attract the artists. Dre was the label's biggest asset.

Suge might have been a master marketer, but Dre had created

the music that had created the resources that allowed Suge to spend on the label's visibility the way he did. Dre was the business reason that Death Row had what it had. Regardless, in the face of this, Suge made the determination that Death Row's success was largely his, which was the same conclusion that Eazy E had made about Dre before him. With the arrival of Tupac, whose Death Row recordings would feature the production work of mostly people other than Dr. Dre, Suge extrapolated that Death Row was a bus he could operate by himself. He grew to see Dre as nothing other than an irrelevant building block and enlisted Tupac as the public mouthpiece to trash him.

In *Othello*, Iago set out to destroy and discredit his former ally in much the same way. Additionally, Iago falsely proffered the concept of love to induce a desired action, before deciding to betray the object of his flattery.

Then there was the issue of Michel'le Toussant, a Death Row artist with whom Dre has a child, that Suge married in 1999. Was this an act of love, on Suge's part? Or an act of alpha-inspired brinksmanship.

Putting aside the Suge / Dre relationship, there was the issue of Suge's colossal misguided stewardship of the label as evidenced by his decision to bring Crips and Bloods into the office atmosphere and the joy he appeared to summon in presiding over violence that was inflicted on artists and others in his employ. Steve Housden, Jeff Scheftel and I wrestled with how deeply to pursue this story thread. Some of the violence, like an incident with producer / rapper Sam Sneed, a Dre loyalist who was savagely beaten in the wake of Dre's departure, was so dark that I was concerned it would overwhelm the film.

But when Death Row photographer, Simone Green, agreed to discuss the beat down she received as Suge participated and David Kenner watched, and then produced the photographs she took of herself afterward, we knew we had to capture this material. It was the ultimate affirmation that at this company, no responsible adult was in charge. Suge had created a situation where everyone was in his sway and there was no one he respected who could stand up to him and say, "*This is wrong.*"

There were three people who we had interviewed who had actively gotten in Suge Knight's face in the wake of the chaos at Death Row. And, in what may strike some as surprising, given the type of music that Death Row was creating, all three of them were women. Lydia Harris had battled Suge Knight, David Kenner and Interscope, each toe to toe, to get what she felt was owed in her partnership with Death Row. Simone Green had fought back against Suge Knight after she was physically abused by him and his minions. Death Row artist, Jewell, had not been shy about personally confronting Suge concerning money due her. Steve Housden, Jeff Scheftel and I would watch these interviews and just shake our heads at how brave these women were. They had brass ovaries. They did not live in fear of Suge Knight. It was clear to them that business was business and nonsense was nonsense. And they were not going to give the mighty Suge Knight a pass.

Lastly, in the face of the label's out-sized success, there was the collective decision by both Suge Knight and his consigliere, David Kenner, to betray their original partner in arms, Michael Harris. Harry O's funds had come at a critical time in the label's genesis when capital was needed to fully finance *The Chronic*, keep Suge Knight out of jail and keep the artists in the fold. But of equal importance was the fact that Harry O understood business and had insights into and understood the gang sensibility much more acutely and incisively than either Suge or Kenner. And in shunning Michael's counseling and choosing to marginalize and demonize him, they helped sow the seeds of the label's destruction.

As I contemplated what we'd captured and updated my notes on what needed to be in the film, I continued to feel more and more that this was the ultimate cautionary tale of an ambitious man who, in a very short period of time, captured lightning in a bottle and then squandered it because of a deep denial about the factors that led to his success in the first place. Over and over, I watched the footage from BET news reporter Stephanie Frederic, where Suge remarks about Dre's departure from Death Row, "*If you own 50% of a label worth a billion dollars and you got a partner that you don't have to give anything to but his walking papers, that's great.*" The message from Suge was, "*This is my creation and my success. And it is success I control. No one else matters.*"

Tupac Shakur's death, when coupled with Dre's departure, and the departure of other key artists like Snoop, would eventually lay Suge Knight bare -- revealing an emperor with no clothes. A long, tortuous, spiral, as epic as his rise to power, would begin.

Tupac

Tupac Shakur was one of the original stars at Interscope. But he proved to be a constant headache for them with his continual arrests and jail sentences. Suge saw an opportunity to sign him to Death Row after Shakur was incarcerated at Riker's Island, and later, the Clinton Correctional Facility in New York on a sexual assault charge. After Suge posted his bail (with financial assistance from Interscope), Tupac joined Death Row and agreed to record three albums. Tupac proved to be a huge financial asset for Death Row. His first album, "All Eyez on Me," would sell nine million copies.

FRANK ALEXANDER: Tupac Shakur was not before his time, but one of a kind for his time and era.

JEFFREY JOLSON COLBURN: He was a movie star, and for him to be doing street stuff gave him a sort of Marlon Brando edge -- the outlaw who was living his life in some romantic, Ernest Hemingway world. Where you lived out your art.

GARY JACKSON: He had that almost uncontrollable, defiant attitude.

TUPAC SHAKUR: (13) I got a big mouth. I can't help it. I talk from my heart. I'm real. You know what I'm saying? Whatever comes, comes. But my controversy problem? It's not my fault. I'm trying to find my way in the world, trying to be somebody, instead of just making money off everybody.

KEVIN POWELL: If anybody embodied the eclecticism of hip hop it was Tupac. When we were interviewing him, we went to South Central L.A., to a burger joint. He was giving people love. People were giving him love. It was that Malcolm X kind of thing going on. Next minute, he would be quoting Shakespeare or Machiavelli or Beethoven. He had that high art thing going on as well.

ALLEN GORDON: Tupac's gift was to take somebody else's pain and story and translate it.

DOUG YOUNG: I've been in two drive-bys and felt both of 'em. You feel that type of stuff.

TUPAC SHAKUR: (14) We, as rappers, we brought that violence. We brought that violence, that we seen on the street, and we put it in our records. We put it on our records for years. After three or four years, people finally started to see it. Because of all the statistics that's going on in the streets. If we stopped talking about it, they wouldn't notice (the statistics). And when they stop takin' statistics, then White people wouldn't care no more.

LIONEL RANDOLPH: He would definitely give you something to think about.

ALLEN GORDON: Today for somebody to become a superstar in the rap world, you need an incredibly engaging personality. (Either) charming to the tenth degree or the most disgusting person to the tenth degree. There's no room for being in the middle. Overly nice or extremely threatening. Because people are attracted to personalities.

TUPAC SHAKUR: (13) I know some of you White folks and some of you Black folks don't appreciate what we're talking about. But this is the only way we got to make money. And if you don't let me make my money (rapping) about the streets, I guarantee you, I will make my money on the streets.

TONE DEF: A lot of people say the same thing or have said the same things as Pac. But Tupac made it believable.

DOUG YOUNG: That *Me Against the World* record? If you was really down in the streets, you knew that record was huge.

ALLEN GORDON: *Me Against the World*? That's the Tupac you fell in love with. Because everything on there somebody felt at some time. There was something about that album that was just magical.

JEWELL: He was crazy like me. We're four days apart. He's June 16th and I'm June 12th. So we just clicked.

LIONEL RANDOLPH: His words were magical. But the music was magical, too. Because a lot of rappers just use drum bass kick and a few samples. He had guitars, live bass piano and singing.

FREDDIE RHONE: He bridged R&B with gangsta rap. I think that's what made a lot of people feel him.

B LEGIT: He said the reason he got good at rapping so fast, was that he didn't have the budget to come back the next day and record it. He had to make the beat, record it, and then mix it the same day.

DOUG YOUNG: At first I thought he was a crazy, arrogant, little idiot. But I didn't know how deep he was.

TUPAC SHAKUR: (14) We have to be honest about the tools we use to survive. Why is a Black life any more recoupable than a White life? You know what I'm saying? We know they don't put the same security in the ghetto that they do in the White neighborhoods.

ATRON GREGORY: I met a Northern California promoter who told me she had a group called *Strictly Dope*. And it was Tupac, Ray Love, and D.J.. Tupac auditioned for Shock of the Digital Underground and Shock liked him and offered him a job as a dancer and roadie. He was like, *"Whatever it takes. But I want to be on one of your records."* So we collectively made that agreement.

Later, Digital did some songs for a feature film with Chevy Chase and Dan Aykroyd. One of those songs was called *Same Song,* and that was the first time that Tupac did anything on a record, CD, or cassette.

DOUG YOUNG: I met Tupac back when he was a dancer for Digital Underground. Actually met Tupac through his first manager, Atron Gregory, who was tellin' me how brilliant this brother was. He got Tupac his first solo deal at Interscope. I remember [Gregory] approaching me sayin', *"I'm gonna have a Tupac record -- I need you to promote it."* And he gave me an advance copy of it. I thought it was pretty dope. I thought he was kinda rough around the edges, but I really liked that *Brenda's Got a Baby* song. So I did some promotion on it. I remember being at a store, AMC in San Bernardino, that didn't have any Tupac albums in it. And it was one of my *firestarter stores*, where if your record really starts selling, you're about to have somethin' big. And they told me the Tupac album was sold out -- and I was like, sold out? And I remember asking Alvin (the owner) what single does everybody like on that Tupac album? And he told me *Brenda's Got a Baby.* So I remember racin' home, callin' Atron. I said, *"Atron you got somethin' in that Tupac kid. That Brenda Got a Baby is goin' through the roof."*

ATRON GREGORY: What I saw in Tupac was someone who had a desire to be successful and he only had two or three avenues. One was rapping, one was acting and one was going into the (political) movement that his family came out of.

FRANK ALEXANDER: His mother was a Black Panther. All of the anger, frustration, and everything that she was dealing with, and what was going on at that time in her life, was feeding right into him. When Tupac was a kid, for punishment, she would make him read the *New York Times* cover to cover, and then, at the end of the day, he would be quizzed on everything he read out of the paper. Tupac, well aware of what his mother had gone through, brought that into the 90s because nothing had changed in the 60s to the 90s, as far as what he saw as his race of people.

GARY JACKSON: Having a mother that was in the Black Panthers and having to raise him herself -- she had such a strong influence on him. *Dear Mama* was dedicated to her.

ALLEN GORDON: The Black power movement did not pay for bills. The whole thing was about self-empowerment for inner city Black kids and nobody was empowered. Bobby Seale was speaking at colleges and Bobby Rush was an Alderman in Chicago. They took regular jobs. So (Tupac) got disillusioned. He had internal conflicts with his mother (who) was addicted to crack cocaine at the time.

ATRON GREGORY: He wanted to be known as a good rap artist, a good lyricist, a good actor, and the child of revolutionaries.

TUPAC SHAKUR: (15) I don't know how to be responsible for what every Black male did. I don't know. I guess I'm gonna say I'm a thug. That's because I came from the gutter, and I'm still here. I'm not saying I'm a thug because I want to rob you or rape people or things. I'm a businessman. I mean, you know I'm a businessman, because you find me at my place of business.

GEORGE PRYCE: He's from a very revolutionary upbringing. What he was taught as a child, with his mother and the foster homes is the need for equality. He was angry.

ATRON GREGORY: He was controversial, lyrically. He was also in the movies. Any time you're on the big screen, that kind of changes things.

JEFFREY JOLSON COLBURN: Tupac was a good looking guy. He was a movie star. Everybody looks good when they're 14 feet high on the screen. But he was especially good looking. And for him to be doin' the street stuff, gave him an edge. And that's attractive to women.

ADINA HOWARD: There was no need for him to bite his tongue. That's why a lot of people, especially women, like his music. Because he wasn't gonna lie. He was gonna tell you what he wanted.

DOUG YOUNG: I remember the movie, *Juice*. Hank Shocklee and I promoted that soundtrack. And he gave me an advance cut and let me see the movie. I thought Tupac was an incredible actor. I said, "*If this guy never raps another lyric in his life, he can act.*"

ATRON GREGORY: He had the energy. But as much as the energy and the writing, he had the desire. He was one of those people that wasn't gonna quit until he got to the top. Period. Whatever it took, he was willing to do.

LIONEL RANDOLPH: He wrote that song, *Keep Your Head Up*. Talked about a bunch of stuff that females were goin' through, havin' all those babies and no daddy there and stuff like that. He was givin' them a message on how to be strong.

ADINA HOWARD: Pac loved women. He wanted to do a calendar with real Black women. Not the Tyra Banks and Naomi Campbell type women. He wanted to get fabulous Black women with big butts and hips. He didn't want a stick figure Black woman. He wanted to show you -- this is the *real* Black woman.

JEFFREY JOLSON COLBURN: Tupac was considered a hunk. Women would scream when they saw him. Snoop is rather tall and gangly, but Tupac looked like he could do like fashion ads. He was a good lookin' guy.

Tupac signed with Interscope Records in 1991. His debut album, 2Pacalypse Now, generated controversy after a teenager in Texas shot a state trooper and his defense attorney claimed he was influenced by the song's commentary on police brutality. In 1993, after a series of very public incidents, which usually involved the police, Shakur was accused of sexually assaulting and sodomizing a twenty-one year old woman in his hotel room.

A jury found him guilty on three counts of sexual abuse and he faced up to four and half years in prison. After spending more than a year in prison, initially at Rikers Island, and later, at the Clinton Correction Facility in upstate New York, Tupac signed with Death Row Records after the label fronted the bail money that secured his release. Within days of his release, Tupac recorded the first track for the album that became All Eyez on Me and soon became Death Row's most significant artist by virtue of album sales.

ALLEN GORDON: In some cases, bad press is good press for an artist. But how far do you go? In Tupac's case, bad press definitely boosted his sales. Tupac was actually a mediocre rapper, but (with bad press) you felt more emotion for Tupac, goin' through his trials, being shot, being put in prison, getting beaten by the police. The little kid that died in the park back in 1993, you know, when he had dropped a gun and it went off and shot a kid in the heart. It's those type of events that make people to want to buy your album.

FRANK ALEXANDER: Tupac was definitely his music. That's how he expressed himself. That's how he got out his anger and his pain, was through his music. *Me Against the World;* when he came out with that album, Tupac Shakur was born.

ADINA HOWARD: Whenever you spoke to him, he always spoke with sense. He always knew what he was talking about. Every now and then his temper would flare up. He's a Gemini.

JEFFREY JOLSON COLBURN: Tupac was a star at Interscope and Interscope had their hands full with him. He was in jail and in trouble. And here you had Death Row that was experienced in dealing with troublesome rap acts in jail. Or in court.

RATED R: He had just got beat up by the police. He had a lawsuit going with them that he won. And he was just getting harassed for anything. I mean they just started throwing him on the news as the bad guy of rap when he really wasn't that person.

TUPAC SHAKUR: (15) (to the cameras) I appreciate the present you're giving me, for giving me a fair trial and a fair shot at justice. I thank you from the bottom of my heart for just destroying everything I've worked for for the past twenty three years. And a happy New Year to you, too.

MILLER LONDON: Tupac was in the news every day. I mean you can't buy that kind of publicity. It's unfortunate the kind of media coverage they got. But it added to sales.

RATED R: People didn't know Pac had like fifteen cases in different states in America. We would go to a show and Pac would go straight to court as soon as we'd get off the airplane.

TUPAC SHAKUR: (13) Don't block my way and don't hit my lawyer.

VIRGIL ROBERTS: Great artists are almost always out of step with what's going on in society, because they see the world differently and they act differently.

JEWELL: The last situation he got into, Interscope kind of left him for dead. They weren't really fucking with Pac like that. Pac felt like Interscope betrayed him.

Shakur and another man were accused of sexually assaulting and sodomizing a 21- year old woman in their hotel room in 1994.

TUPAC SHAKUR: (15) It's not a crime for me to be with any girl I want to be with. It's a crime for that girl to turn that into a rape charge. It was her who sodomized me. It wasn't me who went down in a dance club and ate her out. It was her in a dance club who had oral sex. *She* should be charged. Not me.

RICK JAMES a.k.a. PRETTY RICKY: Tupac didn't rape that girl. Tupac had sex with that girl. That girl wanted to spend time with Tupac. She went and lied. Somebody told her to do that.

Just after midnight on Nov. 30, 1994, at 723 7ᵗʰ Ave., Tupac Shakur and members of his party were robbed and shot.

KEVIN POWELL: What we know happened at Quad Studios is that a bunch of people were recording. Biggie was in the building. Puffy was in the building. I believe Andre Harrell was in the building. Someone was supposedly calling Tupac, paging him a lot. Tupac told me he was getting like seven thousand dollars. That's how he operated. No contract. *"Give me cash and I'll drop some vocals for you."* He gets to the studio, on the ground level and there are some guys in camouflage. Anyone from NYC knows that people in camouflage are from Brooklyn. Apparent (Tupac) and the homeboy he was with got in a scuffle and Tupac got shot. The bullet went through his scrotum and I think another bullet grazed his head. The word on the street was that it was a warning to Tupac. Who was it coming from? Hey, listen to Machiavelli.

Tupac Shakur erroneously blamed Sean Puffy Combs, the CEO of Bad Boy Records and Combs's biggest act, Notorious B.I.G. a.k.a. Biggie Smalls, for having prior knowledge that the attack was going to happen. Both men had been involved in a recording session at Quad Studios the night of the incident. And a war of words between Death Row and Bad Boy Records would begin.

KEVIN POWELL: Biggie and Tupac were friends for a little while. They did a track or two together. Keep in mind, during this time, Tupac was filming *Above the Rim*. He was spending a lot of time in New York because that's where the film (was being made). Tupac was a people person, so he gravitated towards a lot of people. He and Biggie performed together on stage and recorded together. There was a friendship.

After three days of deliberation, the jury found Tupac Shakur guilty on three counts of sexual abuse. He was then facing 1 1/2 to 4 1/2 years in prison.

MICHAEL WARREN / ATTORNEY: (16) The main impetus for the incarceration of Mr. Shakur was from City Hall, Mr. Giuliani himself.

KAREN LEE / TUPAC'S PUBLICIST: (16)   Being 23, being Black, his last name being Shakur - in America, he never had a chance.

FRANK ALEXANDER: Tupac was in jail and he wanted out of jail and he wanted out of jail <u>badly</u>. No one, including Interscope, was putting up any bail money to get him out. His bail was set at $1.4 million.

Thug Life was a group that Tupac Shakur sponsored. The group released one album,
Thug Life: Volume 1 in 1994.

THUG LIFE GROUP MEMBER: He always talked about jail. But he'd never been there. He wanted to be there and see what was goin' on with the shit. And then when he got there, he didn't like it. Aww!

KEVIN POWELL: A lot of people on the East Coast and New York dissed him hard. No one wanted to go visit him.   Death Row Records had wanted to get Tupac for some time.

LAMONT BRUMFIELD: He had a lotta hype behind him and

bein' a bad guy and Death Row being a bad label at the time. And then he got into it with Puffy and Big. He needed some back up.

ALLEN GORDON: There was talk of Suge Knight wanting Tupac on Death Row well before he went to jail. But he stayed away because he was a star

KEVIN POWELL: Even though Snoop was a huge star, he didn't have what Tupac had -- that kind of iconic presence like James Dean or Elvis.

ATRON GREGORY: He wanted to be number one again. So where else do you go but to where the other number one people are.

DOUG YOUNG: Suge caught Tupac at the right time. I don't know anyone that wants to be in jail. Go to L.A. County jail for a week and you're ready to get the hell out of there. So you can imagine what it's like at Rikers Island.   And he's on the East Coast, too. Tupac got all the people talkin' how they were gonna rape him for Biggie. Had to be a hellhole.

HANK CALDWELL: Who could fault Suge for being a good businessman? Tupac was a talent.

LAMONT BRUMFIELD: The record industry is cold-blooded. They'll come at you, make your artist leave you, make your artist sell you out on different levels of the game. I learned every last one of 'em dealing with Death Row. I learned from the best.

DOUG YOUNG: That was the main reason that (broke) Atron and Tupac up. Him sitting in jail and Atron telling (him) that he didn't want nothing to do with Death Row. Tupac was trying to get him to go to Suge to get the money and Atron wasn't with it. He was like, *"I'm not doing business with no Suge."* (But) Atron was already feeling what was going down.

ALLEN GORDON: If you've got Suge Knight dangling freedom, money, power, and respect in front of you, what else you gonna go for? You've got a scared young man, first time behind bars. And he's supposed to be there for four years.

ATRON GREGORY: Interscope always said they would put up the money -- that he needed protection.

DOUG YOUNG: I don't know what it cost to bail him out of jail.

ATRON GREGORY: To get Tupac out of prison, his lawyers had to appeal his sentence. His sentence was stayed, pending appeal. And this cost money. It wasn't Suge -- the money was put up by Interscope, with Tupac's future royalties guaranteeing it.

DOUG YOUNG: Tupac had to do what he had to do fast. 'Cause he was in the penitentiary. He wasn't just in jail.

FRANK ALEXANDER: Tupac promised Suge a return, *"You get me out of here and I'll put Death Row on the map. My first CD will sell six million copies."*

JEWELL: Now I heard (Suge) had Pac sign a contract on toilet paper. I don't know how true that is. But I know that when Pac came back, he was ready.

FRANK ALEXANDER: Tupac got out in September of '95. He went to Death Row Records the day he got off the plane and they laid down their first track for *All Eyes on Me* in fifteen minutes.

TUPAC SHAKUR: (*All Eyes On Me*) is more celebratory of life, upbeat, energetic, fun, I think. But it's also harsher in terms of the language, because I've been in jail for eleven and a half months.

GARY JACKSON: Tupac really knew how to glorify his own life. Some of those stories on *All Eyez on Me* -- your jaw drops when you hear it.

THUG LIFE GROUP MEMBER: He went to Death Row cause they were gang bangin' on the highest level. He wanted to see that life. He wanted to see the gang bangin' mentality in South Central. He wanted to live the thug life. It looked fun to him. You know, just like a little kid wants ice cream. *"You mean to tell me I could gang bang, and claim Bloods and Crips and ride in a rad Corniche? I gotta get this image so I'm gonna start livin' this lifestyle."*

FRANK ALEXANDER: Most of the time I went anywhere with Pac, I would say 50 percent of the time, Suge was with him. Pac and Suge were always together.

SUGE KNIGHT: It wasn't like I had love for him because he made great records. 'Cause, you know, you can have great artists like Michael Jackson. I wouldn't hang out with him.

HANK CALDWELL: A lot of the younger kids really fed off the fact that you had someone like a Tupac at the label - that would always help them creatively.

TONE DEF: Tupac brought that feeling of "I was nothing, now I'm something, and I want everybody else to be something, too. If I can do it, you can do it."

GEORGE PRYCE: He stirred up the group and got them working. He made sure every artist at Death Row had some part of his double CD. It was his way of saying *"Look, I'm part of the family."* Which he didn't have to do.

STUDIO TONE: I remember doing a session with him and it seemed like he was just running around, having fun, partying, you know, having a good time. But the man was done. We thought that he didn't even write them (the lyrics). We thought he just came with his lyrics already. But no, he wrote them that day. And that's just how sharp he was, man.

HANK CALDWELL: I didn't notice anything out of the ordinary once Tupac came on board. Anything that did take place was just the professional jealousies that you would have at any label, whether it be between Tupac and whomever, or Streisand and Celine Dion. No different. And I think the younger kids really fed off the fact that you had someone like a Tupac at the label. That would always help them creatively.

THUG LIFE GROUP MEMBER: Tupac was talkin' about knockin' people out in his songs, but he never actually did. So when we used to go out, he tried to prove it to us. *"Yeah, nigga. I'm a thug, too."* You know what I'm saying? So when we have our thug conversations, he can come in and talk. Man, if you're not a thug and we're all talking about thug shit and you can't, you have no business being around. You're sittin' there lookin' stupid. You know what I'm saying? So basically he just wanted the experiences.

JEWELL: That's somethin' he don't know nothin' about 'cause he was predominately from the East Coast. And see, the niggers out here, they didn't play that. You can't be joined in. You gotta be born in. But I think he always wanted that respect.

THUG LIFE GROUP MEMBER: Ray and I were the real thugs. We tattooed up. We got the (graphics) on our back arms and on our back. Tupac wasn't doin' all that. When I showed Pac my back in the studio, he went crazy. He wanted to live that. He was just like amazed. *"Oh my God! Look at your back! Oh! Oh!"*

JEWELL: (He'd) come in the studio and do three songs back to back. Cigarette in one hand, drink in another.

SUGE KNIGHT: (5) You have people in our studio saying, *"Man, we gotta get like Pac. Pac just goes in there, kick em in, kick em out, kick em in, kick em out."* And that's all they talk about. And that's exactly what they're doing.

SONSHINE: The thing I loved about working with Tupac -- you would get in the studio with this guy and he wouldn't just say, *"Do your vocals."* He would basically say, *"This is what I want you to do,"* and he would do the note and he would stay there and produce you. *"Okay, one more time, Sonshine. Hit it!"* But Tupac coached you. He coached you on. He'd say, *"Stop the tape -- stop. I didn't like that. One more time."* He was really into you.

SUGE KNIGHT: (5) He was the hardest worker I've ever seen in the studio in my entire life. He don't have to do takes. He don't have to punch in. He just makes it happen.

GEORGE PRYCE: He raised the level of competition, which is a good thing. He brought that level up. Any of the artists will tell you that what Tupac put into them was this business of a work ethic, where you can do more if you just work at it.

FLIPSIDE: When Tupac came, it was like Suge wasn't worried about nobody else. Not Snoop. Nobody at the time. Nobody.

GEORGE PRYCE: There were several artists, for instance, the young R & B singer, Danny Boy; Suge treated him like he was his son. He didn't understand when Tupac came and Suge (had to) diminish the relationship which bothered Danny Boy a great deal.

FRANK ALEXANDER: If (Tupac) wanted anything, Suge bought it for him. You know, cars, homes, jewelry. Pac, every week, would request a $5,000 day. And he would get $5,000 by messenger. That's the extent of the money I saw.

MICHAEL HARRIS: (Suge) didn't care about the other artists. He says all he needs is Tupac. He says Tupac is a genius and a workaholic. He didn't want no girls. All he wanted was go to the studio and work. He wanted to take his experiences and share them with the world.

JEWELL: He felt like he couldn't trust nobody. And Suge was the only hand that leaned in to help him. He was trying to pay Suge back for helping him out.

The Interview

Welcome to Death Row had been in production for two years and we felt like we were in the slammer for documentary films with no finish line in sight. While we had the rudimentary structure and chapter construct in place, with people speaking freely on film as had never been captured in the press, we were still missing key pieces of information, not to mention an editor. So basically we had a $1,000,000 home movie. And we still hadn't licensed any music.

In the documentary film world, there are a small coterie of film editors who are known to have exceptional skills in the area of story assembly. In the same way that you can admire how Dr. Dre can synthesize various musical elements to create the tracks on albums like *The Chronic,* you have to look at brilliant documentaries like *Capturing the Friedmans, When They Were Kings,* or more recently, *Print The Legend,* and *The Great Invisible* and understand that there is a common thread. In the film world, the Dr. Dre equivalent is often the editor as much as the director. A director can envision a story or a pacing solution. But in most cases, the editor has to figure out the mechanics of it. And more often than not, a great editor finds a solution better than the director's original concept.

Tyler Hubby would end up being my Dr. Dre. Steve Housden knew about Tyler. He called him *The Great Hubbini.* We met with Tyler, showed him where we were in the cut, and he agreed to come on. Steve, Jeff and I decided to keep his hiring a secret. We also decided not to mention to Tyler about what had happened to Karl Slater. He'll find out if he reads this book.

The funds conveyed in the Darden incident would provide the *quid pro quo* for the long, talked about, but long withheld interview with Harry O. Sometime in the spring of 2000, we finally had Michael in the proper frame of mind, and had assembled a workable construct to secure his interview. There are prisons in California that have little or no problem with film crews bringing cameras on the premises. Lancaster wasn't one of them. The only way anyone could get a camera in there was if they were a lawyer filming a deposition.

Jeff Scheftel and I had batted around a fake deposition scenario where we brought a camera and a criminal lawyer with us. (Lydia had suggested that this was a cover David Kenner had once employed.) But we dropped the idea as too unwieldy. Michael's cell phone had been confiscated, so we had figure out a way to get him on a prison pay phone for the two plus hours we needed. Lydia said she needed $2,500 to pay off a decoy inside the prison so that Michael could talk on the phone for that length of time. So that was arranged. Jeff arranged for the call to go into a recording studio and I mapped out every possible question I could ask him.

The first attempt was aborted due to an issue inside the prison. But the second attempt took. The call came into the studio and Michael was up for the task, explaining things about Death Row Records that only he could know and demonstrating above all else, that there was a kind of smooth, if somewhat haunting, brilliance to him. *Butter.*

Yes, Harry O was finally in the house.

East vs West

A rivalry and war of words between East Coast and West Coast rappers began with a misunderstanding over Biggie Small's alleged involvement in Tupac's shooting at Quad studios, intensified into a no-holds-barred, brawl between Death Row Records and East Coast based Bad Boy Records and its CEO, Sean Puffy Combs. Tensions peaked when Tupac -- who thrived on the media attention -- claimed to have slept with Faith Evans, Biggie Small's wife. Later, there is gunfire involving Snoop and Tha Dogg Pound in New York.

HANK CALDWELL: As you're successful in this business, you're building Frankenstein monsters.

KEVIN POWELL: Around the time Tupac got out of jail, Sean *Puffy* Combs was about to become, I would say, the East Coast version of Suge Knight, with Bad Boy Records. His first big artist was Notorious B.I.G.

S. LEIGH SAVIDGE: As Death Row began to grow, Suge Knight had developed a lucrative side business as the manager for Mary J. Blige and Jodeci, two acts associated with New York based, Uptown Records. Suge had managed to improve both artist's arrangements with Uptown in the wake of what many people said were violent encounters between himself and Uptown label chief, Andre Harrell. Shortly thereafter, Sean Combs, who had been instrumental in developing both acts and had his own conflicts with Harrell, would leave Uptown and form Bad Boy Records.

KEVIN POWELL: The famous legend about (Puffy) is that at 19 (he was) an intern for Andre Harrell, the founder of Uptown Records, who had put out people like Heavy D and other very successful platinum acts by the early 90s. Not only was Puffy a top executive at Uptown, he was now beginning to formulate what would become Bad Boy Records. Craig Mack and Notorious B.I.G. were two of the first people he put out on Bad Boy Records.

DOUG YOUNG: I think what Biggie and Puffy conjured up was brilliant. Jeff House was working over at Arista. I remember Jeff giving me an advance copy on Bad Boy. Craig Mack was on one side -- six songs and Biggie's was on the other side -- six songs. I said, *"Oh, my God, Puffy's about to take over New York."* He had that East Coast flow with them samples. Just the samples. The loops. The timing for what Bad Boy did was perfect.

NATE DOGG: This bullshit about East Coast and the West Coast started when we went out to New York to do the Source Awards and Mr. Knight went onstage. And he's in New York City. And we all know that Puffy's from New York City.

SUGE KNIGHT: (at the Source Awards) Any artists out there who want to be our artists and stay a star and won't have to worry about the executive producer trying to be all in the videos, all on the record, dancing, come to Death Row.

NATE DOGG: The whole crowd started booing and I thought to myself, *"Why would you do that?"*

SNOOP DOGG: (at the Source Awards) The East Coast don't love Dr. Dre and Snoop Dogg? The East Coast ain't got no love for Dr. Dre and Snoop Dogg and Death Row? You all don't love us? Well, let it be known then! We know you're all East Coast!

SEAN COMBS: (at the Source Awards) I'm the executive producer that comment was made about a bit earlier. Check this out - contrary to what other people may feel, I'm very proud of Dr. Dre, of Death Row and Suge Knight for their accomplishments. And all this East and West needs to stop.

JEWELL: I mean for me to go into it, I would really have to get into it. It was so personal and it hurt so many people. But the beef came from jealousy. Puffy was a good friend of mine.

KEVIN POWELL: There's enough room in this business for two young Black males who are entrepreneurs to exist. I mean, can you imagine if Al Bell and Berry Gordy were fighting? Or if The Temptations had beef with The Four Tops? I mean, it sounds fucking retarded when you think about it. *"The Four Tops got a beef with The Temptations. Marvin Gaye and Smokey Robinson were fighting at the Grammy Awards last night."* Think about that for a second.

MICHAEL HARRIS: The East Coast / West Coast situation was truly motivated by an economic situation rather than personal vendettas. The East Coast created rap and the West Coast turned it into stupid, crazy money.

DOUG YOUNG: A lot of people on the West Coast felt that we always had love for the East Coast. They come here and break their records, they come here and play at the clubs -- they come here and do in-stores. We do the whole nine with them East Coast cats. And we go out there and don't get that same love.

SUGE KNIGHT: (5) It was people hustling other people out of money on the East Coast. *"You don't have no team. You need us. We're from the East Coast. Pay us X amount of dollars for protection."* And some of these idiots were doing it.

GREEDY GREG: I hate to say this but it seemed like the East Coast raps more about fantasy than reality. And I think rappers on the West Coast rap more about reality.

DOUG YOUNG: It was really people who were in charge of playing stuff. If they wasn't gonna play your stuff, it wasn't no artist's fault. You had a lot of power brokers on the East Coast that couldn't find something on the West Coast to play. People from the West Coast knew they didn't need the East Coast to sell no records. But the East Coast needed the West Coast to sell records.

KEVIN POWELL: I remember New York DJs at parties refusing to play West Coast records. *"They're country, they're bammers, they wear Jheri curls, they can't rhyme. They're wack. It's not danceable."*

DR. DRE: (3) It was the media that blew it up. You're seeing certain things that somebody said highlighted in magazines about the West Coast and vice versa and it just boiled over from there.

TUPAC SHAKUR: (17) All these people talking about an East Coast, West Coast war, they're like Judas was to Jesus. They're only here to 'cause confusion.

MASTER P: It made rap music look bad. It made rap music look like it was just another part of the dope game. It made outsiders look at rap music like they didn't want to be part of it.

DOUG YOUNG: The West Coast made it so that people in middle America could understand hip hop. It wasn't a bunch of New York rough sounding beats, where you had to totally understand rap to get it.

NATE DOGG: Controversy is what Death Row started living off of, instead of talent.

TUPAC SHAKUR: (17) If this was chess, we'd be yelling *checkmate* three motherfucking years ago, because we've done beat these motherfuckers. Overthrow the government you all got right now, which is Bad Boy and Nas and all that bullshit and we will bring a new government here that will feed every person in New York.

DOUG YOUNG: The disrespect just started getting worse and worse between the East Coast and the West Coast.

FRANK ALEXANDER: If (Tupac) had something to say he said it and he didn't care who heard it. He didn't care if it hurt somebody.

DOUG YOUNG: And then you had the Tupac and B.I.G. situation flaming it even more.

TUPAC SHAKUR: (18) I possess (Biggie's) soul. His and Puffy's. They know that I was the truest nigger involved with Biggie's success. I was the biggest help. I was the truest nigger. I was the biggest help. He knows how I'd stop my shows and let him touch the show. Let him blow up and do his whole show in the middle of my show. How I used to buy him shit and give him shit and never ask for it back. How I used to share my experiences in the game and my lessons and my rules and my knowledge on the game with him. You know what I mean? He owes me more. He owes me more than to turn his head and act like he didn't know a nigger's about to blow my fucking head off! He knew. But for me to know, like, three weeks ago this happened, and three weeks later your album's coming out and you're a fucking Don on your album. But you don't know who shot me in your own fucking hometown? You think it's from your neighborhood? And I gotta find out by myself. And I don't even call myself a Don. I'm just a Capo. From the west side. And I'm on the east side in jail and I know who touched me and I know everything that happened.

S. LEIGH SAVIDGE: Atron Gregory and Kevin Powell both told me that Tupac simply got the issue of Biggie's involvement in the Quad Studio's shooting wrong. The Bad Boy camp certainly knew who the alleged perpetrator was. But no information has been disclosed that would indicate that Biggie had any idea that an attack on Tupac was in the offing. Tupac's attacks on Biggie would take the East Coast / West Coast war up to another level.

KEVIN POWELL: Tupac was wrong in not blaming whoever the

individual figures were, who actually had something to do with it in New York and making it in a whole New York City thing and then this whole East Coast, West Coast thing. He definitely had someone in his ear, probably Suge, exacerbating it. It sells records. It continues to get media attention, which sells more records.

JEFFREY JOLSON COLBURN: Tupac claimed to have gone out with Biggie's wife, Faith Evans. This was a great humiliation, reportedly, for Biggie. (Then) It was all over and accepted as truth.

FRANK ALEXANDER: We were in Manhattan shooting a video. Biggie Smalls had gotten on the radio station and Biggie said, "*I can't believe that New York is allowing Tupac and Tha Dogg Pound to shoot a video in our city, right in the heart of Times Square.*" The words out of Biggie's mouth was Tupac and Tha Dogg Pound. And it wasn't. It was *Snoop* and Tha Dogg Pound. Tupac was not with us. Snoop was having his hair braided. All of the artists was in the trailer and all of a sudden, *gunfire*. Someone shot into the trailer. They weren't shooting in there to say, "*Get out.*" They were shooting to kill someone.

JEFFREY JOLSON COLBURN: There was a shift in Tupac Shakur's lyrical content. At first he was more political and then, at some point, he became more *street*. It was West Coast vs. East Coast.

FRANK ALEXANDER: The lyrics started getting dangerous. More threatening.

DOUG YOUNG: Tupac always had that Jekyll and Hyde type of personality. I remember another story I heard that he was out on the road in D.C. and cussed out his fans in D.C. Told 'em he didn't even know why he was in this little messed up city, doin' a show for them bastards. And the whole crowd rushed the stage on him.

KEVIN POWELL: The person at Rikers was very reflective. He was going to change his life and everything. This new person was like, *"Fuck New York. Fuck the East Coast. Suge is The Man, he takes care of me."* He's flashing money in front of the MTV cameras. It was like, *"Wow. It's Jekyll and Hyde."*

JEFFREY JOLSON COLBURN: The Soul Train Music Awards. I was covering them and both Tupac and Biggie were up for awards. I was out back having a cigarette and Tupac and Suge come riding up in this Black Humvee. They get out and Biggie Smalls is in the lot with Puff. So you've got two carloads full of bodyguards from the West Coast. You got another ten guys from the East Coast. This is the first time Biggie and Tupac have seen one another since the shooting in New York, which Tupac blamed Biggie for setting up. And they start yelling at one another on that subject almost immediately. And this wasn't just two guys in a schoolyard. These are two guys with a large number of bodyguards trained to pull the trigger at the first sight of another gun. And so there is this face-off. It was like the *Gunfight at the O.K. Corral* with like six guys with their hands on their guns. I saw the bravest thing I've ever seen. The Knights of Islam, the little bow-tie wearing, suit guys, marched right up between these two rival factions and stand there stoic staring them both in their faces. It was the craziest thing I ever saw.

FRANK ALEXANDER: One of his songs was a song called *Hit 'Em Up*. It talked about killing the Bad Boy camp, you know, different artists. It was a lot of threats. I go, *"Pac, did you hear what you said?"* He was like, *"Yeah, nigger, I wrote it."* (I said) *"Okay, we're gonna need more security and you need to start wearing a vest."*

MASTER P: I was taught never to rap about a person on a record. If you got problems, go see that person and handle it with each other.

B-LEGIT: Pac was a mess. He was just scared of nothing. He was being a man about what he was representing. He knew both sides of the game. He was for the struggle. But he was also in it.

DOUG YOUNG: Even with his hypocrisy, he walked it the way he talked it. Tupac was no punk. He was the type of brother when you got into it, there wasn't gonna be no talking your way out of it. I remember one time I saw Tupac get beat up by some Crips in Hollywood by Sunset and Poinsettia, by that old Ralphs store they tore down. I remember three dudes jumped Tupac and beat him up. I had an apartment on that street. Tupac came back with some 40s and some 20s looking for 'em. Got's the whole nine. Tupac was always crazy.

JEWELL: Tupac turned into somebody else. I had to talk to him one day. I said, *"Nigger, why you claiming MOB? I remember when you were dancing with the Digital Underground."*

KEVIN POWELL: Just because he's this famous hip hop icon, doesn't mean he hadn't rectified some of those things inside of him. Tupac was only 25 years old when he was assassinated.

"The Whitest Mutherfucker"

With his interview in hand, the last tool in the shed with which Michael and Lydia could ransom me with had been used up. We were on slightly different footing now and I could sense that Michael knew that. In one of my last visits to see him, I told him that Karl had been let go, Tyler Hubby had been hired and that I was taking the film underground in the sense that I was not going to let Lydia interfere with it anymore. I told him that as we perfected each sequence, I would give Lydia a DVD copy of it so she could see that we were making progress.

I sat back and braced myself for yet another ugly exchange.

There was one issue for which Michael had always felt little or no sympathy: The fact that the project was taking all of my company's financial reserves to complete. Michael and I had spent hours talking about business and I had made it clear to him on numerous occasions that the capital we were using to finance the film was very hard earned -- the product of 90 hour work weeks and many, mostly small financial transactions. It was capital that I wasn't taking for myself, redistributing as employee bonuses, or putting into new film acquisitions that would have an immediate benefit for the company. This wasn't Interscope with *fuck you* capital to burn on his wife's passion project. This capital was everything I had spent 12 years accumulating and this project was bleeding us and had put Xenon's growth on hold. Bank of America's representatives were horrified to discover that their credit line, which was guaranteed by my personal assets, was being used to finance a project about Death Row Records.

I would ask Michael constantly, *"Why do you want to fuck with the guy that is putting it all on the line for you? Why is that in your nature?"*

There was a side to Michael -- the hard core street side -- that seemed to enjoy the fact that he'd lured me into a situation where I'd have to keep advancing money to his wife to obtain their ongoing assistance -- like it represented validation that his street instincts were still on the cutting edge. I never viewed it in racial terms. For him, this was simply business. Our contract and its stated terms was just a conceptual idea to him -- something to be modified whenever his needs dictated. His wife had gotten used to the money he once had as well as advances from record companies on projects that had never seen the light of day. She'd used a lot of those funds to finance a certain lifestyle for herself.

Those funds had dried up and I'd been the next guy through the door.

Michael was very Machiavellian so he understood when to message aphorisms of support. Channeling Iago from *Othello*, he told me he loved me any number of times. However, at his core, Michael was a gladiator. And each conversation I had with him, either on the phone or face to face at Lancaster, was a duel of sorts. My prior deeds or our previous agreements did not inform his agenda in new conversations, unless I'd done something in the past that he didn't like. He played chess in every conversation.

As I suspected he would, Michael refused to view my decision to take the film underground as something that was necessitated by his wife's ongoing destructive behavior. Our new editor, Tyler Hubby, was the kind of guy who attended Cindy Sherman openings at the Gagosian Gallery in Beverly Hills and read magazines like *Dwell* and *Architectural Digest*. He was from the Bay Area and very sophisticated, with a pronounced intellectual curiosity. He believed in the project. He wanted his name on it. But the minute Lydia Harris got in his face, he'd be out the door. He was not going to indulge anyone in misguided drama, least of all someone as toxic as Lydia.

Even so, Michael viewed what I was doing as gamesmanship, that somehow in this whole crazy scenario I had outplayed him. There was a disconnect with his normally keen business sense. And it angered me to the core - the whole street mindfuck thing he always employed - trading in all this pathology and mistrust when it was clear my efforts here were straight-forward and sincere.

"Why you trying to play me?" he asked.

"Look, I'm not playing you. I'm not Suge Knight and I'm not David Kenner. Don't put that shit on me. I'm doing what I told you I'd do and I'm risking my life and everything I have personally to do it. I'm sitting here with you face to face after driving two fucking hours to get here, getting my butt checked for crack for the umpteenth time and spending three fucking hours in the waiting room for my name to be called. So here it is. Your wife is fucking crazy. I have to do it this way."

Michael often took great satisfaction when I got angry with him. At some point in this conversation, he broke into one of his flashbulb grins.

"Do you know why I'm with Lydia?"

I was used to trick questions from Michael, where his intent was to induce me into saying something about his wife that he would actually be offended by. There were subtle nuances here. I could get away with saying, *"Your wife is fucking crazy."* At some level, I think he understood that. But that was about as far as I could go. If I went further than that, he would take it more as a reflection on *him* rather than *her*. So I responded by saying, *"I think so. But you tell me."*

At the beginning of the project, Michael had shown me pictures of some of the women he'd been with prior to Lydia. At least one of them, I'd actually met in person. Most of them made Halle Berry look like the woman next door.

"You've seen the pictures of the women I was with back in the day. What's the comparison?"

There it was on a silver platter. This was a grade A, Harry O, displacement mindfuck. He knew I resented his wife more than anyone I'd ever met in my life and I knew that, at that juncture, they were still loyal to each other. For her part, a lot of the toxic energy she threw my way was probably rooted in the fact that she hated being his dutiful servant most of the time -- banging the walls to get him out of prison. But that's of little solace when someone's draining your bank account. I was not going to be manipulated by the trap he was setting for me. I was not going to say anything to him that would invite the wrath of C. Delores Tucker. I was not going to say, *"You'd be doing a lot better than Lydia if you were on the outside."*

When I would not answer the question, he broke into a hailstorm of laughter. It was as big and as cathartic a laugh as I've ever witnessed. It was overlong; just kept going and going. When he finally pulled himself together, he said, *"Leigh, did I ever tell you that you are the whitest mutherfucker in the history of whiteness?"*

There were a myriad of possible interpretations to this comment. As a joke Michael used to say, *"I'll put some street in you one way or another."* When I told him I'd written some lyrics to a prospective rap song called *"Laying in the Cut,"* he practically wet himself.

But in this instance, it was his way of saying, *"You're not saying anything. But I know what you're thinking."*

When I refused to disclose the location of the editing facility where Tyler and I were working, the Cold War with the Harrises' quickly resumed. For months, I simply refused to make myself available. If Tyler and Lydia were going to meet, it was going to be at a screening of the completed film -- not before. For weeks,

298

Michael left message after message on my home answering machine. If Lydia came by the office unannounced and I was there, I'd simply run out the back door of our offices.

I kept getting death threats. But there wasn't a pattern or coherence to them. They'd be totally random coming at different times of day and from different people. I was pretty sure they were coming from people connected with Death Row -- Who else would do it? Someone would call the company and say they were calling from a company like Sony Music. I'd take the call and someone who was clearly calling from a pay phone would get on the line and say things like, *"You're gonna die, mutherfucker. You are fucking dead."* I got the sense that the existence of these calls was getting around town. One day, producer, Topper Carew, called me on what I thought was a follow up to a recent conversation we had had. When I answered the call he said, *"I'm just calling to see if you're still alive."*

Later, there was another incident that was just plain bizarre. One day, what looked like a 1960s style ice cream truck pulled up in front of our offices. A man with a megaphone began shouting, *"Hey Xenon, pay your bills. Leigh Savidge. Pay your bills, You owe us money."* This went on for about five minutes. Then the truck drove away. Kent Little, Xenon's CFO, came into my office and just shook his head. He said, *"It's gotta be the latest salvo from the Harrises'."*

At some point during this period, my office received a call from someone who described himself as an emissary of sorts who had been appointed by the Harrises to communicate with us on their behalf. I did not know what to make of this -- whether it signaled a capitulation of sorts or just represented more trouble. Steve Housden and I discussed what to do and we determined that our best strategy was to take the meeting, but advise the Santa Monica Police Department of the its timing. We advised them that we'd call them if a negative incident ensued.

On the agreed upon day, the Harris associate arrived and was ushered into a small office where Steve Housden and I met with him. The Darden incident had left a permanent impression on Steve and, on this go around, he may or may not have had a 12 gauge shotgun concealed under his desk. It was a very tense situation. The man began with a pitch about how the Harrises felt disrespected by Xenon. I cut him off and told him that our job was now to protect the project from any further disruptions from the people he supposedly represented. Miraculously, the man's demeanor seemed to change. He identified himself as someone from *The Bottoms*, the area in South Central Los Angeles where Michael Harris was from. He suggested he was a friend of theirs who just wanted to help get communication between the parties back on track again. *"They just want to see what you've done,"* he explained. I agreed to make the current iteration of the film available to them under the condition that Lydia Harris agreed never to come to the office again and would leave me alone until the film was finished. The man told us he would take that message back to them and left.

The Harrises had another intermediary who we'd interviewed for the film who I dealt with extensively during this period. His name was Mark Friedman.

Friedman's roots were in Los Angeles and Las Vegas, where his family had owned the Frontier Hotel before selling it to Howard Hughes in the 60s. An ex-con who'd met Harry O during dishwashing duty at the Terminal Island Penitentiary, Friedman had reinvented himself as a bail bondsman to the stars and seemed to know every important criminal lawyer in town, including men like Dick Sherman, James Blatt and Donald Re who were considered the crème de la crème. His family's roots in Vegas had remained strong as well. At a Mayweather or Klitschko fight, you'd always see Mark in the third row.

At various times over the years, Friedman had acted as a go-between between Suge Knight and Michael Harris and between

Michael and David Kenner. Now he was a go-between between me and the Harrises. In time, I learned to trust Friedman. Unlike Norman Winter, Friedman had the ability to balance his loyalties. I could tell him that the Harrises were bleeding me financially or making it impossible for us to work and he understood and kept the information to himself. He'd always say, *"Just keep your head down. I know what's happening. Deep down, they know that no one else would have done this. I have your back."*

Later, the Harrises' demands for money seemed to let up a little. Soon, I learned why. Friedman had started lending them money. When I asked him why he said, *"Something big is going down."*

Exodus

With the arrival of Tupac, the relationship between Suge Knight and Dr. Dre began to break at the seams. Uncomfortable with the label's gang-like atmosphere and Suge Knight's stewardship in general, Dr. Dre stopped coming to work. All Eyez On Me utilized mostly other producers in the Death Row stable and Suge begins using Tupac as a vehicle to publicly bad-mouth Dr. Dre. Tupac was vocal about Dre's absence, suggesting that he's gay and questions why he was still receiving producing credit on certain tracks. In 1996, after a still mysterious confrontation between Knight and Dre, Dre left Death Row and formed Aftermath Entertainment in conjunction with Jimmy Iovine and Interscope.

HANK CALDWELL: The frame of mind I was in when I left was -- it started to deviate from what I had seen going on creatively. And now the focus was on the violence.

NATE DOGG: We used to have Death Row meetings and everybody would be there. Dre would be there first, most of the time. Now we call a meeting and Dre never showed up. I got into the game as far as even being with Death Row because of Dr. Dre. Albums started being produced and Dre had less to do with 'em. And it was like, *"I wonder if Dre is gonna do a beat for my album?"*

MARIO JOHNSON a.k.a. CHOCOLATE: From what I knew, niggas was walking up to Dre sayin', *"I signed to Suge."* Dre didn't even know they was signed. (He) didn't even know. *"Who? Who is he?" "Yeah, nigga. We signed."*

ALLEN GORDON: Suge getting involved and controlling the quality of the product caused Dre problems. To take a whole soundtrack for the *Above the Rim* movie and executive produce it -- which (Dre) doesn't want to do.

KEVIN POWELL: When you think about Dr Dre, here's a cat that always had some sort of big brother or father figure around. Early on, it was Alonzo Williams. Then it was Eazy-E / Jerry Heller. Then it becomes Suge Knight. And so Dre was always one of those cats who always needed guidance from someone else. Because Dre's a really artistic person. He's an artist. He's a true artist.

JOHN KING: Seemed like after a while, somebody was pulling his strings. You know, like Dre had to answer to somebody.

INTERVIEWER: Who do you think that was?

JOHN KING: We all know who that was.

SAM GIDEON ANSON: You almost see a pattern of Suge helping people, getting close to them, and leaving them behind.

MICHAEL HARRIS: A man that is not intimidated by others would never take that position. That's what happened with Dre. That's what happened with everybody.

KEVIN POWELL: The King i.e. Suge Knight felt the need to have a court around him and I don't think Dre felt comfortable with that. What I got from the interview I did with him was *"I'm half of Death Row. Who are these folks?"*

SIMONE GREEN: Dre did not like the distraction. He's all about work. When he gets in that studio, whoever's in there with him is going to work. If it's two to eleven or four to twelve, you're gonna work. He didn't like all that other stuff going on around him.

DR DRE: (3) I've got all these people around me. How many of them do I really need?

FRANK ALEXANDER: Tupac and Dr. Dre was fine, in the beginning. Everything was great. You didn't see any problems. (But) From the time I worked there in '95 up to '96, Dr. Dre had been in the studio twice. Pac took offense to that.

TUPAC SHAKUR: (18) [Dre] wasn't producing shit. All the niggers were producing the beats on my album. All the niggers were doing the beats and Dre was getting the credit.

FRANK ALEXANDER: Whether anyone liked Tupac, Suge didn't care. But everyone doesn't get along with everyone and there's problems.

KEVIN POWELL: Suge basically took on the role for Tupac that he had taken on earlier for Dre and I don't think it's a coincidence that, at a certain point, Tupac started becoming the mouthpiece for Suge and started dissing Dre.

TUPAC SHAKUR: (18) He is a dope producer. But he ain't worked in years. I'm out here in the streets, whooping niggers asses, starting wars and shit, putting it down, dropping albums, doing my shit and this nigger's taking three years to do one song."

NATE DOGG: That was all Suge Knight. I watched Tupac and Dre. Tupac loved Dre.

SUGE KNIGHT: (5) Daz and all the other little producers, and Sass, and all the ones we have, they did the tracks. Dre wasn't doing the tracks and Dre didn't write the lyrics.

KEVIN POWELL: The story goes that, at some point, Tupac tried to have people physically attack Dre. Suge was the general and Tupac became his soldier, this fearless soldier for Suge Knight and Death Row Records. I think it was unnerving to Dre. It was unnerving to Snoop Dogg and the other artists that Tupac had just come right in and become the favored son.

FRANK ALEXANDER: I didn't see any changes in Dre because I didn't see Dre. It was obvious that him and Suge Knight had some disagreements and he was no longer in the picture.

S. LEIGH SAVIDGE: Dr. Dre's enmity for Tupac apparently exists to this day. One of the producers of the *Straight Outta Compton* film told me that there was a day on the set when someone started playing a Tupac song. Dre got visibly angry and demanded that the person turn it off.

ALLEN GORDON: Remember creative people are on their own time. They don't really meet deadlines. And, you know, they want control of their product. And you know Dre also had a drinking problem at times.

ANGELA WALLACE: Dre never did a day in jail. The only time when he was subjected to jail time was when Kenner represented him during a DUI.

MICHAEL HARRIS: Dre was petrified during his lock-up period. He never lived the life he was able to profit from.

SNOOP DOGG: I seen a change right after we finished *Murder is the Case* and we moved into Can-Am studios and started working on the *Dogg Food* album. I just seen that he wasn't as inspired. It was too many thugs and too many niggers up there that didn't have anything to do with nothin'.

JEFFREY JOLSON COLBURN: You can talk about it. You can report on the street. You weren't really supposed to live it. One has to say, "*You've taken this too far.*" I think Dre realized this.

MICHAEL HARRIS: Dre could be a vicious as Suge. It's not fair for Dre to be viewed as a victim. He knew what was going on.

DR DRE: (3) I just didn't like some of the things that were going on. There was nothing being done to stop it.

SNOOP DOGG: It was not a work atmosphere anymore. It became fun and games and the success had kicked in. We were stars and motherfuckers just loved being around us. And bringing bullshit around us. Dre wasn't for that.

ALLEN GORDON: His dream was shattered. And if you ruin the dream of somebody who's very creative, they're not gonna be creative.

NATE DOGG: Dre gave all he could to start that company. Dre gave his best beats.

JEWELL: Dre agreed to do some tracks for Tupac and go.

DOUG YOUNG: I remember I saw Suge at a Mary J. Blige concert and I had quit. He bum rushed this concert at Universal City, gang of Bloods with him. And I knew they didn't have no passes, no nothing. I just snapped back into my role at Death Row and made sure I got everybody backstage without them beatin' up this guard. I knew them guards was gonna get beat up. Suge saw me handle that and said, *"Man, it's like you ain't never missed a beat."*

JEWELL: Suge took over the company. It was no mystery to nobody. I don't think Dre wanted to be a *yes man* for somebody. He wanted his own situation again. So he bailed out.

SNOOP DOGG: Dre likes to work in an environment where he can create and everybody's on the creative atmosphere and it's not about what's goin' on in the 'hood, how many niggers you shot and how much shit you did. He didn't want that.

LAMONT BRUMFIELD: I predicted it. He was unhappy. He wasn't around. Couldn't get a beep from him. He just disappeared. Suge went on and used everybody else.

JEFF JOLSON COLBURN: He says, "Wait. *I want out of this world. I want to form Aftermath, where I'm not part of Death Row anymore. I want to live.*"

In Randall Sullivan's book Labyrinth, the author suggests that Suge showed up to Dre's house unannounced with eight other men and demanded master recordings that he supposedly kept there. The terms of his departure were worked out at a meeting at the Gladstone's restaurant on Pacific Coast Highway a few weeks later.

ALLEN GORDON: Even though he wouldn't admit it, there were physical altercations. In the Mob, if the Don slaps you, you take it. So he's in the Mob and whatever happened, it was enough for him to move on.

HANK CALDWELL: When Dre left, it hurt. Anytime you have this much synergy between two or more people and they make things happen, when you start breaking that up, things are never the same.

NATE DOGG: When Dre left Death Row Records, that was the biggest shock to me. Because I was real confused at how you start a label and then leave the label. I always figured if you had a problem with somebody on your label, you make them leave and you go on with what you're doing. I guess that was the way of learning that it wasn't his all his label.

SUGE KNIGHT: (5) Dre's departure wasn't a loss. I mean, if you've got a multi-million dollar company maybe worth a billion dollars or so and you own one hundred percent and don't have a partner and you don't have to give him nothing but his walking papers - that's great.

NATE DOGG: That was all Suge Knight. We had a meeting and he was in there talkin' all that, "*Dr. Dre left y'all. Dr Dre left y'all hangin. Dr Dre gay."* I came over here to be part of a family. Now we're not a family.

KEVIN POWELL: Dre made Death Row Records. This is absurd that he's going from one situation to another situation where he's feels like he's being undercompensated.

Though many of the details of Dre's departure are unknown, when Jimmy Iovine learned of Dre's unhappiness with Suge and Death Row, he set him up with his own label, Aftermath to be distributed by Interscope. Though press reports indicated that Dre had given up his share of equity in Death Row, there was a substantial financial settlement between Dre and Death Row for the equity Dre was giving up. Additionally, it is likely that the money he was owed from producing so much of Death Row's music was worth more than the value of his equity given the lack of controls in place with Death Row's business operations. As the remitter of the lion's share of the funds coming into Death Row, Interscope was in a position to make sure funds owed to Dre got paid to him.

ALLEN GORDON: To give up fifty percent of your label and move from a dangerous situation, which Death Row was becoming, was a smart move for him.

DOUG YOUNG: Of course Suge owed Dre money, but you ain't really got no money until the royalty checks come in. And, then a lot of times, if your manager is paying your rent, paying your telephone bill, giving your baby mama some money so she stays off your butt, buying you a car (all that has to be deducted from what you're owed). All of that stuff is money with interest on it.

MICHAEL HARRIS: A lot of people weren't being recognized for what they did. That's the way the system worked. Once I get the exposure, I can go somewhere else. Warren G figured that out.

ALLEN GORDON: What appears to be the destruction of Death Row is Dre's leaving. Dre is a very creative individual. He can take your idea and make it ten times better. So you've allowed an opening for a bunch of hacks to come in and try to patchwork something and make it sound as good. And it doesn't work.

Kevin Powell

For the next seven months we worked tirelessly. Tyler Hubby spent weeks organizing the mammoth amount of footage that we'd either collected or sourced and we cut and recut and recut again so that slowly but surely the film began to flow. Tyler had no background in hip hop, but he was clearly energized by the story. One of his many important contributions, was to tie Harry O's frequent communications with Suge on the phone that was dedicated to him with the beat down of the Stanley Brothers over their use of the same phone. A filmmaker himself, Tyler was very diversified in his skill sets. At one point, he flew to Las Vegas and shot point-of-view footage of the route that Suge and Tupac had traveled before Tupac was shot.

It was the final leg of a long, brutal journey - just a couple guys in a room with an assistant finally realizing the potential of what we had…with no distractions.

By the fall of 2000, we had a rough assembly that I felt was showable. But there were still holes. There were factual pieces to the story that no one we had footage on had addressed. We needed a journalist who audiences would see as credible, who knew that information. But given the wide scope of our story, finding a person with that knowledge would be a very difficult task. Jeff, Steve, and I batted around a few names like Chuck Phillips and Cheo Coker of *The Los Angeles Times*.

But the guy that seemed to make the most sense was a New Yorker named Kevin Powell.

Kevin Powell was known to audiences of his generation as probably the most controversial housemate on the first season of MTV's, *The Real World*. He'd been the lone Black guy in the house, and had used the show as a vehicle to present his views on race relations and what life was like coming from the inner city. After that, he had segued into hip hop journalism eventually landing at places like *Vibe Magazine* and *Rolling Stone*, where he'd written high profile stories on Eazy E, Death Row Records, and Tupac Shakur.

I contacted Kevin by e-mail and discussed the project and his possible participation and immediately I could tell there was a pronounced hesitancy on his part. He'd been interviewed and had appeared in a fair amount of hip hop oriented documentaries and was tired of it. Mentally and spiritually, hip hop, and a lot of the machinations associated with it, had burnt him out. He was in a new place. He'd become an activist and was touring prisons where he was being invited to lecture on Black history, among other subjects. He was also a published author with six books under his belt and was working on number seven. Additionally, he wasn't wild about the money I could offer and didn't want to be part of anything that wasn't *balanced*.

I offered to fly out to see him and show him what I had and he accepted.

Kevin lived in Brooklyn in a walk-down apartment right next to a subway stop. When I got there, he was in the middle of preparing for a lecture. I sat down in his living room and immediately got a lucky break when I noticed a DVD copy of *Dr. Martin Luther King Jr: A Historical Perspective* sitting on his bookshelf. When I told him I produced it, he said, *"Get the fuck outta here."* Then he picked up the DVD and saw my name on it. Things got better from there. We discussed the Death Row story, the holes, and the intent of the film and then we watched the rough cut. When it was done, I could tell he was energized. He was a silent for a minute and then said, *"There's a part of me that really hates the fact that you brought this to me. Because I really don't want to, but I have to be in this thing."*

Jeff Scheftel got me a cameraman and we shot the Kevin Powell interview in New York City the next day. Kevin was as good as it gets. We had finally plugged the holes.

We had a movie.

After the visit from the mysterious man from The Bottoms, semi-normalized communications with the Harrises resumed until Tyler and I got the film locked. Music producer Tommy Coster, whose father had been a guitarist for Carlos Santana and who had worked with both Dr Dre and Eminem, delivered a brilliant dramatic score. After a huge back and forth negotiation, we were granted the use of thirty seconds of *187 On an Undercover Cop* from the Deep Cover Soundtrack. It was no bargain. Between Dick Griffey's sync rights, and the publishing rights, which required Dr Dre's personal approval, the cost was equivalent to the entire budget of many documentaries: $50,000. It was the only music from either Ruthless or Death Row that we'd get. On the Ruthless front, Priority Records, at the insistence of Suge Knight, had said *no*, even though the music was actually controlled by other parties.

It was time to show people what we'd done.

Vegas

In September of 1996, Tupac and Suge were in Las Vegas attending a Mike Tyson fight. After the fight, while walking through the lobby of the MGM Grand Hotel, Suge and Tupac spotted and attacked Orlando Anderson, an alleged Crips gang member. The attack was later seen as retribution for an altercation that had happened months earlier between an associate of Tupac's and Anderson over a Death Row medallion. Later that night, on the a way to a party at 662, a nightclub owned by Suge Knight, Tupac was shot by an unidentified assailant while seated in the passenger side of Suge's car. Tupac Shakur died six days later in a Las Vegas hospital.

"That shit ain't funny cause if I die before June, I swear to God, I'm gonna hurt you all"

Tupac Shakur

FRANK ALEXANDER: On September 7th, we were just leaving the fight. Tupac, Mike Tyson, friends, were at the fight. Immediately, after coming from backstage, one of Suge's homeboys came up and whispered in Tupac's ear. Pac took off running. There was a gentleman standing with an MGM security guard by a pillar, as Tupac was approaching him. Now that I think about it, the guy was standing there waiting. And Pac ran up on him and a fight broke out.

S. LEIGH SAVIDGE: Multiple sources including the *Los Angeles Times*, and Greg Kading, the lead investigator in a multi-jurisdiction investigation into the incident, identified the man who whispered into Tupac's ear as Travon Lane. Lane was a member of the Blood street gang, a Death Row employee, and a close associate of Tupac Shakur. Orlando Anderson was a member of a rival street gang, the Southside Crips. According to Frank Alexander, Tupac was wearing a medallion that had the word *Euthanasia* inscribed on it. Euthanasia was to be the name

313

of Tupac's new record label.

FRANK ALEXANDER: Orlando Anderson and a couple of Suge's homeboys had gotten into a fight at the Lakewood Mall in California back in April of '96 over a Death Row (neck) chain, because there was a bounty on the Death Row chains. The same person that had gotten into an altercation with Orlando Anderson in the mall whispered into Tupac's ear, and he calls this a fight. They were beating Orlando Anderson up on the ground. As Tupac is fighting Anderson, the (medallion) breaks. When (Tupac) goes down to grab it, I go down and grab him.

S. LEIGH SAVIDGE: In his book *Murder Rap,* which is widely acknowledged as the definitive source on the murders of both Biggie Smalls and Tupac Shakur, author Greg Kading reveals that Orlando Anderson had come to the fight from Los Angeles with his uncle, a Southside Crip named Duane *Keffe D* Davis and two other associates in a rental car. The rental car was a white Cadillac.

FRANK ALEXANDER: (Afterwards) Tupac, Suge, and the rest of the entourage were pretty much bragging about what had happened. We get back to the Luxor Hotel, we go to Tupac's room, he changes clothes, comes back downstairs. We're all just standing around. All the women are coming out. Everybody's ready to go to 662 (Club) the after party, to party.

S. LEIGH SAVIDGE: According to *Murder Rap,* when Orlando Anderson told Keffe D about the kicking episode, they convened briefly in a restaurant and then got in the white Cadillac and set out to find Tupac and Suge.

FRANK ALEXANDER: So (Tupac) turns to me and says, "*No. Don't ride with us.*" He hands me the keys and says, "*You drive the little homies 'cause we're going to the club(662), we're gonna be partying and you're gonna drive them.*" So I say, "*Okay.*" Pac and Suge get into the BMW. We go back onto the Vegas strip, and

Suge's the lead car. I'm right behind him and then there's just cars all behind us. So we turn right off Las Vegas Boulevard onto Flamingo, to go down (toward) 662.

S. LEIGH SAVIDGE: According to the testimony that Keffe D gave Greg Kading, which appears in *Murder Rap*, it was just a coincidence that Anderson, Keffe D and the two others in the white Cadillac happened to see Suge and Tupac's car leading the rest of the entourage to 662. They were driving in the opposite direction. Next, the white Cadillac quickly made a U turn and positioned itself in the far right lane and began moving up fast on the passenger side of Suge's BMW.

FRANK ALEXANDER: As we approach the next stoplight, which is Koval and Flamingo, there's a car coming down the open lane that is next to myself and the BMW. As the car's approaching, I turned and looked to my right and I see the car and it's a white Cadillac. It had moved over and I would say closer to the BMW. Probably about that close. And an arm comes out and starts firing.

S. LEIGH SAVIDGE: In *Murder Rap*, it is revealed that Orlando Anderson shot across another passenger who was sitting in the back seat next to the window as the white Cadillac pulled up next to the passenger side of Suge's car where Tupac was sitting.

SUGE KNIGHT: (5) I heard the shots being fired. Pac stood up and tried to get in the back seat, to get out of the way of the shots. That's why he got shot in the hip, which hit one of the bones and traveled and hit his lung. I grabbed him and said, "*Get down!*" and covered him. When I pulled him down, that's when I got shot in my head. I said, "*Are you hit?*" He said, "*I'm hit.*" So I'm driving like a madman to the hospital. And he said, laughingly, jokingly, loudly, "*I need a hospital? You're the one that's been shot in the head.*"

FRANK ALEXANDER: Suge should have been able to look over

and see who was there.

S. LEIGH SAVIDGE: The white Cadillac was later retrieved. It had been abandoned in the California desert. According to *Murder Rap*, Keffe D, Orlando Anderson and a number of Southside Crips had had a long association with Sean Combs. *Murder Rap* provides pretty compelling evidence that Combs had close relations with both Keefe D and Orlando Anderson, put the plot in motion and may have used intermediaries to provide payment to Keffe D for the shooting. Kading's evidence is backed up by audio taped confessions which he allowed me to listen to.

KEVIN POWELL: I was flown to Vegas by *Rolling Stone* two days after Tupac got shot. So I was out here until he died. It was the strangest thing because I was cool with Tupac and the Shakur family. I was trying my best to get to the hospital. I was warned by people, *"Don't go to the hospital because there are Bloods everywhere and they don't drive red cars."*

Tupac Shakur died on September 13, 1996.

KEVIN POWELL: On the day they announced Tupac had died, myself, and another reporter are inside the lobby area of the hospital and Suge Knight drives up. We all move out of the way and he gets out with a cigar he's smoking. And there's such a nonchalance about the whole situation. It was surreal, like there was no emotional connection there. You have all these fans all around you, who never touched Tupac Shakur, who are crying. That will always stay with me about Suge - how there was no emotion.

FRANK ALEXANDER: Do I think Suge had anything to do with it? No. If you want to have someone killed, you're not going to be with them the day it's going down -- especially in a car.

PAUL PALLADINO: The first thing I started hearing were

rumors that Suge had had Tupac shot because Tupac was thinking of leaving the industry. And I started to laugh when I heard that. I said, "*You know the problem with this is, Why would someone like Suge have the shooter shoot across the car so that the bullets would hit him?*"

VIRGIL ROBERTS: There are so many different layers to this story and it's so tragic. Tupac Shakur is really one of those kids who's one of the great creative forces of our ages. He wasn't just a rapper. He was a kid who was really insightful.

GARY JACKSON: He's absolutely the James Dean of the Black community. The guy just didn't stop working. There're still, from what I understand, 120 songs that have not been released on him.

FRANK ALEXANDER: (Tupac) said, "*I didn't want to go to Vegas anyway.*" He almost didn't come. But that day was gonna happen. It was the destiny of his life. He had thought of not going. But he went. Because his destiny was to die the next day.

JEWELL   And it's a shame that another brother gets lost as a victim of his music.

S. LEIGH SAVIDGE: Rick James a.k.a. Pretty Ricky lived with Tupac during the recording of *All Eyez on Me* and was one of his preferred running buddies, because James was astute at dealing with the troublesome situations Tupac often got into. But when Tupac asked him to come to Vegas for the fight, James declined because Suge Knight had recently told him he did not want to release his music.

RICK JAMES a.k.a. PRETTY RICKY: I shoulda jumped in the car and went to Vegas with him to the fight. Jewell, Michel'le, everybody on Death Row, when Tupac got shot, that's all everybody said, "*If Rick James was there, that shit wouldna even happened.*"

FRANK ALEXANDER: I'm not going to say he was unhappy. But he wasn't as happy as he once was. He called an audit on Death Row. And I think that's when it all started coming to a head.

SUGE KNIGHT: (5) There's not going to be a day when I don't think of him. I put his name on my body -- on my arm.

DOUG YOUNG: Tupac's mom went on Prime Time (Live) and said Suge wouldn't take her calls and how (Tupac) was tryin' to get out of the contract. I guess his mother would know 'cause I tell my mother all my business. There's no reason for her to lie. I tried my best to stay on Suge's team. But the minute I heard he didn't take Tupac's mama calls -- I was cool. Her son is dead. And then everybody was talkin' about how Tupac's cars were leased in Death Row's name. The house was leased in Death Row's name. Suge was sayin' that Tupac was in debt to them and everybody knew that's ludicrous. He sold six million copies of *All Eyez on Me*. He sold four million of *Makaveli*. At a dollar a copy that's ten million dollars if he only made that. We know you made at least ten a copy. Let's round 'em off.

FRANK ALEXANDER: Pac's music related to him -- what he was going through. And when I listen to that today and I visualize and I start thinking about when we were together and when those songs were released, I start to miss him. I miss Tupac. I miss him a lot.

3 a.m. with Haitian Jack

In January 2001, we began showing *Welcome to Death Row* to select audiences and the reaction was very strong. Immediately, lawyers representing the Death Row label attempted to suppress further screenings by writing letters to theatre owners. By offering to indemnify them, the screenings moved forward.

Reactions to those screenings continued to be strong. After one showing BET reporter Stephanie Frederic approached me and just shook her head. *"You guys have major fucking cojones."* Some of the attendees were loyalists of Suge Knight. Several people who had attended the initial screenings also attended subsequent screenings just to see it again. Wyclef John attended one screening and afterward he bowed his head to me and said, *"Thank you."* Michael Harris told me that Wyclef came to visit him a week later.

The most important pre-release screening for press would take place in New York, a few weeks later. Our publicists, Damian and Edna Bruce, had advised us that we needed to hire major security and that it would be prudent to frisk most of the attendees. But as fate would have it, Dionne Warwick was the very first person to show up and when the security detail went to frisk her, there were audible gasps from the people behind her. As a result, the security detail stopped checking for firearms altogether. It was suggested to me later that a significant percentage of people who attended that night were probably armed.

Even so, the screening went well and afterward a number of journalists, including Nelson George suggested to me and others that the film was "a major work." Eames Yates, a former CNN reporter, and Mike Wallace's stepson signed on to present the film to HBO. Jean Riggins, a top executive at Universal Music, and one of the highest ranking women in the music business at the time told Edna Sims that she was blown away by the film but confided to her that her boss, Universal Music CEO Doug Morris, would hate it. Everywhere I looked there was a sea of smiles.

When I saw Kevin Powell, I went over and thanked him again for participating. But there was something wrong. I could sense an unease within him. Nearby, I noticed a light skinned, Black man that appeared to be watching him. I would find out soon enough that the man in question was Jacques Agnant, who was known on the streets of New York as *Haitian Jack*.

If Haitian Jack didn't exist, it would be left to a Hollywood screenwriter to dream him up. Reportedly the son of high level government operatives in the Dominican Republic and a blood relative of Wyclef John, Agnant immigrated to Brooklyn in his early life and quickly gained status as a prominent club promoter. In that capacity, he created ties with any number of gangsters throughout New York City and Brooklyn. His club connections and gangster ties made him a gate keeper in terms of what music got played at area clubs. He became a shot caller in New York music circles, with the power to break or suppress new acts and had developed the reputation as a fearsome adversary for anyone who might decide to cross him. Mike Tyson was known to be scared to death of him, as were people like Puffy Combs who reportedly paid him thousands of dollars a month just to keep the peace with him. Many people, including detective William Courtney, who investigated the shooting and robbery of Tupac Shakur at Quad studios, have suggested that Haitian Jack also had another occupation: government informant.

Tupac Shakur and Haitian Jack had been friends until the aftermath of the incident at the Parker Meridian Hotel, which led to Tupac's rape conviction. Haitian Jack was in the hotel room when the incident occurred, but was not charged with a crime and Tupac felt that he'd taken the fall when Haitian Jack was the one who had set the incident in motion. The shooting incident at Quad Studios had happened shortly after Tupac had made his feelings about Haitian Jack known to a reporter for the New York Post. After the attack, Tupac extrapolated from this event that he'd been set up by both Haitian Jack and Biggie Smalls, who had been recording at Quad Studios on the evening the shooting occurred. This event would factor heavily into the East Coast / West Coast War that would ensue and lead Tupac to call out Haitian Jack by name in subsequent recordings including a track called *Against All Odds* from his Makaveli album.

After the screening, Steve Housden, myself, and Edna and Damian had gone to a bar in midtown Manhattan and gotten stupid drunk, while discussing our next moves with the film. When I returned to my hotel, there were several messages from Kevin Powell, each more frantic than the one before it. He was positively terrified. *"You've got to call Haitian Jack and tell him you're cutting that Makavelli line. You've gotta fix this situation. I'm fucking begging you. This guy is crazy."*

I called Kevin right away. After taking in what he had to say, it forced me to replay the tape in my mind of his struggle in making the decision to talk to me in the first place. This is why he had moved away from hip hop journalism and reinvented himself as a lecturer. *Because of this kind of shit.*

In the cut of *Welcome to Death Row* which had screened that evening, when I asked Kevin Powell who shot Tupac at Quad Studios, he suggested that the incident was a warning to Tupac. *"Who was it coming from? Listen to the Makaveli album."* He hadn't mentioned Haitian Jack by name. But the reference would lead anyone hearing it to him.

I hung up with Kevin and looked at the clock. It was 3 am. I called Lydia Harris' cell phone. When she picked up, I told her that she needed to get me in touch with Haitian Jack right away. Without a trace of irony she said, *"He's right here,"* and handed her phone to him. It was a short conversation and Haitian Jack got right to the point. *"I don't need that shit. That doesn't help me."* I told him the line was out -- that it wasn't needed to tell the story. Kevin's safety was far more important. He said thanks and hung up.

The irony in all of this is that according to police investigator and *Murder Rap* author Greg Kading, who met with me shortly before this book's publication, forensic evidence obtained by the New York Police department in their investigation of the Quad Studios shooting suggested that some and likely almost all of Tupac's gunshot wounds were created by his own gun. The forensic evidence suggested that the positioning of some of Tupac's bullet wounds were such that they only could have been created by the accidental discharge of the gun he was carrying in his waistband. Kading further suggested that after his surgery, Tupac had gone to great lengths to conceal this fact from the public -- fearful that this disclosure would paint him as a *drama geek* and tarnish his reputation as a rapper with street credibility. Kading told me that Tupac found two doctors who were willing to sign an affidavit attesting to the fact that he was shot by someone other than himself.

But none of what Kading told me addressed the issue of the wound to Tupac's head. If that wound had come from a bullet, it had to have come from the gun of one of his assailants. Tupac was an individual of many talents. But he couldn't have shot upwards and downwards at the same time.

I called Kevin Powell and the issue settled down.

Empire Undone

After the death of Tupac Shakur, Death Row Records quickly went into a downward spiral. Suge was convicted of a parole violation connected with the kicking incident at the MGM Grand and was sentenced to several years in prison. In 1997, the federal government opened an investigation into Death Row, alleging among others things, that the label had engaged in money laundering and fraud. Of particular interest to the government was the extent to which drug money had funded the label. During Suge's incarceration, a mass exodus of the remaining artists took place.

JEFFREY JOLSON COLBURN: It was a company that celebrated violence. You had at least one of their members, one of their biggest artists, die by violence. This was not the record business that most people were used to. You've got people getting shot. You've got people going to jail. This was not pleasant record business with the occasional o.d. This was people firing on one another. And nobody quite understood it unless you were from Compton.

DOUG YOUNG: If you had any street sense, knowledge about yourself, you knew that company was gonna come crashing down face first.

MICHAEL HARRIS: Death Row went as far as it could go with the leadership that it had.

KEVIN POWELL: This is the classic tale of a Black boy coming out of the inner city, out of the ghetto and wanting to empower himself. And power can be very corrupting.

LYDIA HARRIS: What took over was the greed, the power, and the money.

LAMONT BRUMFIELD: Kurupt filed for bankruptcy in '96 or

'97. He filed for bankruptcy because he wasn't getting any money from Death Row.

NATE DOGG: People let the fame go to their heads and the egos took over and the next thing you knew, there wasn't nowhere to go but down.

PAUL PALLADINO: I don't know if *vendetta* is the right word. But it wouldn't surprise me that because of the high profile of Suge Knight, and the things that surrounded him -- would they like to see him in jail? Yes.

NATE DOGG: God decided to pull out his belt. It was time for Death Row Records to take a whipping.

S. LEIGH SAVIDGE: Court TV described Suge Knight's defense team in the trial surrounding the MGM kicking incident as *The Dream Team*. In addition to Kenner, the criminal defense team included Don Re, and Las Vegas attorney, David Chesnoff. As part of Suge's defense, Kenner introduced the notion that Suge had tried to break up the fight and had *"slipped toward the pile."*

DAVID KENNER (during the trial): (19) The question now is do we deal with Mr. Knight in the manner of a political prisoner? Or, do we deal with him as a person with enormous resources to do enormous good for the community?

DISTRICT ATTORNEY WILLIAM HODGMAN (during the trial): (19) I note that in his criminal career, the defendant has received six particular grants of probation. And your honor, I ask you, how many bites at the probation apple does this defendant get?

JEWELL: That man made a choice to ignore his conscience. It was only him that could reconcile that and change it. We can't. We can just move on, give our contribution to the music industry and hope that nothing like this ever happens again.

JUDGE L. STEPHEN CZULEGER (during the trial): (19) I think he was an active participant in this assault and I do find a violation of probation. Also, keep in mind, I think the way he left the scene evidenced a consciousness of guilt. I think he had been involved in an assault and the way he left the scene causes me to believe that he knew exactly what he was doing and what he was involved in. Your prior record indicates one of violence. You are a danger to the community. Your prior performance on probation was not satisfactory. You committed other crimes while you were on probation. You're not a suitable candidate for probation, in other words. And so therefore, probation is denied.

DAVID KENNER: (19) I don't think anybody here has a question that if we were dealing with anyone other than Mr. Knight, that what we saw on that videotape, first of all, would not be sufficient to constitute a probation violation and secondly, and most importantly, even if somebody thought it was, it's certainly not the kind of violation and the kind of activity that warrants a nine-year sentence.

During sentencing, Judge Stephen Czuleger had this to say: "Mr. Knight, you blew it. You have a need to explain away your problems -- to not take responsibility for your actions. I am sentencing you to nine years."

MICHAEL HARRIS: He was a good kid gone bad. He became a bully. He starts feeling his oats -- 325 pounds and it starts to feel good to him.

JAY KING: How can Suge be in jail? How can one of the most powerful people in the record business, not just *Black* people, but one of the most important *people*, in the record business be in jail for something as silly as stopping a fight or even, kicking somebody?

PAUL PALLADINO: The interesting thing about it was that the focus didn't become the murder of Tupac, but rather how can the government incarcerate Suge as a result of the kicking episode that preceded the Tupac shooting?

DAVID KENNER: (19) In my opinion, this is a miscarriage of justice. The decision is a reaction to the overall animosity that exists for Mr. Knight's label -- Death Row Records.

DOUG YOUNG: Suge, I would imagine in the minds of White, corporate America, record business, he had to be stopped. He had to be stopped.

MICHAEL HARRIS: It really troubled me to see him turn into a monster. I wanted young people to understand they didn't have to sell dope no more. They could sell music.

WILLIE MOSS: The executives at the top were too scared to come to this record company and lean on them. They had to figure out a way to get rid of Suge. That's why Suge is sittin' where he's sittin' right now with a ridiculous sentence. But what goes around comes, comes around. And the major corporations (were saying) we can't work with (him). We've gotta slide 'em out of the picture.

JEFFREY JOLSON COLBURN: I can't say it didn't bother Interscope. But it surprised them when people started dying. People were getting killed. If there isn't a rule that says, "*Don't kill off your artists*" there should be.

GEORGE PRYCE: Suge Knight was and is Death Row. And for me, without Suge Knight, there is no Death Row.

JEFFREY JOLSON COLBURN: Even when he went to jail, with a $150 million a year coming in, they should have been able to build an organization that would survive and still be breeding great young rap acts on the West Coast. This whole thing let the balance of power shift to the East Coast.

GEORGE PRYCE: Almost immediately, after (Suge's) departure, it changed for me. The people that had been chosen to carry on his work, I didn't feel that their actions were benefiting the company. I no longer could be a part of it.

PAUL PALLADINO: If Suge has grasped all that has happened to him, I think that he could come out again and start up Death Row Records and start a record company that would be more viable than ever.

ALONZO WILLIAMS: They'll be legends no matter what happens. If they'd been allowed to go on, there's no telling what influence they could have had on the inner city youth of America. When you have guys that have the ears, not only of Black America, but White America also, you can call some shots. Anybody that can sell four million records, five million records, anybody that can sell out concerts around the world - whatever they put their names and faces on will sell. Whatever they endorse will be backed up one hundred percent.

JEFFREY JOLSON COLBURN: The Death Row Records story was one of the great stories I had the opportunity to cover while being a daily music journalist. It told the tale of three major record labels, almost brought one of them down, rattled another to its core and set the framework for a whole new way of doing business in the music business. This story wasn't just about a bunch of guys from Compton. It was a story that affected the whole music business, and ultimately, the business world.

MICHAEL HARRIS: Death Row was able to generate $500,000,000 and move Interscope into a position of prominence in the entertainment industry. It gave Master P and Puffy their reason for being. And it all started with three guys in an attorney room.

JEWELL: I had nothing before Death Row. I helped nurture and build that company. So it's part of my life.

MASTER P: I learned from their mistakes. I think God blessed me because I think I probably would have made the same mistakes.

KEVIN POWELL: It's about empowerment, it's about greed, it's about ego, it's about sex, it's about violence, it's about fame, it's about failure. I mean, you don't get any more American than that.

SAM GIDEON ANSON: In some ways you hate to talk about it, simply as a cautionary tale that is full of hubris. Suge Knight had tremendous success in his grasp and for whatever reason, let it slip away.

JEFFREY JOLSON COLBURN: (Death Row Records) created a new genre in music, and it became the most successful rap label the country's ever seen and perhaps ever will.

VIRGIL ROBERTS: The legacy that Death Row Records has left is both positive and negative. I think the positive legacy is that, if you have talent and you're prepared to work, you can create a business and be successful. People always say, "*You remember how ole' Suge started his company from nothing? We can do that!*" We're going to hear this music forever. It's going to forever mark an era in American culture and American history.

JAY KING: This urban scene, this rap music business, started back in the 20s and 30s. As Black folk, this whole element was always here. We just didn't have control of it. We are finally at a stage in this business where we have control over what's happening to us culturally and for us culturally.

NATE DOGG: I think the legacy of Death Row Records would be that they were known for great music -- legendary songs that people always remember. The negative is that they'll always be known for somebody that God gave the world to and they decided to give it back.

VIRGIL ROBERTS: It's an example of the building of a real empire and also a human tragedy, because there was a tremendous potential for doing good and creating a very large enterprise, owned and directed by an African-American, based upon African American culture. It always pains me to watch what has been the demise of Death Row, because I felt I was there at the birth.

SNOOP DOGG: My first album, I was happy. I was fresh out of the hood working with Dr. Dre. The second album, *The Doggfather*, I had a murder case, I had a son, I had no money. Tupac had been shot and killed. Death Row was going downhill. Dre wasn't there. DOC wasn't there. RBX wasn't there. It told you where Suge Knight was going to end up.

ALONZO WILLIAMS: As an old school hip hop cat, I would like to see hip hop get off of this gang stupidity. I mean you can only wear so many Rolexes. You can only drive so many Lexuses.

HANK CALDWELL: The best thing about my experience with Death Row was the music. I had a chance to be on the set when Dr. Dre was creating, watching this music and it was a second education for me. I'm really beholden to the whole experience that I had at Death Row. I could have done it forever, because it was like a rejuvenation as far as my career was concerned, and it enabled me to understand what these kids are doing creatively. Believe me, that's worth a million itself.

GEORGE PRYCE: My experiences at Death Row afforded me something I had very little knowledge of. I didn't get bored. It was a stressful job, long hours, 24 / 7 as they say. We were always at (Suge's) beck and call. I don't care if it was four in the morning. Sometimes I'd have to get up and go to Compton to work out something. But it was something I enjoyed because I believed in it.

DICK GRIFFEY: Now, the sad part about this whole thing is that Jimmy Iovine and Ted Fields sold Interscope for four hundred million dollars. I still have the article in the Wall Street Journal that says *Warner Ups Its Stakes in Rap Music.* So what they were buying was Death Row. They paid four hundred million for it. So Jimmy Iovine and Ted Fields got four hundred million, Tupac's dead, and Suge's in jail. And Dick Griffey had to sue to get his pennies.

S. LEIGH SAVIDGE: There is no question that Interscope did many things to enable the success of Death Row Records, both financially, especially in the case of funds lent to secure the release of Tupac and in the marketing guidance and a lot of behind the scenes strategy they provided. But this was not information that we could present because unfortunately, no one from Interscope would speak to us.

JAY KING: Who's in jail? Michael Harris. Suge Knight. Where's the money? Who controls the money? What happened to the power all these Black folks controlled?

SAM GIDEON ANSON: I spent quite a bit of time looking into David Kenner and his role in the rise and fall of Death Row. And when you look at some of the problems around Death Row -- with the federal investigation, they're looking into Suge's dealings in Las Vegas. David had a large role in that. They're looking into his dealings with Michael Harris. David had a large role in that. Death Row was a named party in scores of lawsuits over its financial management and mis-management. David had the largest role in that. I think you have to ask yourself, "*Was David really looking out for Suge's best interests all this time?*"

MICHAEL HARRIS: Kenner knew that Suge would eventually be incarcerated -- and I was incarcerated -- which would eventually put him in control.

RICK JAMES a.k.a. PRETTY RICKY: The FBI bothered me cause they knew I used to stay with (Suge). They arrested me tellin' me that they had drug charges on me. They questioned me about Tupac's murder and about Suge hanging people out of windows and making people drink piss and stuff like that. I had to go to trial and fight the case and the jury seen how they set me up. So I got acquitted of all charges.

PAUL PALLADINO: Ever since the federal investigation was thrown out there, basically everybody was at a loss, because the first thing that people started hearing was the money laundering charge. And from what I saw, it was hard to conceive of money laundering in a company that was rolling in money coming in from legitimate sources. What was the need to launder money?

MICHAEL HARRIS: At no point was my money considered illegal. There was no evidence to prove that I ever participated in money laundering.

S. LEIGH SAVIDGE: Michael told me that he was contacted by an FBI investigator named Wayne McMullen during the Federal Investigation into Death Row. He told me he declined to give him information that would help him with his investigation.

MICHAEL HARRIS: He was doing his job. But he realized I was not going to assist the government in their duties. What happened between me and Suge was between me and Suge.

PAUL PALLADINO: Michael has an attempted murder charge over his head and drug case over his head. If the government offered Michael an opportunity to get out of jail to testify against David Kenner or Suge Knight or Andre Young, there's a good chance Michael would take it.

S. LEIGH SAVIDGE: The rumors that Michael was co-operating

with the government would continue to be fomented by Suge and Death Row for some time -- that he'd become a snitch -- which in the eyes of both the Mafia and in inner city street culture, is the worst thing you could ever be.

MICHAEL HARRIS: They felt I was taking that position and in their mind they felt that if they could destroy my name in the street, that that would somehow shut me down.

S. LEIGH SAVIDGE: In our meeting with police investigator and *Murder Rap* author, Greg Kading, he indicated that Michael had spoken to Federal authorities about Death Row's formulation. Later, Michael would tell me that it was one thing to speak to them and quite another to give them any information that would actually assist them. When he'd spoken Wayne McMullen, Michael said he told him "*You gotta talk to Kenner. He can give you all the details.*" When that message got back to Kenner, Kenner and Suge went into battle mode. In Michael's words "*That's when they tried to put a snitch jacket on me.*" Whatever information Harris chose to disclose didn't result in an indictment of Death Row or a lessening of his back to back sentences. Though Michael had made a critical contribution to seed Death Row, a number of other investors had put early-stage funds in as well. In the case of Michael's funds, since they were made in cash and flushed through Kenner, their origin was likely impossible to trace. The government would later drop its investigation into Death Row's activities.

MICHAEL HARRIS: I don't work for the government. I only work for myself, my family and my friends. I would stay in prison before I would live as a rat in society.

LYDIA HARRIS: But David knows Michael is not an informant. He knows Michael inside and out.

PAUL PALLADINO: That's easy for (Lydia) to say. Anybody in the criminal arena knows that snitches trade dollars for days.

LYDIA HARRIS: (Kenner) turned on me and Michael with the Death Row situation. Michael introduced him to Suge Knight. He turned on us. I thought that David was a friend. We trusted David. So when you say Michael is a snitch…

PAUL PALLADINO: I'm not saying Michael's a snitch. I'm saying that is something that they have to anticipate that could happen.

MICHAEL HARRIS: I could have shut down Death Row. But that's not my nature. I wanted it to reach its full potential.

JAY KING: You got this attorney, this guy who's pretty brilliant. So, you know, this isn't a regular attorney. He's got pull somewhere. Because he's got somebody from the D.A.'s office involved in this thing and you're saying to yourself, *"What kind of situation did he set Suge up in?"* I mean, Dave Kenner was a big man in our business. On all levels. And you have to ask yourself, *"Did the money get to him? Did the power get to him?"* You gotta ask yourself, is Suge sitting in jail saying, *"Is this guy really on my side?*

JEFFREY JOLSON COLBURN: Kenner had to answer to Suge before he did anything. So, if you're like Suge and you've made all the decisions and you don't have a strong lieutenant to make them in your absence, the company will fail. When the boss makes himself the sole decision maker, this is a problem. Even when they go on vacation, it becomes a problem. Not to mention a long jail stint.

ALLEN GORDON: The only people that got rich were David Kenner, Suge Knight, Jimmy Iovine, Ted Field, the jewelers, American Express, the limo companies, the champagne companies, the cigarette companies, plus anybody who was selling them weed. Dre had money. But he didn't have a warehouse full of antique cars and new Lamborghinis. For Suge to have that, something's wrong. Snoop was broke until he started getting money from Master P to appear on a few tracks. A couple of artists in the industry who knew what was going on purposely asked Snoop to record a track -- even though they knew it couldn't be released, just to give him some money. But until his signing with No Limit Records, he was flat broke. And the only thing he had was his house and a couple of cars. I shouldn't say flat broke -- he had 20 – 30,000 dollars, but for a guy that generated like thirty million dollars in sales, that's bananas.

LAMONT BRUMFIELD: We started right back here in this garage, from dirt and we come up with hit songs -- so it all comes from right here. Why does somebody else reap the majority of the benefits? We out here dodging bullets for this.

RICK JAMES a.k.a. PRETTY RICKY: When we start taking the money we make in the streets - how we live is in hustling bottles, selling bottle tops, selling a bag of weed on the corner. How we do it. We do it and start realizing, *"You know what? Let me find something legal to do."* That's when it becomes a problem. They don't want us legal. They feel like you're selling dope, you ain't never gonna get rich unless you're the man sitting next to the goddamn *Man*. It would be hard to dig up and find who did what with what kind of legal money. But they wouldn't want to do that. If they were to take Death Row from Suge Knight -- What about Atlantic Group? What about Interscope Records? They made more money off of Death Row than Death Row did. If Death Row is founded by drug money, and Death Row made money at Interscope, Atlantic Group made money, then you take everybody's record company. You don't just take the Black man's.

HANK CALDWELL: I would find it very interesting if somewhere in doing something like this and really getting the story of Death Row, if, in fact you can interview Jimmy Iovine and Ted Field. Because normally, as is the case in our society, these are the guys that ultimately made a fortune off Death Row. And they were never really tagged with any of the stigmas that were put on Death Row. I'd like to have someone direct very pertinent questions to them about what did they know, what was going on, what they were willing to accept and not accept.

RICK JAMES a.k.a. PRETTY RICKY: I don't use drugs. I don't sell drugs. I don't gang bang. I went to college -- took four years of marine biology. My first kid was born in '89. I got a record company. My record company ain't blowed up. But I can stand on the street corner and sell 100 tapes for 10 dollars apiece and make a 1,000 dollars. All I gotta do is pay my taxes.

MICHAEL HARRIS: When I think about the things that I've missed the most or things that I would like to do, what comes to mind most of the time, is that your hands are tied. You're not able to take care of your children or your mother from the vultures and vipers out there. People that used to be your friends, play off your incarceration and try to use it to their advantage. It's these things that haunt you. I consider myself a businessman. I have seen everything in life from the ghetto to Beverly Hills. These walls do not stop me and do not dim my dream. People do.

Aftermath

After screenings in Los Angeles, San Francisco and New York and several film festival appearances, *Welcome to Death Row* was released into the home entertainment market two weeks after the 9/11 attacks on September 25, 2001. Prior to the film's release, a lawyer representing Death Row Records named Jeff Lowy, wrote letters to nearly every important retailer in the home entertainment space looking to suppress it. But letters of indemnity from Xenon allowed the release to go forward.

By any normal standard, the film would have been considered both a critical and financial success. But financially, the die had been cast a long time ago. All in, Xenon had laid out $2 million dollars to get the film made and marketed, which had maxed out our credit lines and wiped out our cash reserves. I did take solace in the fact that the film appeared to connect with many people on an emotional level. Snoop Dogg's representatives called to say that Snoop had watched the film seven times consecutively.

These days *Welcome to Death Row* plays regularly on U.S. cable television, is widely available in the digital sphere and has its place on many lists as one of the top documentaries ever made chronicling the hip hop music movement in America.

There would be even more contention with Michael and Lydia when it became apparent that *Welcome to Death Row* would never turn a profit sufficient to produce additional royalties to them. We had achieved fairly significant sales in the home entertainment market. But many important broadcasters including HBO, MTV, and BET refused to show the film. Only limited information came my way as to why. But it was clear that the subject matter in the film was politically toxic for all of them.

For example, both BET and MTV were dependent on Interscope Records for video content for their programming at that time. In one meeting, an MTV executive asked me point blank if I was willing to cut the material relating to Interscope and Jimmy Iovine. When I told him that I didn't know how the film would make any sense if we did, the meeting ended. With HBO, the film reportedly went all the way to Jeff Bewkes, who, at the time was the head of HBO and is now the CEO of Time Warner. It probably made sense that a unit of Time Warner did not want to broadcast a film that featured C. Delores Tucker, Michael Fuchs, and one of the most embarrassing hours in the company's corporate history. Bewkes's comment as filtered back through intermediaries was *"We survived this. Our kids are safe. We don't need this."*

When the Harrises got their first royalty statement, they immediately called for an audit. When their auditor, Anthony Padilla, found that Xenon's numbers were accurate, Michael reacted by accusing me of assaulting his wife. In doing so, he was trading on the same kind of misinformation that had run rampant at Death Row Records and had contributed to its downfall. For me to assault Lydia Harris was as an absurd a concept as Simone Green bad-mouthing a car she'd been given by Suge Knight. It represented the height of desperation for Lydia. Michael, apparently needing to show loyalty to his wife, had gone crazy on me. The Santa Monica Police Department called to advise me that Lydia had filed assault charges against me. This gave me little choice but to file for yet another restraining order against Lydia and keep the Santa Monica Police Department apprised of any contact she had with me or had initiated.

Later, Lydia Harris would sue Xenon for fraud. I burned up another $50k in a needless back and forth process with a lawyer who had taken their case on a contingency basis. Several months later, in a deal brokered by Mark Friedman, Xenon would settle with Lydia, once and for all, for an amount less than what it would have cost to prove at a trial that her claims were baseless.

Michael and Lydia Harris continued their pursuit of lost profits from their interest in Death Row Records and years later, in the face of a legally non-responsive Suge Knight, the Harrises' lawyers eventually secured a $107 million judgment against the company. Shortly thereafter, in a move that would shock everyone close to the settlement proceedings, Suge Knight contacted Lydia and persuaded her to accept $1,000,000 in full settlement of the Harrises' claim. This was done against the will of Michael Harris and set the stage for divorce proceedings and acrimony between the two. The settlement also came as a surprise to many of the parties that comprised the Harrises' legal team, some of whom were left holding a largely empty financial bag. Mark Friedman, who had lent Lydia Harris nearly $600,000, up to and through the legal proceedings, would lose his house to foreclosure.

In earlier times, Lydia had fought hard to execute business moves with Michael's direction using her own self-styled, by-any-means-necessary approach. But what couldn't be separated from the story was that Michael had brought her to a table she would have never gotten near otherwise. She'd been an obscure, would-be singer who Michael had plucked out of Houston and brought into Los Angeles-based entertainment circles that he had developed. Lydia had married Michael after he went to prison and in the process had availed herself of his remaining money and connections, meeting the likes of Dr. Dre, Suge Knight, Snoop and executives at Interscope. Michael had been the raison d'etre for her whole identity, allowing her to take on the persona of a label executive, and live that life without having to hustle in the same ways that are common in the music business. Then, when she was persuaded by Suge Knight that he was presenting her with the last dollar that would ever come from the Death Row money train, she grabbed what she felt she could and ran.

One of the few people *not* surprised by this outcome was me.

As fatigued as I was of the Death Row Records story at that point in time, I couldn't help but feel badly about what had happened to the Harrises, especially this eleventh-hour decision and the resulting betrayal. Even though he'd done a dance on my head for several years, there was a part of me that felt very bad for Michael Ray Harris. I looked at the string of betrayals in his life; beginning with James Lester, who'd stolen from him and then testified against him, to David Kenner, his would-be savior on his attempted murder appeal who would turn his back on him and might have tried to poison him, to Suge Knight who would take his money and later tell people that Michael was a nobody and a snitch and finally, Lydia, who, on the threshold of getting some real money for all their efforts with Death Row, would sell him out for a million bucks.

I felt bad for him. I really did.

Sometimes, in our darkest hours, we grow to understand the deepest truths about the society we live in. I've been lucky. For most of my life, I've had good people around me. I've had my share of unpleasant exchanges in the business world. But betrayals on the order of what Michael Harris had experienced were beyond my comprehension. Over the next 14 years, I thought of Michael often. My time with him had challenged me in ways I'd never imagined.

Part of my process in salvaging something from the *Welcome to Death Row* project was to write a screenplay which, after many later revisions, became the film, *Straight Outta Compton*.

Jerry Heller was a big fan of *Welcome to Death Row* and a meeting with Jerry, orchestrated by Alonzo Williams, was arranged. Jerry liked the fact that I was in the business of distributing Black audience content and invited me to speak at a class he was teaching at UCLA. Eventually, Jerry would generously agree to lend me many hours of his time, disclosing how he came to be partners with Eazy E, revealing many of the key details and story beats that would make it into *Straight Outta Compton*. His book,

Ruthless, released years later in 2006, would contain some of the same information.

I had two meetings with Suge Knight, one in a lawyer's office and another at the Four Seasons in Beverly Hills. Surprisingly, he made no mention of the Herculean effort he'd made to flummox *Welcome to Death Row*'s creation and release. In the second meeting, there was even a quasi-serious attempt to play nice. But as I suspected, Suge was a jellyfish. Both meetings had a theatre-of-the-bizarre quality to them and only served to underscore why he has become such a difficult person to work with or understand. What really came across to me was that Suge was not prepared to reconcile his role or complicity in many of the things that had happened to him.

I met with other players in the story as well including DJ Yella. Eventually, after 20 or so drafts, the script, co-written with Alan Wenkus, got to Eazy E's widow, Tomica Woods-Wright. My emissary to Tomica was Madeleine Smith, the ex-wife of Audio Achievement's owner Donovan Smith, who had handled Ruthless-related publishing issues for Tomica for many years and had once run N.W.A.'s fan club.

A few weeks later, while recovering from knee surgery, my cell phone rang from a number I didn't recognize. When I answered it, a voice on the other line said, *"This is Tomica Wright. I don't know who you are or where you came from. But you captured Eazy. So this must be God's will."*

It was one of those moments in life that you never forget.

Tomica and I had a few discussions which led to a lengthy eight-hour, one-on-one meeting where she would shed light on information from Eazy E's life that I'd never previously had access to. Once she got into the zone of what she wanted to say, there was no stopping her. It appeared to me that for Tomica, speaking about all this was a catharsis of sorts. There were facts to get straight. But this was also an unburdening of sorts. Even though it had been over a decade since Eazy's passing, the scars from her many battles relating to both her relationship with Eazy E and its aftermath and the complexities of taking over Ruthless Records in the wake of his death were clearly still alive.

Next, Alan Wenkus and I wrote yet another draft which Tomica agreed to put her music publishing rights to. Xenon and her lawyers at Brittenham and Branca then executed what's known as a "shopping agreement" where Tomica pledged allegiance to the Xenon-owned script but still made it incumbent upon the studio to work out a separate rights agreement with her.

But her endorsement of the script was all I needed. As soon as *Straight Outta Compton* went out on an auction basis to the major Hollywood studios, New Line Cinema made a pre-emptive bid to buy it before the end of the first day.

Laying the initial track for *Straight Outta Compton* pretty much ended my role in the film. Alan Wenkus and I did two more drafts for New Line, which they referred to internally as *The Tomica drafts* and then we were told that the studio would take it from there. Later, Ice Cube and Dr. Dre signed on as producers with F. Gary Gray directing and other writers, including Andrea Berloff and later, Jonathan Herman, were brought in. Though the final shooting script would contain many of the key story beats from our drafts, the story would morph from a story about Eazy E and his relationship with Jerry Heller to a more N.W.A. focused story which gave equal weight to the characters of Eazy, Dr. Dre and Ice Cube. It would take many years and the persuasive leadership of Donna Langley at Universal Pictures before all the issues -- budget, script, rights and otherwise -- could be resolved so that the film could go into production.

The Legend of Harry O

I began writing this book around the time *Straight Outta Compton* had completed production in October of 2014 and as the film headed for theatres nationwide, I began to think, once again, about Harry O. I started to ask around. Mark Friedman put me in touch with Alvin Brown, who was Michael's closest associate. I listened to a podcast hosted by Jay King which featured Michael. He sounded good. I liked what I heard. I hadn't spoken to him in nearly a decade and a half and wasn't sure it made sense to resume any kind of communication with him. But the word came back to me that Michael wanted to speak to me. He wanted to clear the air on a few things.

Everybody said the same thing: *"You should talk to him. You'll recognize him. But you won't."*

When we finally reconnected on the phone, what came through immediately was that Michael's unbridled ambition had been tempered only by the fact that he was a mature man who was now focused on utilizing the time he had left in the best way possible. He told me, *"The doctors here say I have the blood of a twenty-five year old."* His message to me came out full-stop: *I am healthy and I have not been diminished by what has happened to me. I will be a warrior until the day I die.*

When I told him about my involvement in *Straight Outta Compton*, he was stunned. It took him several minutes to digest the fact that part of the work we'd done together would soon capture the imagination of the world. And it was in the face of this disclosure that I saw that the legendary Harry O had moved to a different mental station. There was no *"where's my cut"* or *"you owe me, mutherfucker"* from a decade and a half ago. He had something bigger in mind and it didn't involve picking my pocket.

"I want you to come see me. I need to talk to you."

The third act in the life of Michael Harris had begun during the last leg of his attempted murder charge when he'd been moved to San Quentin State Prison in northern California. He'd become the editor of the prison newspaper, *The San Quentin News*, and had attracted the attention of several important people in the Silicon Valley who had begun working with him to establish foundations to assist the transition of inner city kids into meaningful jobs in America and to assist soon-to-be-released prisoners in their transition to become productive members of American society. His work and connectivity with these people had led him to Van Jones, a graduate of Yale Law School and President Obama's former Green Czar, who was now a journalist for CNN.

Cynics will say, *"Okay, I've heard this story before. A leopard doesn't change his spots. Remember what happened in the 80s with Norman Mailer and Jack Henry Abbott?"*

The most interesting thing about Michael is that he has always been a fugitive from the law of averages. In life it's often so easy for people to extrapolate that this is this and that equals that. Assessing nuance requires patience that many people don't have the time or capacity for. As a crack dealer Michael had built a fearsome reputation for himself. But unlike Suge Knight, Michael's gangster image was bigger than the reality. He cultivated it and used it. But he was loathe to go too far with it. He was too smart for that. He'd never joined a gang. In the drug game, he learned to move to virgin territory rather fight for turf, which is where most of the problems happened. At his core, Michael was an ambitious businessman who knew how to deal with people from all walks of life. With me, he'd played a lot of cards. But race wasn't one of them. This is part of why I risked my life to go into business with him. Even if his point of view didn't jibe with mine, Michael was always about business. And this is why I felt I had to determine for myself what was really inside his head.

In 2012, Michael achieved an early parole after serving 25 years of his 28-year sentence for attempted murder.

The parole hearing had contained an especially dramatic event. James Lester, the man whose testimony in 1987 had sealed Michael's fate on the attempted murder charge had shown up of his own volition and presented the parole board with a statement that said that Michael had not been the triggerman in his shooting. Then Lester fell to his knees, began sobbing and begged the parole board to commute Michael's sentence, "*He shouldn't be in here,*" He kept repeating, "*He didn't do it. He didn't do it.*"

I asked Michael to send me any documents he had that pertained to his parole hearings and a stack of documents the size of a phone book arrived at my office a few days later.

Lester's message for the parole board was that his appearance on this day was to reconfirm what he'd said in a series of prior statements that had been submitted for previous hearings: Michael was in some way attached to the acts that had resulted in his kidnapping and shooting. He certainly knew at least one of the two perpetrators, Buford Bates Jr., a Southside Crip with a violent history. But it was unclear what Michael's role in his kidnapping had actually been.

Each of the four declarations that were sent to me which dated back to 1992 indicated that James Lester had confessed to lying in court when he put Michael at the scene of the crime and the gun in his hand on that fateful day in June of 1987. In reality, Lester had never met his kidnappers before. The statements indicated that there were two reasons that he'd presented the testimony that he had. Number one, Lester lived in mortal fear of retribution from Buford Bates Jr., who he identified as the man who shot him. Secondly, he maintained that a detective Segars from the Los Angeles Sheriff's department had applied severe pressure on him to identify Harry O as the shooter even as Lester told him it was Buford Bates Jr. Segars had history with Michael. He'd dealt with him in L.A. on a prior gun charge and had traveled outside his jurisdiction to help the prosecutors win their attempted murder case against him.

News of Lester's statements caused a kaleidoscope of thoughts to crash through my head. *This is what Michael was trying to get Kenner to achieve on his behalf.* Lydia had gone toe-to-toe with me to get the money for Darden to get at this. Snoop Dogg would have a very personal connection to this information having survived a murder case where the D.A. had gotten the facts wrong.

Harry O's legend now fully embodied one of the central themes that had emerged from N.W.A.'s music and from the film *Straight Outta Compton*. As the film careened toward global theatres, life was imitating art and art was imitating life.

So to what extent was Michael actually attached to what had happened? Had he ordered a hit? Had he simply wanted to rough Lester up to send a message to him not to steal? Or did he simply make the mistake of reacting angrily to associates in the wake of being ripped off and not taken the proper care to prevent the kidnappers from taking the actions they did? In his testimony to the parole board, Michael maintained that it was the latter scenario. Distracted by the demands of his various legitimate businesses, his crime lay in not doing more to protect James Lester from associates in a business he was moving away from.

The concept of dealing with a strong hand in the face of recalcitrant behavior but pulling up short of really hurting someone was something that Harry O had lived by in the treacherous shark tank of crack cocaine distribution. It was a street concept he had attempted unsuccessfully to convey to

Suge Knight. The material he sent me contained a prior arrest record that was lightweight enough as to be downright embarrassing for a major drug kingpin. Prior to the attempted murder charge, there had been a robbery charge, a concealed weapon charge that had brought him to the attention of detective Segars and a drug charge that had been dismissed. That represented a slow month for his old nemesis - the guy some people called *Sugar Bear*.

There were other notable details in Lester's declarations and Michael's testimony to the parole board. The money that Lester had taken from Michael wasn't from a *rock house* as had been suggested in the press. It was money belonging to Michael's brother David and had been stolen from his mother's house. Michael had owned an electrical contracting business. At around the time that the money had been stolen, one of Michael's workers in the contracting business had been working there had seen Lester leaving the house. A month later, Lester was observed by the same worker lurking around the home Michael lived in and had called him and said *"The same guy who I saw leaving your mother's house a month ago just showed up here."* In response to this, Michael had rushed to his house and confronted Lester. *"Why are you at my house?"* His response had been *"I came here because I wanted to ask you for a job."* Lester's brothers had been involved in the drug trade and Lester had told Michael that he didn't want to follow in their footsteps. Michael told Lester *"I can't give you a job because you stole money from my mother's home."*

Michael was known to be especially close to his mother, a hardworking woman who often held multiple jobs and had raised Michael and his family as a single parent. A major issue for Michael had always been his mother's safety -- and the idea that someone known to him would break into her house and steal from her was not something he could easily abide. Even so, at previous parole hearings, Lester had been questioned repeatedly about whether he'd been in some way forced, coerced or threatened by Michael into changing his story. Reading

346

Lester's declarations, I got the sense of his exasperation with this line of questioning. In the wake of a terrifying experience, he'd been cajoled by Segars and the prosecutors into putting Michael at the scene and the gun in his hand. He didn't even know his kidnappers. He'd told them the shooter was Bates but they didn't want Bates. They wanted Harry O.

Now it was time to get the facts straight.

Lester's disclosure, when coupled with letters from scores of Michael's new supporters, including the police chief of nearby Richmond, California, all of whom attested to the work Michael had done in service of both disadvantaged youth and prisoner education made his early parole a *fait accompli*.

Even so, despite the fact that he'd served nearly three decades in prison in case where his former accuser had spent 23 years pushing for his release, no one in a position of authority and oversight connected with Michael's federal drug conviction seemed to think that he had sufficiently paid his debt to society.

In the wake of the San Quentin parole decision, Michael had been moved to a low security federal prison in Lompoc, California, home to people like Earthlink co-founder, Reed Slatkin, and he was now on year-four of a 20-year sentence on the federal drug charge. In today's environment, given his prior deeds and time-served, Michael would be out on the street. That was certainly the case with his former associates like Mario Villabona and Beau Bennett, who'd gotten out years earlier and actually had bigger roles in his drug business nearly three decades hence. But Michael's sentences had been successive rather than concurrent, an especially harsh punishment that had been meted out in the Reagan era during the reign of the notoriously gonzo Los Angeles police chief, Darryl Gates.

On July 26, 2015, after fully digesting the material Michael had sent me, I made the three and a half-hour drive from Los

Angeles to the Federal Correctional Institute in Lompoc, California. And when I got there, it would take me another two hours before I'd get in to see Michael Harris.

Lompoc

Prior to my arrival in Lompoc, I'd filled out a visitation form that had contained Michael's prisoner identification number on it. Lompoc has its own visitation rules and some of them were different from those when Michael and I had had our dealings at Lancaster, which was a state-run institution. At Lompoc, which is a federal facility, with regard to the low security unit that Michael was in, unless you'd had a lengthy prior relationship with the inmate, you couldn't get in to see him. This was obviously an overly restrictive rule. It meant that any new relationships that Michael might seek to make would have to be forged through e-mail and his somewhat limited access to a phone. But since Michael and Lydia had once been business partners of mine on a prior film project, my visit had been approved by prison officials.

Somewhat naively I thought I was going to show up and skate right in. I should have remembered that when it comes to the U.S. prison system, nothing is easy.

At Lancaster, prison officials had adhered to very strict bureaucratic codes and Lompoc was reading from the same script. When I got to the front desk, I was advised that there was a new form that needed to be filled out which required Michael's prisoner identification number. But I hadn't memorized it or brought it with me. I'd made the assumption that everything was copacetic. My visitation paperwork was clearly on file there but the workers told me that they were under strict orders not to be helpful with this issue. They told me they could not re-examine the paperwork that had led to my approval. I called Michael's friend, Alvin Brown. But his cell box was full. Then I realized that he'd likely gotten in ahead of me and if that was the case, he would have been required to leave his phone in his car. After several interactions with the front desk, I was given a phone number with a Washington, D.C. area code for the bureau of prisons (BOP) and told to leave the premises until I was able to come up with Michael's identification number.

From here, I would continue to be given a tutorial on why even close relatives get tired of visiting a family member who might be in a state or federal facility. Inside the prison, I couldn't wear clothes that were light brown, white or blue and with the exception of up to $20 in cash and I could have nothing else in my physical possession. Not even a pen. Outside the prison there was no wireless set-up. It was a Sunday and there was nobody working at the BOP. I couldn't reach anybody at Xenon so I drove back into Lompoc, found a coffee shop that had a wireless infrastructure and punched in the name Michael Ray Harris into the system. Nothing came up. The number was in my office. I called or e-mailed seven different people. Nothing. Then I called Mark Friedman. "*I think I have it in my car.*" Five minutes later Friedman called back with the number.

I started to get misty for the good ole days where all somebody had to do was stick a finger in my ass. Eventually, I persuaded the man to let me in.

I was led through two steel doors, the back of my hand was stamped and I was admitted to an outdoor yard area. Then the yard door was locked behind me. Across the yard sat Michael Harris with his closest associate, Alvin Brown -- a childhood friend who has dedicated his life to securing Michael's freedom.

When I got to the table where he was sitting, Michael stood up and the two of us embraced -- something that in all our previous history had never happened. Michael looked good. He hadn't aged in the manner that some people do going from age 38 to age 53. He was up. He was ready to go. He pointed to an area of the prison called *The Farm*. The Lompoc facility has four units and The Farm is the prison's version of *club fed* -- the section which has the fewest number of restrictions. Michael told me he was getting moved to The Farm in two weeks. "*That's where all the billionaires are."*

It was time to get down to business.

First, I asked why Lydia would take $1,000,000 in the wake of the $107 million settlement.

Michael explained to me that the prospect of a huge payday to the Harrises had finally put Suge Knight on the ropes. By refusing to pay attention to the Harrises' legal claim, he now knew he'd clutched a major defeat from the jaws of victory. In the wake of this, Suge's first move was to send his lawyers to see Michael at the Salinas Valley State Prison in Soledad, California to try and work out a deal. But when they got there, Michael had told them *no dice*. He wasn't going to make a deal with them. He was only going to make a deal with the man they answered to because somehow Suge's emissaries always got the story twisted. He'd already had his David Kenner experience. This time around, he wasn't going to listen to stories about the *steroid dude* who was fucking somebody's wife.

Suge Knight was going to have to go *mano-a-mano* with Harry O.

Concurrent with the visit from Suge's lawyers, there were two other huge issues at play. In the wake of the $107 million judgment, Lydia had suddenly powered down her communication with Michael. She'd gone *awol*. Word had trickled back to Michael through Alvin Brown and others that Lydia might be looking to grab some or all of the settlement and run. In a matter of days, he was about to be moved from Soledad to San Quentin, so if this situation with Lydia was true, he'd need to file for divorce as a way of nullifying anything she might do or any decision she might make that was against his will. His move to San Quentin would mean that he'd be domiciled in a different county in California. This would have financial implications for his marriage. New paperwork had to be drawn up. That would take time -- time Michael felt in his bones that he didn't have.

He was sure he needed to make a pre-emptive strike.

On the Friday in 2005 that Michael was moved to San Quentin, Alvin Brown walked into a Monterey County courthouse and filed divorce papers on behalf of Michael Harris. This meant among other things that the $107 judgment was now subject to a divorce proceeding. It also meant that if Lydia was going to get her legal share of the proceeds, she was going to have to resume communication with her soon-to-be ex-husband.

Once Michael was in place at San Quentin, a meeting between him and Suge Knight was finally arranged. But to Alvin Brown, who Michael had enlisted to make sure that Suge got to the church on time, Suge Knight didn't appear to be preparing for the meeting with any palpable level of seriousness. The meeting was set for the day after a Mayweather fight in Vegas. The plan called for Brown to meet Suge in Vegas and fly him to Oakland where they'd meet some friends of Suge and then drive to San Quentin. The morning after the fight, when Brown came to pick him up it was clear that Suge had been partying all night. Brown told me Suge was literally wobbling. His eyes were so bloodshot he was wearing dark sunglasses to cover them up. Brown had to pour Suge into the rental car. At the airport, the whole process was a nightmare. Suge was completely disoriented. It took forever to get him on the plane. When they finally got to San Quentin, Suge discovered that he'd left his driver's license on the airplane.

Then a miracle of all miracles happened. Even with no driver's license in Suge Knight's possession, prison officials had let the meeting between Michael and Suge go forward.

When the meeting started, as Alvin Brown put it, "*Suge was still trying to wake up.*" Not even a minute had passed before Michael had laid out his terms: "*My number is $30 million. That's the* *number it's gonna take to get your sorry ass off my back."*

Apparently, the $30 million got Suge's attention.

Michael hadn't come to this figure by accident. Death Row had a boatload of other claims to contend with. His financial advisors had calculated that given the other claims and what was probably in Death Row's immediate financial pipeline from Interscope and other parties, this was probably the largest figure he could extract from Suge.

In the negotiation, Michael would use the same tactic on Suge as Suge had on Vanilla Ice. *"You're going to accept my terms. It's not what you're gonna do for me. It's what I'm gonna do for you."* Michael told me that throughout the meeting, Suge told him over and over how sorry he was. He said it was embarrassing to watch Suge grovel like some school kid waiting for his spanking. For the first time ever in their relationship, Suge's words simply moved past him like water off a duck's ass. When Suge tried to strike a conciliatory note, Michael would say *"Both of us know who you are."* This was business and his number was $30 million with a capital *M*. Alvin Brown told me that by the time they shook hands on the deal, Suge Knight was *"sweating like a pig on a stick."*

But Suge Knight hadn't built one of the most successful rap labels in history by being stupid. In the interview footage we had of him he'd said about Dr. Dre, *"It wasn't no puzzle. I know how to talk to a brother."* Apparently, with his back against the wall, Suge knew how to talk to a sister as well. His first move was to contact Lydia and unload a bombshell, *"Your husband's gonna kill you and take the settlement for himself."* According to Michael, Suge knew that after years of trying to get justice for their claims, a lot of tension had developed between Michael and Lydia and he had used that knowledge to his advantage. When he learned of the divorce proceeding, he called Lydia and played it to the hilt. According to Michael, Lydia internalized Suge's message as the gospel truth, signed a contract which Suge represented was a

$1,000,000 deposit against the $30 million that he'd promised her husband and got the hell out of dodge. Michael told me that Lydia signed the settlement without having it vetted by a lawyer. He said further that Suge had actually told the third party sources he'd gotten the funds from that he needed $2 million to get the deal done, then got her to bite on $1 million and kept $1 million for himself.

With his divorce proceeding in place, Harry O was still in the game. Since it was done without his approval, he could still contest the settlement and its terms. But then Suge Knight did the unthinkable. He filed for bankruptcy. This set the stage for a judge and an ocean of lawyers to preside over the distribution of Death Row's assets. Suddenly, the Harrises' $107 judgment went into a giant creditor pot with all the other claims the label had to contend with -- with a gang of legal fees and court costs ahead of it. The contretemps among the various parties that followed would fill a separate book.

Suge Knight's greatest business skill had been to divide and conquer. He'd done it to Eazy and Jerry Heller to get Dr. Dre into Death Row. He'd done it with Jimmy Iovine to move Dick Griffey out of the picture and try to get rid of Michael Harris the first time. He'd done it in concert with Tupac to get rid of Dr. Dre from Death Row.

Now he'd done it with Lydia to get rid of Michael Harris once and for all.

Upon hearing all the crazy details, all I could do was shake my head. *Wow.* This was a story with the longest tail I'd ever seen. It just kept going and going. But I could tell by the look in his eyes, Michael was not yet finished with Death Row Records. Not by a long shot.

Next up, Michael and I discussed the $3.5 million that Mario Villabona had told his lawyers that Michael owed him before he was arrested. Michael's reaction was *"That piece of shit."* He was visibly upset by this disclosure. I couldn't believe he'd get that upset. This new guy was much more studied and serene when he spoke. This was stuff from three decades ago. Wasn't there some currency for him in the knowledge that he'd played a Columbian drug lord for that kind of cash? But for Michael it was a matter of process and principle. First of all, there was no way you could get into a Colombian for that kind of money. But there was a pride issue as well. As a businessman, his ego was connected to paying his bills. Back in the day, that's why people liked him -- because he was a tough businessman who paid his bills. *"He said that because he knew it would get back to me and he knew it would piss me off. I paid that dude every fucking cent I owed him."*

Finally, we discussed the circumstances of his attempted murder conviction. Amid the endless battles we'd had on *Welcome to Death Row*, this was something we'd never talked about before. Michael told me that the key to understanding the case was to understand the life and methods of Buford Bates Jr.

For many years, Bates had been in the business of kidnapping, robbery and extortion. His rap sheet lit up like a king-sized boil on local law enforcement screens. Bates was just another guy who bought drugs from Michael when he had the cash. Michael told me *"I didn't even like the dude."* When Bates got wind of a rumor that Lester had ripped off Harry O and his brother David and that Lester, in the absence of a job was suddenly driving around in a new car, he made his move. Bates and an associate went to Lester's house robbed him of the cash that he'd taken from Michael's mother's house, kidnapped him and took him out to the desert, shot him several times and left him for dead.

During the police investigation, as represented in his various statements to the people at Michael's various parole hearings, Lester told Segars that Buford Bates Jr. was the man who shot him. But Segars didn't want Bates. He'd traveled out of his jurisdiction to secure a bigger prize for himself. He wanted Harry O, a drug kingpin with virtually no criminal record on whom he'd gotten a gun charge to stick a couple of years back. And to achieve that end, Segars told Lester how difficult he'd make his life if he didn't get with the program. For the L.A. prosecutors, Segars was the kind of strident *company man* they needed to make their case. In the face of this, Lester had switched his story and put Michael at the scene and the gun in his hand. Michael told me that in his pursuit to put him behind bars, detective Segars had interrogated a number of people including Michael's cousin, Richard Dawson. Dawson had been accused of being one of the kidnappers and was offered a reduced sentence if he'd give them what they wanted on Harry O. He didn't and would end up paying a hefty price. Dawson would serve nearly three decades in prison before being released.

As I looked into Michael Harris' eyes, I could see that memory of Dawson standing up to Segars was one of the great acts of integrity he'd ever witnessed. *"They wanted Richard because he was close to me. He didn't do anything. He didn't do anything at all."*

Michael told me that when he went to his house and confronted Lester, who he called *Junior*, he told him he was disappointed in him and to get out of his life. But that was it. He had businesses to run and this was $100,000 which, at that point in his life, was pocket change. Besides it wasn't even his money. It was his brother David's money. Given the assets he'd accumulated and the fact that he was moving away from the drug business anyway, why would he participate in or instruct people to orchestrate a kidnapping and murder plot? He knew Junior. His other family members knew Junior. Okay, Junior had ripped off his brother. But what was the upside in hurting him or getting rid of him? He'd never done anything like that before. That wasn't how he operated. He didn't settle things that way. He knew the cops wanted him. Why would he risk everything he had to send a message to Lester or to the people who knew him that you shouldn't fuck with Harry O?

With regard to his trial, Michael told me his biggest mistake had been his choice of legal counsel. His lawyer, Clay Jacke, had neglected to present critical evidence that would have aided his defense. Michael had not even been in the state at the time of Lester's kidnapping. He'd been in Houston pursuing his relationship with Rap-a-Lot Records. Ten different people had signed affidavits attesting to this fact. He told me that this evidence was never presented to the court. Also, commensurate with the time of the kidnapping, *he'd gotten a traffic ticket in Houston.*

Before entering Lompoc, I'd had a small measure of skepticism about what had really happened. But now it appeared to me that Harry O's only crime was that he'd been a drug dealer who happened to know Buford Bates Jr.

Things would not end well for Buford Bates Jr. After one robbery too many, his bad seed *modus operandi* would finally catch up with him. On October 24, 2000, police would recover his bullet-ridden body in mid-city Los Angeles.

But since Michael had been convicted of attempted murder, for many years he'd been in parole hearings where the people charged with evaluating him wanted to see and hear that he'd taken responsibility for what he'd done. Since Michael didn't feel he was responsible for what had happened to James Lester, his reluctance in the eyes of his evaluators to properly atone for his sins had had the effect of forestalling his prospect for an early release. This where he had needed Kenner to battle on his behalf -- to get an investigator at the level of Paul Palladino to track down witnesses who could speak on his behalf -- like the two of them had done for Snoop. This is where he needed Chris Darden -- who he told me straight up -- *"took the money and didn't do shit."*

After years of fighting the idea that he had to cop to responsibility for something he felt he had nothing to do with, in

2012 he finally told the people at the parole hearing that given the dynamics of his life at that point, he should have taken more care to protect the life of James Lester. In the wake of the robbery at his mother's house, he should have recognized that Bufford Bates Jr. might do something to Lester and worked harder to insure that Bates didn't go near him.

It had been the bitterest pill he'd ever had to swallow. And yet, at the end of the day, when everything else was considered, it was this part of his testimony that had secured his parole.

Before me was a strong, prideful man, still tall and powerful in countenance despite the fact that he'd been in prison -- stuck in a quagmire of dehumanizing rules and regulations, away from family and friends, away from the dream of building his own business -- for 29 years. And to get to get three measly years commuted from his attempted murder charge so he could start serving another twenty on a federal drug charge, he'd had to sublimate his pride and claim to be responsible for someone who'd broken into his mother's house and stolen money that belonged to his brother.

****

At one point in our meeting, Michael marveled at the whole Harry O image and what it had represented to people. He told me *"I'll never understand why people were so afraid of me."*

Michael has never been one to run from his legacy and, as our discussion progressed, it appeared to me that he had adjusted his goals to utilize his life and prior decisions to make a new name for himself as a force of good. As he had stated to me years before, he hated what crack had done to his community and he hated that he'd had a role in that. One of the most frustrating things for him to reconcile was that, at the time, he felt that the crack business represented the only mechanism available to him to secure the funds necessary to transition into the world of legitimate business. No bank or private citizen was going to back him. The government was spending a fortune enabling detractors of rogue governments overseas and on tanks and munitions in preparation for foreign wars. But there was simply no mandate through the government, private individuals, private foundations or a combination thereof to help Black people in the ghetto who had the predisposition to build businesses. A mechanism that could enable that process simply did not exist.

Michael certainly hadn't lost his taste for business and business process. But gone was the bluster and hubris and out-sized concepts that had characterized many of our prior conversations. The transmutation of Harry O into a man who these days only wanted to be known as Michael Ray Harris now involved simple pragmatism: If you're an inner city kid or a prisoner ready to be released into society, who are you going to listen to? A Harvard-educated social worker or a newly actualized former legendary original gangster whose seed money helped build the careers of Snoop Dogg, Dr. Dre and Tupac Shakur? No offense to the people doing God's work in this area -- but if Michael is really walking the walk and talking the talk, it's kind of a no-brainer.

In our meeting, Michael and I discussed two of the best books on people, business and organizations in existence: Ben Horowitz's *The Hard Thing About Hard Things* and Jim Collins's *Good to Great*. In both books, the authors discuss the whole concept of ambition and what it means. They bifurcate between ambitious people who are ambitious solely for themselves and those who inextricably link their ambitions to the success of the people or enterprise they work for. Michael was now firmly in the latter category. He'd been that way during the genesis of Death Row Records and now his energy was being utilized to extend the knowledge he had obtained to others through the power of a coterie of new, more powerful associates, the likes of which had been non-existent in the previous two acts of his life.

I would encourage anyone who really cares about the issues relating to America's inner cities and to the U.S. prison system to contact Michael and take his temperature. As he did with me, if you prove sincere in your desire to help the country with these issues, it's likely he'll welcome the opportunity to speak with you.

My meeting with Michael ended up being more emotional than I anticipated. We talked about the past. But we also talked about his future and how in life, you are only as strong as your weakest link. There's where you start and where you finish and Michael was determined to finish strong.

Most importantly, the two of us were able to achieve closure on past events.

Suge Knight might have gotten the better of Michael in the battle for Death Row Records. But Michael would always be the much bigger man. I left Lompoc that day with the firm sense that best chapter in the legendary life of Michael Ray Harris had yet to play itself out.

Epilogue

Death Row Records would limp along for several more years with Suge Knight directing the company from prison and, for a few years after his release from Mule Creek Penitentiary in August of 2001. Interscope ended its business relationship with the company shortly after Suge went to prison and focused its hip hop music efforts around Dr Dre and his Aftermath label. Some artists like Daz Dillinger and Kurupt stayed on the Death Row label and Suge Knight was able to sign promising new artists like Lisa *Left Eye* Lopes. But with the departure of Snoop Dogg to No Limit Records and other artists like RBX, the label became a shell of its former self.

In 2006, in the wake of the $107 million judgment secured by Michael and Lydia Harris and amid a hailstorm of other lawsuits and declining revenues, Death Row Records filed for bankruptcy. The many issues and complexities involved in the bankruptcy kept a number of viable bidders like Warner Music Group away. Three years later, Death Row's assets were auctioned off to a Canadian entity, Wide Awake Entertainment Group. Former Death Row recording engineer and *Welcome to Death Row* interviewee, John Payne was installed as company president. Later, Wide Awake also became insolvent.

In 2013, the Death Row Records catalog was purchased by the diversified Canadian company, Entertainment One. E-One as it is known in the entertainment industry was the most likely purchaser of the catalogue because the nuances of the issues surrounding the Death Row bankruptcy were well known to them. Previously, E-One had purchased Koch Records which had been a prospective bidder for Death Row's assets in the initial bankruptcy filing and had also provided financial assistance to Wide Awake in its purchase of the label.

Dr. Dre's new life at Interscope Records would restart his now legendary ascent to becoming the most prolific and successful producer in the history of the music business. He would bring artists like Eminem, 50 Cent, and others into the fold at Interscope, helping solidify the label's position as the most important label group in the music industry. MCA would later consolidate other important label groups inside the company with Jimmy Iovine at the helm and rename it Interscope Geffen A & M.

In 2006, Dr. Dre, in partnership with Jimmy Iovine and other partners including the Universal Music Group, founded Beats Electronics, a maker of headphones and speakers that placed a heavy emphasis on the listener's ability to hear a track's bass tones. Marketed under the brand name, *Beats By Dre*, and utilizing the extensive infrastructure of Universal Music Group, Interscope, and Jimmy Iovine's personal connections, including Apple founder Steve Jobs, Beats Electronics grew to capture 64% of the headphone market by 2012 with annual revenue exceeding a billion dollars.

In 2014, Apple, Inc. agreed to buy Beats Electronics for $3.2 billion dollars. The transaction put both Dr. Dre and Jimmy Iovine within a heartbeat of becoming billionaires.

Suge Knight's personal fortunes would go in the opposite direction of his former associates. Bankruptcy court would claim the last of his houses, a seven-bedroom Malibu, California mansion for $4.5. Later, in 2009 the last of Death Row's assets including the iconic electric chair from the label's logo were auctioned off. Subsequent to this, some of Knight's personal possessions were auctioned off in the debut episode of the A & E's series, *Storage Wars*.

Though he would form a new entity, Black Kapital Records, and form associations with artists such as comedian, Katt Williams, in recent years Knight is known more for violent episodes and legal scrapes, than his music creation or artist development.

In August of 2005, Knight was shot in the leg after he crashed a pre-music awards party for recording artist Kanye West in Miami. In 2008, Knight was involved in an altercation reportedly involving money outside a Hollywood, California nightclub. Witnesses on the scene said Knight was knocked out for a few minutes before being treated at a local hospital. Later that year, Knight was arrested on drug and aggravated assault charges after leaving a Las Vegas strip club. Charges in this matter were later dropped. In 2009, Knight was treated for head injuries after an altercation at a private party at the W Hotel in Scottsdale. Later, Knight was implicated in a robbery relating to the incident in Scottsdale. Knight told investigators that the impetus for the robbery was to collect assets in lieu of a debt that was owed to him.

More recently, Knight's name began popping up in the news again. In his book *Murder Rap*, police investigator Greg Kading would present fairly compelling evidence that Suge Knight hired the triggerman that killed Biggie Smalls in Los Angeles in 1997. In August of 2014, Knight was shot six times in the leg at a pre-music awards party in Los Angeles hosted by recording artist, Chris Brown. Knight's injuries required surgery and according to press reports, created a blood clot in his lung which began affecting his breathing. Even so, in keeping with his long-standing custom, he refused to co-operate with the police regarding the incident. Later that year, Knight and Katt Williams were arrested for stealing the camera of a female photographer in Beverly Hills.

On January 29, 2015, Knight was involved in an incident related to the film, *Straight Outta Compton* that many people believe will send him to jail for a significant amount of time. After crashing the set of a promotional shoot for the film, which featured Ice Cube and Dr Dre riding around Compton in a car, Knight had words with Cle Sloan, a part-time actor, who was part of the film's security detail. Sources say Knight wanted to speak with

Dr. Dre about money and why he hadn't been asked to be involved in the film since he was part of the story. Sloan and other members of the film's security detail blocked Knight's entrance to the set and asked him to leave.

Minutes later, Knight, Sloan and Terry Carter, an associate of Ice Cube's who owned a record label called Heavyweight Records, ran an entity that bought and sold low-riders and was well-known as a dispute settler in issues involving rival gang factions in South Central Los Angeles, reconvened at Tam's Burgers, a burger stand roughly a mile from where the filming was taking place. The details surrounding what happened next will now be decided in a court of law. Footage captured from a security camera near the scene of the incident and later broadcast by TMZ, shows an altercation between Sloan and Knight who is sitting in a large red truck. Subsequently, Knight then ran over Sloan and then barreled straight into Terry Carter who was standing roughly fifteen feet away. Knight then fled the scene. The final action in the video showed an unidentified man appearing to grab a gun from Sloan as he lay on the ground.

Terry Carter died shortly thereafter from his injuries and Cle Sloan sustained injuries that will likely affect the way he walks for the rest of his life. The incident soon evolved into a national news story, with Knight being arrested for the murder of Terry Carter. Knight claimed that he ran over the men because they intended to shoot him. His bail was initially set for $25 million dollars but was later reduced to $10 million. Subsequent press reports have disclosed that Cle Sloan is refusing to testify against Knight reportedly for fear of his life, and that boxer, Floyd Mayweather was examining the possibility of posting Knight's bail. David Kenner served briefly as Knight's attorney.

Old habits die hard.

Acknowledgements

This project had been waiting to be addressed for nearly a decade and a half. Steve Housden, a Xenon shareholder and the company's Chief Operations Officer had pushed me to do it for years and, more than anyone other than myself, lived with the story and its players for a very long time. Steve had the temerity and courage to stand tall during the very dangerous period when we were capturing this material and I'll always be grateful to him for that.

Jeff Scheftel, the other producer of *Welcome to Death Row* film and my close friend, conducted most of the interviews that yielded the words in the book's oral history chapters. Jeff also spend many hours reviewing the book's many iterations and gave me sage advice every step of the way.

Next, I'd like to thank four women; Los Angeles area publicist Susan Self, who put together the initial oral history pass that got the book kick started; Dr. Patricia Rust, my primary book editor, who pushed me to go deeper into the memoir side of the book than I had originally planned and Dr. Lael Atkinson who was generous enough to read many of the book's drafts and like Patricia pushed hard for me to give equal balance to both the oral history and memoir sections. Dr. Atkinson is also a 1980 graduate of Lakeside School in Seattle and has spent many years involved with prison outreach and studying issues within the inner city in America. Finally, I'd like to thank Vita Olivo, my partner in life, who read every draft of the book and patiently supported me every step of the way.

Andy Hoffmann's reasoned guidance helped me survive both the film and book projects. His steady hand has always been a constant through thick and thin. Everyone in life should be so lucky to have a friend like him.

A book like this only happens because people choose to speak with you. This book contains many voices and I thank all of those people for their participation. However, certain people decided to give me access to information that really afforded the reader real insights into the many of the issues at play in this story. Those people include Jerry Heller, Snoop Dogg, Allen Gordon, Alonzo Williams, Matt McDaniel, Doug Young, Kevin Powell, Stephanie Fredric, Jewell Payton, Jay King, Lydia Harris, Atron Gregory, Alvin Brown, Simone Green, Greg Kading, George Pryce, Dick Griffey, Hank Caldwell, John Payne, Virgil Roberts, Jeffrey Jolson Colburn, Frank Alexander and Mark Friedman.

Finally, I'd like to thank Michael Ray Harris. Keep the faith, my friend. The best is yet to come.

A PARTIAL LIST OF INTERVIEWEES AND WHERE THEY ARE NOW

Eric "Eazy E" Wright: The legendary Ruthless Records founder and NWA group member died of complications related to AIDS in March of 1995.

Jerry Heller: Heller is considered to be one of the most influential entrepreneurs in the history of both the rock and rap music movements. He released a memoir, appropriated entitled, *Ruthless* in 2006. He remains active in the music business, most recently in the country music sphere.

Frank Alexander: Alexander produced and appeared in multiple documentaries on Tupac Shakur, and remained active for many years as a bodyguard for a number of high profile celebrities, including boxer Manny Pacquiao. He died in May of 2014 of what police believe was a self-inflicted gunshot wound.

Matt McDaniel: McDaniel remains active as both a photographer and a DJ. His *Matt McDaniel Archive* contains the most important visual representation of the West Coast hip hop movement in existence. He was a technical adviser on the film, *Straight Outta Compton*.

Doug Young: Doug Young is one of the few living eyewitnesses to both the Ruthless Records and Death Row stories and, as a promoter for both Ruthless Records and Death Row, is considered one of the most important figures in the history of the West Coast hip hop movement. Today, Young remains active in the music business and has a number of business interests including a chain of outlets that sell medical marijuana. He is a sought after speaker on the subject of hip hop history and promotion.

Rudy Pardee: Was a founding member of the L.A. Dream Team and a close associate of Dr. Dre's throughout his life. He died in a scuba diving accident in 1998, shortly after we interviewed him.

Paul Palladino: Before the work he did on behalf of Death Row Records, Palladino gained his reputation by being part of the team that helped get automaker, John DeLorean acquitted of federal drug trafficking charges. He is a licensed private investigator in Los Angeles.

Kevin Powell: A political activist and the author of twelve books including, *The Black Male Handbook: A Blueprint For Life*, and *Barack Obama, Ronald Reagan and the Ghost of Dr. King*, and the forthcoming book, *The Education of Kevin Powell*. Powell has obtained a high profile as a lecturer on the subject of violence against women. He made a third run for Congress in 2010.

Jeffrey Jolson Colburn: A long time music editor for *The Hollywood Reporter*, Colburn's lineage in music went back to singer Al Jolson, who was a distant relative. He was the editor of *Grammy Magazine* and founded the website, *Hollywood Today*, in 2006. He died of undisclosed causes in 2012.

Allen Gordon: A former editor-in-chief at *Rap Pages*, Gordon is an educator and free-lance sportswriter in Oakland, California.

Alonzo Williams: Williams owns the music publishing concern Lon-Hop Music which owns a wide catalog of songs including works from *The World Class Wrecking Cru*, and remains active in the nightclub business as CEO of Los Angeles based Hall of Fame Entertainment.

Dick Griffey: Dick Griffey will be remembered as one of the most important entrepreneurs in the music business -- as a club owner, musician, songwriter, concert promoter for the likes of Stevie Wonder, Michael Jackson, Aretha Franklin and James Brown, and the founder of SOLAR Records. He died on September 24, 2010.

Virgil Roberts: Roberts is the managing partner of the Los Angeles based law firm of Bobbit and Roberts, where he has represented sports and music figures including the Jackson Family. He is the Chairman of the African-American Board Leadership Institute and a graduate of Harvard Law School.

Lydia Harris: Ms. Harris runs a catering business in the Houston suburb of Sugarland, Texas, and also does life coach counseling. Recently, she has begun signing artists for a new label.

Snoop Dogg: One of the most iconic names in the history of the music business, Snoop has collaborated with numerous artists including Ice Cube, R Kelly, E-40, Katy Perry and Wiz Khalifa. Snoop has released thirteen studio albums most recently, *Bush* which was produced by Pharrell Williams. He was nominated for a Grammy for Best Rap Song for *Young, Wild & Free* in 2012. He is an avid sports fan, and his appearances on the Comedy Central roasts usually steal the show.

Nate Dogg a.k.a. Nathaniel Hale: Hale was featured on a number of Tupac Shakur tracks including, *All About U.* His post Death Row career was highlighted by collaborations with Dr. Dre, Mos Def, Ludacris, 50 Cent, Mark Ronson, and Eminem. He died from complications from multiple strokes on March 15, 2011. A final solo album *Nate Dogg: It's a Wonderful Life*, featuring Eminem, Dr. Dre, Snoop Dogg, Mary J. Blige, and Jay Z is scheduled for release in 2015.

Stephanie Frederic: As a reporter for BET News in the 1990s, Frederic captured interviews with many notable figures in politics and entertainment including two lengthy interviews with Death Row founder Suge Knight. Her FGW Productions imprint has produced numerous documentaries most recently, *Light Girls*, with director Bill Duke.

Atron Gregory: A pioneer in the rap movement with key associations with Alonzo Williams, Jerry Heller, Tupac Shakur and Interscope Records, Gregory is the Chief Operations Officer of Stanley Clarke's Roxboro Entertainment and owns a music publishing and management concern called TNT management. He is working on a documentary on his association with Tupac Shakur.

Hank Caldwell: A former executive with both Epic Records and Dick Griffey and SOLAR Records, Caldwell left Death Row Records in 1994. He remains active as a consultant in the music industry.

Jewell a.k.a. Jewell Caples a.k.a. Jewell Peyton: Jewell was featured on *N.W.A's Niggaz For Life,* and numerous Death Row releases including, *Deep Cover, The Chronic, Doggystyle, Murder Was the Case,* the soundtrack for *Above the Rim, All Eyez on Me* and *Suge Knight Represents: The Chronic 2000.* Since leaving Death Row, Jewell has collaborated with numerous artists including Missy Elliot, Snoop Dogg, Daz Dillinger, Kurupt, Prodigy and Jake Steed. She released a solo CD, *My Blood, My Sweat, My Tears* in 2011. A memoir of the same name about her time with Death Row has yet to be released.

Jay King: King's association with the rap music movement dates back to his involvement as a producer for the Timex Social Club and as a singer, songwriter and producer for Club Nouveau whose rendition of Bill Withers's 70s ballad *Lean On Me* won him a Grammy. Today, King manages multi-platinum artist Karyn White, and owns The Jay King Radio Network where he hosts music-related shows including, *The Music Business: The Way I See It.*

Master P a.k.a. Percy Robert Miller: An actor, rapper, one-time professional basketball player, and entrepreneur, Miller took the blueprint provided by Death Row Records and built No Limit Records into a rap music juggernaut. In 2013, he released his thirteenth studio album, *The Gift.* The same year, Forbes estimated his net worth at $350,000,000.

Norman Winter: Winter's show business roots dated back to his relationship as Frank Sinatra's photographer in the 50s. As a publicist, he represented Janet Jackson, The Who, Barry White, Elton John, George Michael Jackson, Tom Petty and numerous record labels and executives including CBS Record Chief Walter Yetnikoff. He died on August 22, 2013. He was 85

George Pryce: Known alternately as *Papa G* and *Papa Hollywood* in his days as Death Row's communication director, Pryce is an independent public relations and media relations specialist in Los Angeles.

Sam Gideon Anson: Is an investigative journalist based in Los Angeles. His father is legendary investigative journalist Robert Sam Anson.

Dan O'Dowd: O'Dowd is a long time video producer based in Los Angeles.

Simone Green: Simone was Death Row's principal in house photographer. Her photo archive from that era is one of the best in existence. Her Death Row memoir: *Time Served: My Days and Nights on Death Row Records* was released in 2012.

Lorenzo Patterson a.k.a. MC Ren: A group member of N.W.A., a featured performer on Eazy E's *Eazy Duz It,* and a lyricist for many of Dre's early recordings for Ruthless Records, Ren was affiliated with the label until 1999. Over the years, he has collaborated with Snoop Dogg, RBX and former N.W.A. band mate, Ice Cube on various tracks. He is the founder / owner of his own record label called Villian Entertainment.

John Payne: A studio engineer for Death Row who worked with Dr. Dre on both *Deep Cover* and *The Chronic,* Payne later became president of Wide Awake Entertainment, one of the entities that briefly owned the Death Row catalog. He remains active in the music business.

Freddie Rhone: Rhone is a songwriter and film producer based in Los Angeles.

Studio Tone: Studio Tone is a San Francisco-based studio engineer who worked with Tupac Shakur.

Joe Isgro: After working as a salaried promotion man for a number of labels including Motown, Isgro would use his contacts to establish the most powerful promotion network in the music industry during the 1980s. His behind the scenes work was critical to the success of many important artists of that era including Michael Jackson, U2, Phil Collins and Madonna. These days Isgro develops movie projects. He owns life rights to a number of historical figures including Lucky Luciano.

Other Interviewees:

Rick James
Rated R
Thug Life Group Members
Dove C
Sonshine
Lionel Randolph
Tone Def
Ron Newt
Greedy Greg
Battlecat
Diane Frank

Principal Interviews: Jeff Scheftel

Additional Interviews: S. Leigh Savidge, Allen Gordon, Darryl Pitts, Roger Steffens

Cover Design: Ned Suohevêts

References:

1. "Ruthless" by Jerry Heller.
2. Matt McDaniel archive.
3. VH1 News.
4. HipHopDX.com.
5. Stephanie Frederic archive.
6. "Prime Time Live".
7. "America's Most Wanted".
8. CNN.
9. KCBS News.
10. Fox News.
11. Dan O'Dowd archive.
12. Los Angeles Times.
13. MTV News.
14. BET archives.
15. Conus archive.
16. NY1 News.
17. Chum TV / Much Music.
18. Radio inverview / Rob Marriott.
19. CourtTV.